What IS THE *Difficulty?*

What IS THE Difficulty?

Intimate Moments *in the* Personal Service *of*
His Divine Grace
A. C. Bhaktivedanta Swami Prahupāda

Śrutakīrti Dāsa

Bookwrights Press
Charlottesville, Virginia

Readers interested in the contents of this book are invited to correspond with the author.
email: srutakirti.acbsp@pamho.net / sruto@yahoo.com

Paperback ISBN: 978-1-88040433-1

Hardback edition published by

Dharma Publications
Mayapura House, 2a Station Road Radlett, Herts WD7 8JX

First printing: 3000 copies
Second printing: 1500 copies
Third printing: 1000 copies

This paperback edition published by

Bookwrights Press
Charlottesville, Virginia
The publishing arm of
The Bhaktivedanta Center, Inc.
publisher@bookwrightspress.com

Contents at a Glance

Contents

An Appreciation

Dear Śrutakīrti Prabhu,

I want to thank you for how much you've been a source of inspiration for me. Whenever I've been around you and heard you share pastimes about Śrīla Prabhupada, I have not only been helped by them but when I hear you speak there's a simplicity and honesty that seems to come through that makes me feel, 'this Śrutakīrti, I really like him, he seems to radiate such kindness'.

I am glad that you are travelling and sharing your association and realizations because you've been so blessed. You will constantly have to deal with lots of big challenges. Those who are given much; much is expected from them. You should surely always see me as a grateful friend.

Yours in Śrīla Prabhupada's service,
With love,
Bhakti-tīrtha Swami
May 2005

Foreword

Śrīla Prabhupada was coming; devotees gathered from across America and the anticipation was reaching a crescendo. It was August 1972, in New Vrindaban, West Virginia. His Divine Grace AC Bhaktivedanta Swami Prabhupada was to deliver a historical lecture series entitled, "Bhagavat Dharma Discourses." The culmination would be Lord Kṛṣṇa's appearance day (Janmastami), followed by Śrīla Prabhupada's appearance day (Sri Vyasa Puja) a day later. Everyone greeted him with tears of joy and gratitude.

For the next two weeks we were all blissfully submerged in the ocean of his Divine Presence. All except one humble soul. While celebrations, festivals, kirtans and amazing lectures were relished by all like the essence of life itself, this one devotee was a prisoner in a smoke-filled primitive kitchen covered with black soot, choking on the smoke of burning wood. As we gazed upon His Divine Grace with tear filled eyes, the young devotee toiled in the kitchen weeping in separation as he cooked each meal for the multitude of devotees. Two weeks passed and he had not heard a single lecture or even seen his beloved spiritual master, yet he carried on as the servant of the servant of the servant.

Śrīla Bhaktisiddhānta Sarasvatī Ṭhākura has taught us, "do

not try to see Kṛṣṇa but try to serve Kṛṣṇa in such a way that he is pleased to see you." Kṛṣṇa Himself has spoken in the Adi Purana, "service to my devotees is more dear to Me than service to Myself." Although this simple soul was heartbroken, being so close but so far from his spiritual master, he personified this holy quality. On Śrīla Prabhupada's last day at New Vrindaban, this selfless soul received a message: "Śrīla Prabhupada is departing tomorrow morning, he requests you to travel the world with him as his personal servant!"

From that day on, many years would see our beloved god-brother Śrutakīrti prabhu at Śrīla Prabhupada's side as his longest-standing personal servant. Śrīla Prabhupada loved Śrutakīrti prabhu dearly. His unassuming nature made him dear to all of our hearts. There was no place for political ambitions in his surrendered life. He simply wanted to please his beloved Gurudeva with his heart and soul. In doing so he was given entrance into the intimate personal life of an unalloyed lover of God. Śrutakīrti Prabhu witnessed Śrīla Prabhupada humbly offering all credit to his Guru Mahārāja and to his own disciples for unprecedented victories as he spread Kṛṣṇa Consciousness all over the world. He gratefully observed the love, humor and fearless determination of a global acarya. Late at night while massaging Śrīla Prabhupada under a mosquito net, he often heard candid tales of his master's early life. Śrutakīrti Prabhu was an intimate part of Śrīla Prabhupada's daily life. He often bore witness to the personal character of Śrīla Prabhupada who steadfastly responded to attacks, confrontations and sad betrayal. As Śrutakīrti prabhu dutifully performed his service, he was naturally privy to the inside truths of how ISKCON had developed in its formative years.

In October 2003, at Śrīmatī Rādhārāṇī's birthplace, over 2,000 devotees had gathered. His Grace Śrutakīrti Prabhu inaugurated our Vraja Yatra with his memories of our beloved Śrīla Prabhupada. For five continuous hours he mesmerized the assembled devotees with enthralling stories. The multitude of devotees sat spell-bound by his every word, laughing and crying in spontaneous gratitude. Many expressed that they had never felt Śrīla Prabhupada's presence so deeply affect their hearts as it did through Śrutakīrti's heartfelt narration.

It is our great joy that Śrutakīrti Prabhu is now releasing his precious memories to the world in this long awaited book. I sincerely pray that all readers for generations to come may find supreme shelter of Śrīla Prabhupada's compassion through Śrutakīrti's heart-felt words.

Rādhānatha Swami
Mumbai, India

Preface

In November, as we started the final push to finish this book, I sent an email to Śrutakīrti expressing my joyful feelings about his wonderful memories of Srila Prabhupada. He wrote back to say that my reaction echoed the sentiments of the many readers and he asked me to share some of those thoughts here to represent all who have written over the years.

Śrutakīrti's memories of Srila Prabhupada are pure joy – they make my love for Prabhupada deeper and sweeter. My consciousness of Srila Prabhupada is transformed from seeing him as a wonderful yet distant leader and guide, into an affectionate father. I'm so grateful to Śrutakīrti for being who he is – simple, loving, a servant of Prabhupada. He has witnessed, and is sharing, wonderful moments which we will relish for millennia.

Many followers did not get the chance to personally associate with or serve Srila Prabhupada. Srutakirti has captured the essence of love in action, in service to Prabhupada. The reader is offered a window into Srila Prabhupada's personality, his intimate thoughts and actions, his concern for every living entity, and some of his likes and dislikes. Śrutakīrti's memories reveal Srila Prabhupada's caring and loving nature for all future generations to appreciate.

By loving Prabhupada we can all learn how to love Krishna. That's why Srila Prabhupada came to us. Śrutakīrti writes an exposition on love, reciprocated love. He has poured his heart into these memories. He has thrown open the storehouse of love for Srila Prabhupada.

Please join us and feel the intimacy of his relationship with Srila Prabhupada. I also urge you to share this wonderful book with friends. It is sadhu sanga, it will sweeten your devotional life and inspire you to act in loving service.

Thank you very much, Śrutakīrti, from all of us.

Vidyānanda dāsa
New Raman Reti, Florida, USA

Introduction

nama oṁ viṣṇu-pādāya kṛṣṇa-preṣṭhāya bhū-tale
śrīmate bhaktivedānta-svāmin iti nāmine

I offer my respectful obeisances unto His Divine Grace A.C. Bhaktivedanta Swami Prabhupāda, who is very dear to Lord Kṛṣṇa, having taken shelter at His lotus feet.

namas te sārasvate deve gaura-vāṇī-pracāriṇe
nirviśeṣa-śūnyavādi-pāścātya-deśa-tāriṇe

Our respectful obeisances are unto you, O spiritual master, servant of Sarasvatī Gosvāmī. You are kindly preaching the message of Lord Caitanyadeva and delivering the Western countries, which are filled with impersonalism and voidism.

"All glories to Śrīla Prabhupāda"

In continuing my writing of Prabhupāda nectar, I have realised my lack of qualifications and the insufficiency of my endeavour. Who can properly glorify the Lord or His pure devotee?

My intention is to glorify His Divine Grace and share with you some Prabhupāda nectar. My desire is to share Śrīla Prabhupāda's glorious enthusiasm in serving the Lord.

I feel it is my duty to tell my memories of His Divine Grace. I was never very philosophical, but I loved the way Śrīla Prabhupāda conducted every minute of his life. He was literally my father. My own father died when I was three. Until I was nineteen and met Śrīla Prabhupāda, I had no significant male influence in my life. I think that is one reason why my stories of Śrīla Prabhupāda tend to reflect the softer side of his personality. There were so many facets of Śrīla Prabhupāda's character, but I only remember his sweetness, compassion and mercy, along with his childlike innocence and kindness. In giving class over the years, it is apparent that the devotees are also anxious to hear about these qualities.

In 1978, Satsvarūpa Mahārāja recorded my memories for more than five days. Śrīla Prabhupāda said so many things. He managed a worldwide transcendental society with his young western followers. He was, and still is, the "Kṛṣṇa Consciousness" within ISKCON.

In my writing I have said, "All glories to Śrīla Prabhupāda," dozens of times, repeating these beautiful words without full awareness, attention, or comprehension. I repeat them like a robot. I need to rejoice in the full meaning of this mantra.

ALL GLORIES TO ŚRĪLA PRABHUPADA!

This phrase "All Glories to Śrīla Prabhupāda!" has personally taken on more meaning then ever before. I can see Śrīla Prabhupāda smiling now. It is a beautiful smile, one I have seen many times before and pray to see again.

ALL GLORIES TO ŚRĪLA PRABHUPADA!

I stand humbled before all who have taken shelter at the

lotus feet of His Divine Grace A.C. Bhaktivedanta Swami Prabhupāda. I hope to receive the mercy of the devotees, so I may become passionate in my love for Śrīla Prabhupāda.

Śrīla Prabhupāda would rise at two or three in the morning and do translating work so that his disciples could have, for all time, his transcendental ecstasies in print. Sometimes, I was fortunate enough to awaken to the sound of his voice in the next room. He may have been translating words, or slowly and carefully speaking the purport into the dictaphone. Even though I was entrenched in the mode of ignorance, I felt fortunate to have been able to hear transcendental history being recorded.

Now, after 25 years, I have finally risen early to write the only transcendental ecstasy that I have realized by the mercy of my spiritual master. In my writings, I have attempted to describe some of these pastimes of Śrīla Prabhupāda, in the hope of increasing our appreciation of his greatness. I beg forgiveness to all I might offend having shared my imperfect perceptions. If I wait until I become perfect before attempting to glorify our beloved guru, I am afraid all memory may be lost. I recognise my inability to glorify Śrīla Prabhupāda properly. I realise that His Divine Grace, being *nitya-siddha*, isn't susceptible to any material disease. Still he granted us his merciful association, and walked among us in this land of misery. He came to deliver us by voluntarily coming to this material world. This was his causeless mercy.

ALL GLORIES TO ŚRĪLA PRABHUPADA!

Begging to remain Śrīla Prabhupāda's servant,
Begging to remain *dāsadāsānudāsa* - Life after Life!

Śrutakīrti dāsa
London, UK

PART ONE

My First Meetings with Śrīla Prabhupāda

July 19, 1971 to June 14, 1972

1

"What is the difficulty?"

July 19, 1971 ISKCON Brooklyn, New York

I moved into the Pittsburgh Temple in April of 1971. In July of that year, Kīrtanānanda Mahārāja took a few of us to the Brooklyn temple to receive first initiation. Needless to say, we were all very excited.

Being Kīrtanānanda Mahārāja's servant enabled me to be very close to Śrīla Prabhupāda's vyāsāsana during class. The day of my initiation was the first time I was able to be in the personal presence of my eternal spiritual master. It was a moment I will never forget. His effulgence was extraordinary. I stared at his every move. The kīrtan was ecstatic. By the time the chanting stopped the temperature in the temple room must have risen to at least hundred degrees.

Hundreds of devotees squeezed into the temple room and tried to get as close to Śrīla Prabhupāda as possible. After kīrtan, we simultaneously bowed down to offer our obeisances. This made the room even more cramped. I started to get up before the devotee behind me and accidentally placed my posterior on his head. This startled him and he rose very quickly, pushing me forward with great force right onto the side of Śrīla Prabhupāda's vyāsāsana. My hands and head landed directly at his right side.

"What is the difficulty?" he asked me.

I shrank back onto the floor unable to say anything in response.

Śrīla Prabhupāda, many times I heard you ask, "What is the difficulty?" Whenever you asked that question, you knew we could not answer because you mercifully removed all of the difficulty out of this process.

"This process is so simple," you explained. "Just chant Hare Kṛṣṇa and be happy. If you chant sixteen rounds and follow the four regulative principles then at the end of this life you will go back home, back to Godhead."

All Glories to Śrīla Prabhupāda!

2

"And your name is Śrutakīrti Dāsa"

July 22, 1971 ISKCON Brooklyn, New York

I arrived at New York Temple from New Vṛndāvana with Kīrtanānanda Mahārāja and a few other bhaktas to receive initiation. I mentioned my initial contact with him, a few days earlier, when I accidentally landed on his vyāsāsana. My first formal meeting was the day His Divine Grace gave me first initiation. I had met the devotees exactly three months earlier in a park in Philadelphia, Pennsylvania.

There were ten bhaktas initiated each day during his stay at the Brooklyn temple. I vividly remember the initiation ceremony when Śrīla Prabhupāda's secretary called, "Bhakta Vin." I squeezed my way through the crowded temple room to Śrīla Prabhupāda's vyāsāsana and nervously offered my obeisances. His servant at the time, Aravinda, said my name, "Śrutakīrti."

I stood in front of Śrīla Prabhupāda as he looked at me. He said, "Śrutakīrti, one whose activities are world famous." All the devotees chanted, "Jaya, hari-bol." He continued to look at me and said, "And your name is Śrutakīrti dāsa." He placed extra emphasis on the word, 'dāsa'. Motioning with his hand he said, "Come on!" I leaned forward, eager to receive my japa beads upon which he had just chanted. Then he asked me, "What are the rules? I responded, "No meat-eating, no illicit sex, no intoxication, no gambling." It was easy to remember them. I had been repeating these words in my head for the last hour. We were all so nervous at the time of initiation. It was usual for us to forget one or more of the regulative principles.

Again, he looked at me and inquired, "How many rounds you will chant?" I foolishly said with a little pride in my voice, "Around twenty, Prabhupada."

He looked at me knowingly and murmured, "Hmmm." I could tell he was unimpressed with my response. I quickly offered my obeisances and made my way back to my spot in the temple room. When I sat down, someone asked me what name I had been given. "I do not know," I replied. How could I?

I had never heard the word before. There were so many Sanskrit words that I could not pronounce, so much I did not know.

Fortunately, we had the option of reviewing our names on a list tacked to Śrīla Prabhupāda's door after the fire sacrifice. We would go there and write our new names on a piece of paper, with the correct diacritic marks, so we could make sure we had understood our names correctly.

It was a dream come true. I was miserable in the material world, but I never knew why. Before becoming a devotee, at the age of nineteen, I would go to bed at night with tears in my eyes and pray to an unknown God saying, "If you are there and can hear me, please reveal yourself. I am so unhappy and do not know what to do with my life." Within a week my prayer was answered when I met the devotees chanting in a park.

> *Śrīla Prabhupāda, there is nothing more painful in the three worlds than to be without the knowledge of our position as your humble servant. I humbly beg that you always allow me to remember you and, although I am unqualified, please let me associate with your devotees and continue to do some service, however insignificant it may be.*

3

"Where were you during my lecture?"

May 21, 1972 ISKCON Los Angeles, California

While Kīrtanānanda Mahārāja and I were in New Dvārakā for a week, I received brahmana initiation from Śrīla Prabhupāda. Although I was not yet Śrīla Prabhupāda's personal servant, in retrospect, I was being initiated into that mood. Throughout the week whenever I saw Śrīla Prabhupāda's servant, I contemplated his great fortune and stared at him uncontrollably. He would glance back at me and smile slightly. He must have thought I was very strange.

One morning during his lecture, Śrīla Prabhupāda noticed his servant was not by his vyāsāsana, so he inquired as to his whereabouts.

"He is in the kitchen," a devotee said.

His Divine Grace continued with class. After his lecture, Kīrtanānanda Mahārāja and I went into Śrīla Prabhupāda's room. The atmosphere was tense and Śrīla Prabhupāda was visibly unhappy. Then Śrīla Prabhupāda's servant brought in his breakfast.

"Where were you during my lecture?" Śrīla Prabhupāda asked in an angry mood. "I was preparing your breakfast," his servant answered.

"Why?" Śrīla Prabhupāda asked even louder. "Anyone can prepare breakfast. You should be there at the lecture."

His illustrious personal servant gave another reason, but Śrīla Prabhupāda was not pacified.

"You must be there," Śrīla Prabhupāda told him. "There is no reason to be absent."

I sat in the room shaking. It was my first experience seeing and hearing my spiritual master in an angry mood. It was difficult to watch as his servant tried to explain himself.

"Talking back to Śrīla Prabhupāda," I thought to myself, "can't be good."

This was a good lesson for me. I made up my mind I would never do that if Śrīla Prabhupāda chastised me. When Śrīla Prabhupāda left New Dvārakā in August of 1972, Śrīla Prabhupāda's servant remained behind to get married. Śrīla Prabhupāda tried to keep him as his servant saying he was "expert."

In September of 1972, I was Śrīla Prabhupāda's servant in New Dvārakā. He told me to prepare his meals in my quarters, not in the temple kitchen, because there were too many women there. Sixteen months later, history repeated itself. Śrīla Prabhupāda left New Dvārakā and I remained, to be married to a girl I had met in the temple kitchen.

Śrīla Prabhupāda knew the weaknesses of his disciples and mercifully encouraged us to rise above them. When we failed, he continued compassionately to accept our service, on whatever level we were able to perform it. On many occasions, he said that our young age was the cause of our restlessness.

Śrīla Prabhupāda, you tried so hard to protect us. You chastised us for sleeping too much, overeating, gossiping, and for wasting time. There were innumerable reasons why you corrected us, for being inattentive in our service, for being proud. It was always done because of your great love and compassion for us. Sometimes you cried when you heard a disciple had left your shelter. Your love for us is unequalled and unending. There is no safe place in this world except at your lotus feet.

4

"Kṛṣṇa is like a sweet ball."

May 22, 1972 ISKCON Los Angeles, California

Śrīla Prabhupāda's Garden

I went to New Dvārakā for about one week with Kīrtanānanda Mahārāja, to receive brahmana initiation. Each evening at dusk, Śrīla Prabhupāda went to his garden to hear Kṛṣṇa Book. A few fortunate disciples were able to join him.

By Kṛṣṇa's grace, I was asked to read. I spent each day in anticipation of this exhilerating activity. Seated on his asana under the arch of a vine-covered trellis, Śrīla Prabhupāda usually kept his hand in his bead bag. Sometimes we heard him softly chant the Mahā-mantra. He carefully listened to Kṛṣṇa Book, and sometimes smiled as he heard the delightful activities of Kṛṣṇa and His brother Balarāma.

One evening as I read the story "Deliverance of Dvivida Gorilla," Śrīla Prabhupāda smiled broadly while hearing of the mischievous nature of Dvivida. He chuckled when I read the passage, "Often he would go to the hermitages of great saintly persons and sages and cause a great disturbance by smashing their beautiful gardens and orchards."

I sensed the story was going to get better, and it did.

"Not only did he create disturbances in that way," I continued, "but, sometimes he would pass urine and stool on their sacred sacrificial arena."

Śrīla Prabhupāda laughed so hard I stopped reading for a moment. Seeing his reaction we all experienced incredible joy. He cheerfully slapped his leg. He liked hearing about Kṛṣṇa and Balarāma killing the demons.

The next evening when we entered the garden I immediately sat down on the lawn and began to look for a story involving a demon. I was going through the pages for a few seconds when Śrīla Prabhupāda stopped me saying, "Go on. Read from anywhere. Kṛṣṇa is like a sweet ball. Wherever you bite, it tastes good."

I joyfully went to the beginning of the next story and started reading.

Staying close to Kīrtanānanda Mahārāja, I was able to go on morning walks with Śrīla Prabhupāda as well. Each day we waited in the hallway for Śrīla Prabhupāda to come downstairs. Because I had been reading Kṛṣṇa Book in the evenings, Śrīla Prabhupāda kindly noticed me one morning as he walked down the stairs. He looked straight into my eyes.

"Oh!" he said. "Look at this nice young brahmacārī. What is your name?" Struck with awe, I could not answer. He continued walking down the stairs.

"His name is Śrutakīrti, Prabhupada," Kīrtanānanda said.

"Oh! Suta Gosvāmī," Śrīla Prabhupāda said smiling.

Śrīla Prabhupāda walked out the door. I finally had a reason to live because my beloved Gurudeva recognized me as the reciter of Kṛṣṇa's līlā, like Suta Gosvāmī. Overwhelmed with the graceful glance of His Divine Grace, I understood that he appreciated my Kṛṣṇa book reading.

My dear Śrīla Prabhupāda, after becoming your personal servant, I was able to see how appreciative you were of the service rendered by each of your disciples. You were pleased to see the seeds of devotion you planted taking root and becoming strong. You enjoyed seeing your students advance in Kṛṣṇa Consciousness. Many times you said,

"I have turned hippies into happies."

As I remember your beautiful lotus feet, I feel very happy. Serving them is my only shelter. Thank you for giving me this eternal opportunity.

☙ 5 ☙

"A devotee has no ambition"

May 24, 1972 ISKCON Los Angeles, California

Śrīla Prabhupāda's Garden

One afternoon Śrīla Prabhupāda was sitting in his garden with the parents of a young brahmacārī. Having landscaped the garden for Prabhupada, they had had the good fortune to have pleased His Divine Grace. Kīrtanānanda Mahārāja and I were also present.

"A devotee is very proud to be Kṛṣṇa's servant," Śrīla Prabhupāda said. "A devotee has that pride. We are not ashamed that we are Kṛṣṇa's servants."

Then speaking directly to the parents, Śrīla Prabhupāda said, "Your son is a very nice boy and a good devotee."

They were very pleased by the sweet words of His Divine Grace, but stated, "The devotees do not seem very ambitious."

"That is right," Śrīla Prabhupāda said. "A devotee has no ambition. He simply wants to do some humble service for Kṛṣṇa. He is not trying to do anything big. A devotee is not ambitious. We have no ambition."

Seeing the parent's discomfort, Kīrtanānanda Mahārāja quickly added, "What Prabhupada means to say is that the devotees have no material ambition."

"No!" Śrīla Prabhupāda replied. "We have no ambition. The devotee is not at all ambitious. We just want to serve Kṛṣṇa."

Śrīla Prabhupāda always knew the exact point he was making, even if others did not. Sometimes disciples would try to interpret Śrīla Prabhupāda's statements, thinking that cultural differences prevented his guests from understanding Śrīla Prabhupāda.

His Divine Grace always knew whom he was dealing with,

what they meant to say, and exactly what he wanted them to understand.

There are hundreds of devotees all over the world to whom Śrīla Prabhupāda spoke only a few sentences. They will tell you that those few words were exactly what they needed to hear, to sustain them to this day. There are some to whom he never spoke. He just glanced at them and it was enough to keep them in Kṛṣṇa Consciousness. I do not know anything about my spiritual master except that he perfectly presented Kṛṣṇa Consciousness to us and, if one remains faithful to him and his instructions, their life will be successful.

Jai Śrīla Prabhupāda!

6

"This little neglect will snowball."

May 25, 1972 ISKCON Los Angeles, California

While in New Dvārakā, Śrīla Prabhupāda liked to take his morning walk on the beach. Included in the group one morning were Kīrtanānanda Swami, Kulādri, a young bhakta about seventeen years old, and myself. During the walk, the bhakta spotted a large sand crab scurrying along the sand. He stopped to watch it, while the rest of us walked with Śrīla Prabhupāda. The ever-observant Śrīla Prabhupāda said, "This boy is too much attached to material things. This little neglect will snowball. Everything comes, first little things and then big things."

The walk continued with the boy catching up to the rest of us after a minute. No one brought up the incident to the young bhakta. When we arrived back in New Vṛndāvana a week later the boy left the temple and was not seen again, as Śrīla Prabhupāda predicted.

Śrīla Prabhupāda, please stamp my forehead with the words, "Keep at the lotus feet of Jagat Guru." Without your direction, I may also end up walking with crabs.

7

"I still want to run up the stairs..."

June 14, 1972 ISKCON Los Angeles, California

One morning after Śrīla Prabhupāda's walk, a group of five or six devotees stood in the downstairs hallway and watched as he walked upstairs using his cane.

"Jai, Śrīla Prabhupāda!" we gratefully chanted.

He turned toward us with an endearing and beautiful smile.

"I was just thinking," he said. "When I was young, I would run up the stairs. Now that same desire is there. I still want to run up the stairs, but due to this body, now I can't run. I still want to do all these things, like when I was young. I want to be active, but the body is very limiting."

He continued walking up the stairs as we paid our heartfelt obeisances.

Śrīla Prabhupāda had voluntarily accepted so many inconveniences to save us from this foolishly gross bodily conception of life. I witnessed the majesty of Prabhupada's līlā while personally serving him, but there were many painful periods as well.

The fact that Śrīla Prabhupāda experienced these discomforts will never diminish his greatness, but magnify it. This is the unlimited mercy of the pure devotee. Who can be this magnanimous?

PART TWO

Twice Around the World in 481 Days

September 7, 1972 to December 31, 1973

ഗ 8 ഗ

My first service: "Wash this."

September 7, 1972 ISKCON New Vṛndāvana, West Virginia

On the Eve of Becoming Śrīla Prabhupāda's Personal Servant

Śrīla Prabhupāda had been in New Vṛndāvana for a week, and all I had seen was the inside of the Bahulaban kitchen. I was extremely envious of my god-brothers and god-sisters, who had been going up the hill to see Śrīla Prabhupāda and hearing him speak every day. I was cooking for a few hundred devotees from 3:30 am until 9:00 pm. They all came to see Śrīla Prabhupāda during the annual Janmāṣṭamī festival. Since I did not have time to chant my rounds, I was distressed. While visiting Los Angeles, I had grown attached to having Śrīla

Prabhupāda's personal association and reading Kṛṣṇa Book in his garden. Now my self-pity was mounting.

At approximately 9:00 pm I was lamenting my misfortune when Kīrtanānanda Mahārāja came into the kitchen with a huge smile on his face.

"Guess what?" he said. "You are going to be Prabhupada's personal servant. You'll be leaving tomorrow morning with him to go to Pittsburgh."

I was speechless, it happened so quickly that I did not have time to think about it. I was feeling elated, nervous and exhausted, all at the same time.

At 6:00 am, Kīrtanānanda Swami brought me to Madhuvana, which was a small, one-story farmhouse where Śrīla Prabhupāda was staying. I was still in a state of shock. We walked into the small sitting room and I offered my obeisances.

"This is Śrutakīrti, Śrīla Prabhupāda," Kīrtanānanda said. "He cooks very nicely."

"That's very good," Śrīla Prabhupāda said, smiling.

"But, he doesn't know how to massage," Kīrtanānanda continued.

"That's all right," Śrīla Prabhupāda said. "Anybody can massage. It is very easy."

Then, Śrīla Prabhupāda picked up a lota on the floor by his desk and said in a deep voice, "OK. Come with me."

He went out the back door of the farmhouse and walked to the edge of the pavement. He stopped there for a moment and turned to me.

"All right, wait here," he instructed.

Śrīla Prabhupāda walked about another 50 feet into a wooded area. After a few minutes, he returned to the edge of the pavement where I stood according to his instructions. As he walked by me, he handed me the lota and said, "All right. Wash this with some dirt and water." He then walked back into the farmhouse.

It was wonderful how he dealt with me that morning. There was no chit-chat, no "please" or "thank you." He immediately let me know that my position was to be his menial servant, assisting him in whatever way he wanted and taking care of his bodily necessities. I was in complete bliss knowing what my service was. I had been given the most wonderful service of taking care of the transcendental body of the servitor of God.

This was the first day of my life. For the first time I could understand what my body and mind were meant for. Unfortunately, due to my youthful restlessness and inability to take sincerely to the process of Kṛṣṇa Consciousness, I lost my service after a few short years. Now, with great regret, I am begging the Supreme Lord Kṛṣṇa to please give this fool another chance to serve my spiritual father.

Śrīla Prabhupāda, without you, I feel very lost and alone. I do not know what to do with myself. It is very painful. My beloved spiritual master, I regret having wasted so much time in sense gratification. Śrīla Prabhupāda, my desire is to continue being your menial servant. I wish to be with you, cleaning your lota.

9

"...I just wanted to see how quick you are."

September 8, 1972 ISKCON Pittsburgh, Pennsylvania

This was my first full day as Śrīla Prabhupāda's personal servant. My only training had been watching one massage that Sudama Mahārāja had given Śrīla Prabhupāda.

"When Śrīla Prabhupāda rings the bell, go immediately to his room and ask how you can serve him," I was instructed.

It was about 2:00 pm. The bell rang. I nervously trotted into Śrīla Prabhupāda's room and offered my obeisances. Sitting up I asked, "What can I do, Śrīla Prabhupāda?"

He smiled and said, "Oh, nothing. I just wanted to see how quick you are."

After successfully completing my first mission, I went back to my room and relaxed, for the first time in the last twenty-four hours. Śrīla Prabhupāda was expertly putting me at ease with his sense of humour, gentleness and kindness.

It was the first time Śrīla Prabhupāda rang his bell and called me into his room. Over the next two years I walked into his room and offered obeisances thousands of times. From the first day, he let me know it was something that would always be exciting and rewarding. It did not matter whether I went in to take Prabhupada his lunch, or to be chastised for being inattentive in my service. He always exhibited the qualities of a pure devotee, and made me proud to be the servant of the servant of Kṛṣṇa.

10

"...they are better that way, if you can do it."

September 11, 1972 ISKCON Dallas, Texas

Those last few days had been the most wonderful days I had experienced in Kṛṣṇa Consciousness, despite the fact that I did not know what I was doing. I had given Śrīla Prabhupāda three massages and after each one his only comment was, "Thank you very much."

On the previous day he came into the kitchen and showed me how to prepare his lunch in the cooker. He made dahl and vegetables using the same chaunce and showed me how to roll chapatis without a rolling pin. He said they are better that way, if you can do it.

He again cooked his own lunch for my benefit. He made three vegetables, dahl, and rice. I made the chapatis. He told me that in the mornings he desired a little fruit with milk and fruit in the late afternoon -- nothing more. He stressed the fact that he only wants small portions on his plate.

I learned so much in a few days, more than how to make chapatis without a rolling pin and how to spice. I was experiencing what life was like with a pure devotee of the Lord. Every moment was full of lessons. I could understand Lord Caitanya's statement, that by even a moment's association with a pure devotee, one can achieve all perfection. Every word he spoke and every movement made was in the service of his spiritual master. If one follows his example, one will become Kṛṣṇa Conscious.

11

"Sruto"

September 12, 1972 ISKCON Dallas, Texas

Śrīla Prabhupāda rang his bell to call me. I went into his sitting room and offered my obeisances. When I sat up, he smiled and said, "Śrutakīrti, your name is too long. I will call you Sruto." The next few days His Divine Grace playfully called me "Sruto." My affection for him increased immensely. Śrīla Prabhupāda's personalizing my name was so endearing.

Another night, during our stay in Dallas, Śrīla Prabhupāda stayed up until 11:30 pm enlivening us with discussions. I felt tired, but unable to pull myself away from such sweet talks.

Śrīla Prabhupāda, when we left Dallas you never called me 'Sruto' again. It did not matter what name you called me, my great fortune was that you were calling me to your room. In 1975 at Kṛṣṇa Balarāma Mandir, Tamāl Kṛṣṇa Mahārāja told me one day we would all be in the Spiritual world and you would ring your bell and ask, "Where is Śrutakīrti?" I am longing for that day.

12

"... so I take a nap after lunch"

September 12, 1972 ISKCON Dallas, Texas

On different occasions, Śrīla Prabhupāda spoke about sleep. When I first became his servant, he called me into his room after he had taken a short nap following lunch. This was at the Dallas temple when Śrīla Prabhupāda visited the gurukula facility. He asked me if I had taken rest after eating my lunch. I said no. This was not something that was done at that time.

"I am an old man," he said. "I cannot sleep very long at one time, so I take a nap after lunch."

I had been with Śrīla Prabhupāda only a few days, but his humility had already captured my heart. On another occasion, when he was getting ready to take rest in the evening, he said to me, "Whenever I go to take rest, I think; 'now I am going to waste my time.'"

Śrīla Prabhupāda never wasted his time. I was only twenty years old when I was his servant, but I had a difficult time keeping up with him as he travelled around the world enlivening his disciples. Śrīla Prabhupāda was seventy-five years old then.

Sometimes on his morning walks, his disciples would look at each other, shake their heads and wonder when he was going to go back to the temple because they were getting tired of walking.

13

"Everyone is a servant..."

September 19, 1972 ISKCON Los Angeles, California
Śrīla Prabhupāda's Garden

One evening, while seated in his garden, Śrīla Prabhupāda sat with his back very straight and his eyes widened.

"*govindam ādi-puruṣaṁ tam ahaṁ bhajāmi*," he chanted. "This is our pride. We are servants to the most regal person, Kṛṣṇa. Everyone is a servant, but our pride is that we are servants to Kṛṣṇa. *govindam ādi-puruṣaṁ tam ahaṁ bhajāmi.*"

We sat at your feet with our eyes fixed on you, waiting for more words of nectar. You looked at your young American disciples, sitting before you, and smiled. Then with a laugh you stated, "He may or may not be God. It doesn't matter. We love Kṛṣṇa anyway."

They were wonderful words and we loved to hear them. You could make the most profound statements seem simple and elegant. That is the value of a moments association with you. If one is fortunate enough to understand these few words, they can become pure devotees of the Supreme Lord Kṛṣṇa.

Śrīla Prabhupāda, our pride is that we are followers of the dearest servant of Kṛṣṇa. Who could ask for anything more?

14

"Tell them to be quiet!"

September 24, 1972 ISKCON Los Angeles, California

Śrīla Prabhupāda took great pleasure in hearing his disciples chant the Mahā-mantra, but sometimes he wanted them to do it elsewhere. The former temple room in New Dvārakā, which now houses a museum, was beneath Śrīla Prabhupāda's quarters. One afternoon, a male devotee was chanting japa very loudly in the temple room. Śrīla Prabhupāda was resting and so were Śrī Śrī Rukmini Dvārakādisa. Śrīla Prabhupāda did not even ring his bell to call me. He opened the door of his room and shouted down the stairway, "Tell that devotee that the Deities are taking rest and that he should be quiet. Tell them to be quiet."

Śrīla Prabhupāda was very humble. His primary concern was the welfare of the deities and teaching his disciples that Kṛṣṇa is non-different from His deity form. He could have said that he was resting and did not want to be disturbed, but that was not the way he saw it.

15

"I have given you sandeśa, rasgulla and sweet balls."

September 27, 1972 ISKCON Los Angeles, California

The following is an excerpt from a letter I wrote to Kīrtanānanda Mahārāja three weeks after leaving New Vṛndāvana and becoming Śrīla Prabhupāda's personal servant:

"I am beginning to understand that anything in connection with Śrīla Prabhupāda is truly nectarean. It is his causeless mercy that I have finally found a preaching engagement I am really attached to - that is, telling other devotees about the glorious activities of our beloved spiritual master. Every word spoken and every step taken by him is a source of pleasure for thousands of disciples around the world. It is Prabhupada alone who can turn wretched lives into something worthwhile. He accepts the most insignificant service as a great deal.

While engaged in talking about New Vṛndāvana during Prabhupada's massage yesterday I mentioned how we had been doing arati to the cows. At that point, Prabhupada frowned. I asked if that was okay to do and he said, 'No.' I asked if there was anything special to do for the cows. He said, 'Keep them clean, brush them nicely, bathe them, and also you can polish their horns and hooves.'

Prabhupada also received your sandeśa yesterday. I put two on his plate last night at his request, along with pineapple and hot milk. He bit into one and said, 'Kīrtanānanda Mahārāja made first-class sandeśa.' He then said how sandeśa and rasagullā are called 'Bengali sweets' and how they are 'standard.' He has been criticizing L.A.'s making of concocted sweets - sweets with puffed rice, carob, powdered milk, food colouring, and peanut butter - in different combinations that he did not care for. He said, 'I have given you sandeśa, rasagullā, and sweet balls. These are standard sweets and are very good. Why do they go to these different things?'

Consequently, last night I made cheese and turned it into sandeśa this morning. I gave him one of the sandeśa you had made and one I had made with his lunch. He ate both. When he was finished, I asked him how the sandeśa was. His face lit up and he said, 'Did you make them?' I told him what I had done and he said they were very good. I am really happy because sandeśa is one of his favourite sweets."

Śrīla Prabhupāda, absolute truth never changes. Twenty-five years have passed since I wrote this letter to Kīrtanānanda Mahārāja. By your grace, I have rediscovered "a preaching engagement I am really attached to." I pray that I never again let so many empty years pass by without attempting to glorify my magnificent spiritual master. Please give me one more opportunity to prepare sandeśa for your lunch. In this way, I can appreciate how you kindly encouraged me by opening your eyes wide and exclaiming, "This is very good."

16

"The devotees give their services to all for free ..."

October 2, 1972 ISKCON Los Angeles, California

One day in Śrīla Prabhupāda's room in Los Angeles, a psychiatrist criticized the devotees because he felt they forced the public to accept their services. Śrīla Prabhupāda quickly pointed out that this made the devotees better than him. He also said that the devotees give their services to all for free by going to them, but the psychiatrist makes people come to him and then charges them. The psychiatrist fell silent.

The psychiatrist could understand that Śrīla Prabhupāda was not interested in taking anything from anyone. His only desire was to give Kṛṣṇa to everyone he met. He gave others the opportunity to engage in devotional service, the highest welfare work. He is our Ever Well Wisher.

∽ 17 ∽

"Wherever there is Tulasī, it is Vṛndāvana"

October 3, 1972 ISKCON Los Angeles, California

While in New Dvārakā, Śrīla Prabhupāda would go into his garden every evening around sunset. He often stayed for two or three hours. Sometimes I was alone with His Divine Grace and sometimes other devotees and guests joined him as well. Despite being in the midst of smog-filled Los Angeles, Śrīla Prabhupāda's garden seemed to be part of the spiritual world.

He often commented on how much he liked this garden, where more than thirty Tulasī plants flourished. He spoke of this garden as his favourite place despite having travelled the world.

"Wherever there is Tulasī," Śrīla Prabhupāda said, "it is Vṛndāvana."

Wherever Śrīla Prabhupāda travelled was Vṛndāvana. Kṛṣṇa and Vṛndāvana resided in his heart. He did not require anything else. He lived very simply. In his room in every city, his sitting place was on a cushion on the floor. There was always a small desk in front of him. From this spot, he managed the worldwide society ISKCON, and from the same spot, very early in the morning, he would translate his books. Sometimes he would say we should live by the principle 'simple living and high thinking'. He showed by example how to do it. He is our ācārya .

18

"The sky is the colour of Kṛṣṇa."

October 4, 1972 ISKCON Los Angeles, California

Śrīla Prabhupāda's garden

One evening, while in his garden, Śrīla Prabhupāda looked at the sky and said; "So, is the sky the colour of Kṛṣṇa?"

"In Kṛṣṇa Book it says that Kṛṣṇa is dark bluish like a thundercloud," a disciple answered.

"The sky is the colour of Kṛṣṇa," Śrīla Prabhupāda explained. "It is the light from Kṛṣṇa's bodily effulgence that makes the sky blue."

Śrīla Prabhupāda gave us the simplest ways to always remember Kṛṣṇa. One must look at the sky every day. By his mercy, we can look at the sky and immediately remember Kṛṣṇa.

19

"This is the common etiquette"

October 6, 1972 ISKCON Berkeley

Śrīla Prabhupāda stayed in Berkeley for a few days at the cottage of some well-wishers. His disciples showed him around the house.

"Is there any prasādam?" Śrīla Prabhupāda asked, after being seated.

There was nothing available.

"So, bring some fruit," he instructed. "Bring something for washing my feet. Bring a towel and some water. This is common etiquette. You should wash a person's feet when they arrive."

Śrīla Prabhupāda did not need anything from us, but he mercifully showed us the proper way to honour a guest, what to speak of the spiritual master.

The devotees quickly prepared the items.

"Wash up to my knees," Śrīla Prabhupāda told his disciple who was washing his feet. "This kind of foot bath refreshes one's whole body after travelling."

One very hot day in Vṛndāvana, Śrīla Prabhupāda again mentioned this fact after returning to his quarters from an engagement. He immediately went into the bathroom and washed his feet and legs with cool water.

"After going out, doing this, the whole body becomes rejuvenated," he said.

He taught us the ancient standard of Vedic etiquette complete with practical application. He enlivened us with this knowledge. Jai Śrīla Prabhupāda!

20

"What can you say to a person in three minutes?"

October 7, 1972 ISKCON Berkeley

Śrīla Prabhupāda said that our real preaching was distributing books.

"What can you say to a person in three minutes?" he asked. "But if he reads one page of a book it may turn him around. However you have to do it, that is okay. But, if you get the person angry and he doesn't take a book, then that is your foolishness."

"My Guru Mahārāja daily printed a small paper," Śrīla Prabhupāda said. "The paper cost a few cents and whenever a brahmacārī came back from the streets and said he had sold one, Śrīla Bhaktisiddhānta Sarasvatī became very happy and said, 'Oh, that is very nice what you have done. You are a very good boy.'"

Purity is the force. Śrīla Prabhupāda is the pure devotee and we are his humble servants. It is our good fortune to be able to distribute his words in book form. He said, "They are not my words, they are Kṛṣṇa's words. Just by reading even one sentence, it is possible to become Kṛṣṇa Conscious. "Śrīla Prabhupāda lives forever in his books.

21

"Adult's fairyland"

October 7, 1972 Oakland, California

It was a cold October morning when, while walking through Merit Park in downtown Oakland, we passed a small zoo with a large sign in front of it that read, "Children's Fairyland."

"Children's Fairyland," Śrīla Prabhupāda read.

Pointing over to the horizon, at the skyscrapers in the distance he added, "Adult's fairyland." He continued walking as his young disciples looked at each other and smiled.

It was what we lived for on a morning walk with Śrīla Prabhupāda. The words of a transcendentalist. Someone who could cut through our illusion and explain things in simple, concise terms. He said no more about it and he did not need to. In thirty seconds, he exposed the folly of modern civilization.

22

"Oh, this is nice."

October 7, 1972 Berkeley, California

One evening, Śrīla Prabhupāda spoke at the University of California in Berkeley, the heart of the hippie capital. The San Francisco devotees enthusiastically received him and relished his lecture. They prepared barrels of popcorn and distributed it following Śrīla Prabhupāda's lecture.

"What is that?" His Divine Grace asked.

"Popcorn, Śrīla Prabhupāda," Jayānanda explained. "Would you like some?"

"Yes, give me some," Śrīla Prabhupāda said.

The devotees gave him popcorn, which was being distributed, in little bags printed with the Hare Kṛṣṇa mantra. Śrīla Prabhupāda ate the fluffy, spiced kernels with great delight.

"Oh, this is nice," Śrīla Prabhupāda told them.

All the devotees, especially those who had cooked and distributed the prasādam, felt overwhelmed with pleasure. Now they were certain their offering had been accepted and their lives were successful. When Śrīla Prabhupāda finished eating the popcorn, he endeared himself to all the Vaisnavas present by contentedly leaving his hand in the little popcorn bag. It was sweet. The entire devotees' attention focused on every movement of Śrīla Prabhupāda. The childlike actions of His Divine Grace continued to fill the hearts of the devotees with enthusiasm.

Overjoyed, the devotees then performed Hare Nama Sankīrtan on Telegraph Avenue, a place famous for its hippie inhabitants. On the way home, Śrīla Prabhupāda continued to inspire the devotees by slowly driving past the sankīrtan party. They energetically chanted and danced being encouraged by Śrīla Prabhupāda's present supervision.

The next night Śrīla Prabhupāda had another preaching engagement. This time, the devotees brought Śrīla Prabhupāda popcorn and offered it to him.

"No, I am old," Śrīla Prabhupāda said. "I cannot do things like that very often. It is good, but it is very difficult for me to digest." He refused saying, "It is very good. I like it."

They were pleasing words to his young disciples. We knew that Śrīla Prabhupāda could do whatever he wanted and we never considered him old. As we drove back in the car, he explained to me that if he ate something in the evening that was difficult to digest, it would interfere with his rising at 2:00 am to do his translating work.

> *Śrīla Prabhupāda's activities focused on his service and there was an abundance of it. Translating books, initiating and training disciples and opening centres. He kept his bodily maintenance of eating and sleeping to a minimum. Just what was needed to maintain health and perform his devotional service, and he wanted us to do the same, while using our common sense.*
>
> *Jai Śrīla Prabhupāda!*

23

"They are not chips!"

October 7, 1972 ISKCON San Francisco

I had been Śrīla Prabhupāda's personal servant for one month. I was beginning to feel comfortable and knowledgeable in my duties. Little did I know that this qualified me for a major setback.

One evening Śrīla Prabhupāda asked me to prepare puris,

potato chips and hot milk. We were not staying at the temple, but at the cottage of a young couple who were friends of the devotees. Before Śrīla Prabhupāda's arrival, the devotees had spent hours cleaning the cottage.

The kitchen facility was poor. Fortunately, there was ghee on the stove, so a meal could be prepared. Śrīla Prabhupāda had asked for "potato chips." I was anxious to prepare them, but had no experience. Making the puris was easy enough, but took time to prepare. It was getting late and I did not want Śrīla Prabhupāda to have to wait any longer. I peeled some potatoes, sliced them as thin as possible with a potato peeler, and fried them in very hot ghee. They came out resembling potato chips, but not exactly like any chips I had ever seen.

I felt very fortunate to serve the living representative of Kṛṣṇa. Śrīla Prabhupāda was my living deity and he mercifully reciprocated with me. I rushed to His Divine Grace with a dish of potato chips, one hot puri and a cup of hot milk.

"What are these?" Śrīla Prabhupāda firmly inquired pointing to the chips. "Potato chips, Śrīla Prabhupāda," I answered, a bit bewildered.

"They are not chips! This is not what I wanted."

Seeing my pain he said, "Anyway . . . go on. Leave it." I felt terrible. This was the first time I had failed in my service to my Guru Mahārāja. I felt like dying. The offering had been unacceptable. I went back to the kitchen and cooked the next puri. Returning to Śrīla Prabhupāda's quarters, I placed the puri on his plate and offered my obeisances. When I sat up, he looked at me with a big smile.

"These are very good," Śrīla Prabhupāda assured me. "It is all right. They are very nice."

I breathed a sigh of relief and replied, "Oh, good! Thank you, Śrīla Prabhupāda." I was in bliss. I did not know whether he really liked them or he just said it to make me feel better; either way it was wonderful. It felt terrific to have someone care about me so much. I brought him another puri and waited for him to finish. Picking up his plates, I was thrilled to see he had eaten all of the so-called "potato chips." Śrīla Prabhupāda mercifully accepted my bumbling efforts.

Months later, while in India, I realized that "chips" are the British equivalent to American "french fries." Being inexperienced, I had misunderstood. I knew then that Śrīla Prabhupāda had wanted french fries. I again made him chips, but according to his instructions, "thin and cripsy." Note the spelling discrepancy. It is not an error. Śrīla Prabhupāda often used endearing words. I preferred his use of the word "cripsy" for "crispy." It sounded crunchier.

Śrīla Prabhupāda, how you responded to my 'chips' was another example of your kindness towards me. I know that I was so young and foolish when I was serving you. I was twenty-one years old and did not know how to do anything. There were thousands of others similar to me. You dealt with all of us in such a caring, patient manner. It was not difficult to become attached to you. It was difficult not to. Thank you for always showing us how a devotee acts. Once, a devotee entered your room and began to shut the door. He asked you if he should close it. You said, "You can leave it open. We have no secrets." Please help me live my life with an open door.

24

"That Requires a Little Intelligence"

October 12, 1972 Manila, Philippines

We arrived in Manila, Philippines on October 11, 1972. I had been Śrīla Prabhupāda's servant for a month now. It was the first time I had ever been outside of the United States. I did not have to arrange for my passport, visa or airline ticket. It was all done by Śrīla Prabhupāda's secretary, Śyāmasundara. My service was to take care of His Divine Grace's personal needs twenty-four hours a day. I still could not believe my great fortune. While I was his personal servant, it did not matter what country I was in. I travelled around the world with him five times in two years and went to so many countries, visiting big cities and small. The only places I saw were the airport, the temple facilities and wherever Śrīla Prabhupāda went for his morning walk. To this day, I still haven't seen the Taj Mahal. Śrīla Prabhupāda had a 'mission' in every sense of the word. He never deviated from it.

Just before lunch on the 12th, I was massaging Śrīla Prabhupāda in his hotel room. Bhūrijana prabhu was present for the massage. While I was rubbing the mustard oil on his back, Śrīla Prabhupāda said, "My god-brothers criticize me, that I have allowed women to live in our temples. This is not done in India. Only brahmacārīs can live. But I have become successful because I have made this adjustment. Although they criticize me, their Gaudiya Maṭhas are empty. The only time they have people coming is during Gaura Pūrṇimā to Māyāpur for parikramā. And who is coming for parikramā? Widows. Women in white. Because I have made this adjustment I was successful."

He then became quiet. I began to think about the amazing 'adjustment' he had made. He then nodded, which meant I was finished massaging his back and should move to the side to start on his arms and chest. Seated next to him, I continued to think of what he had said. The room was quiet. I rarely asked him a question. So many devotees asked questions. When others were around, he was always busy preaching, solving problems and helping his disciples in so many ways. I considered it a part of my service to allow Śrīla Prabhupāda some peace and quiet, but in one paragraph, he had given his formula for spreading Kṛṣṇa Consciousness in the West, something no one else was able to do. I tried to formulate a question and repeated it to myself several times. This was not unusual for me. I have a tendency to think about what I am going to say and this time I wanted to ask it just right. Finally, convinced it was a worthwhile question, I said, "Prabhupada, how can we tell the difference between making an adjustment and changing a principle?" Śrīla Prabhupāda closed his eyes and I continued to rub his body. Finally, he opened his eyes and responded. "That requires a little intelligence." He did not say anything more on the topic during the massage.

Śrīla Prabhupāda, I consider your words on that day an understatement. It again shows your level of humility. No one but you could have made such a radical decision. To this day sādhus in India will not travel outside its borders considering it to dangerous for their spiritual life. You were "Abhaya Carana," fearless. You were unafraid of the decadence of the West. You did not care for the criticism of your god-brothers. Your only concern was to fulfill the desires of the previous Ācāryas, deliver the fallen souls throughout the world, and bring them to their home in Māyāpur Dhāma, at the lotus feet of Śrī Caitanya Mahāprabhu and Lord Nityānanda.

25

"Now tomorrow you must serve her"

October 16, 1972 Rādhā Dāmodara Temple, Vṛndāvana, India

At this time, I had been cooking for Śrīla Prabhupāda and massaging his transcendental body everyday for five weeks. I never understood why I was given this great fortune, but one day something new occurred to change my service to His Divine Grace. Yamunā Devī was in Śrīla Prabhupāda's kitchen preparing his lunch. This had been one of my main services. After all, His Divine Grace taught me for two days in Dallas how to use the cooker!

That day, after massaging Śrīla Prabhupāda, I bathed and dressed. Since I did not have to prepare his lunch, I did not know what to do with myself, so I walked around the temple compound. I had never been there before and felt a little lost, both in my service and in India. It was very different being in Vṛndāvana. I tried to appreciate my good fortune being in Kṛṣṇa's home, and with His pure devotee.

Finally, I made my way to Śrīla Prabhupāda's kitchen. Upon entering, I offered my obeisances. I never considered how offensive I was to take such liberties. Śrīla Prabhupāda was sitting there taking prasādam. He was in the very spot where he had spent years devising his plan to conquer the world with Kṛṣṇa Consciousness. He looked up with a beautiful glance and asked,

"So, you have taken prasādam?"

"No," I replied. "I have just taken bath."

"Oh, so you haven't taken prasādam," Śrīla Prabhupāda responded charmingly. "Yamunā , fix him a plate of prasādam."

"No, that's all right," I said. "I will wait until you are finished."

"No. Sit down and take prasādam," he told me. I happily complied with his instruction, rascal that I was. It was one of the sweetest moments of my life. I was taking prasādam with Śrīla Prabhupāda, just the two of us. In Vṛndāvana at Rādhā Dāmodara Temple, the mercy of the pure devotee is unlimited.

I was not prepared for what followed. After tasting Yamunā Devī 's cooking, I realized I had never before tasted prasādam. In addition, I realized I had never cooked anything fit to be offered. Yamunā Devī was an empowered devotee of the Lord, sent here to sumptuously feed Śrīla Prabhupāda. Each preparation tasted incredible. She made perfect chapatis. The subjis tasted as if they came from the spiritual world. Seated with Śrīla Prabhupāda I realized what a disservice I had performed by cooking for him. He sometimes said I cooked "nice American prasādam." Now I understood what he meant. Yamunā 's cooking was so transcendental that it seemed like I had never eaten before.

"So, you like?" Śrīla Prabhupāda asked as we were finishing.

"Yes, Śrīla Prabhupāda," I enthusiastically said. "Very much."

He smiled and said, "So, today she has fixed your lunch. Now, tomorrow you cook for her. This is the Vedic custom. Today she has done some service for you, now tomorrow you must serve her."

"Oh, yes, Prabhupada," I said.

At other times Śrīla Prabhupāda said, "One has to always be ready to serve a person, not simply you are always accepting service. You call someone 'prabhu'. Prabhu means master. What is the question of you accepting service from your master? You are servant and you are calling them prabhu and accepting so much service from your master. Therefore, I am calling you 'prabhu'. It means I must render service. This attitude must be there, that I am everyone's servant because I am calling everyone 'prabhu'."

I never did cook for Yamunā Devī . That would not have been of service. It would have been an austerity for her to have to eat my "American prasādam." Mataji, please forgive me for accepting service from you.

Śrīla Prabhupāda, please forgive me for not following your instructions. I pray to be given the ability to serve my spiritual master with the expertise of a surrendered soul, such as Yamunā Devī dasi.

26

"Get someone up here with some Intelligence"

October 16, 1972 Rādhā Dāmodara Temple, Vṛndāvana, India

During the month of Kārtika, Śrīla Prabhupāda gave classes on the Nectar of Devotion every evening in the courtyard near the Bhajana Kutir of Śrīla Rupa Gosvāmī. Before arriving, Śrīla Prabhupāda spoke many times about doing this, and was very excited. He said that, for the benefit of his disciples, all the classes would be in English, not in Hindi. On the plane to Delhi, he told me, "You can read from the *Nectar of Devotion* and then I will give purports." I was very happy to be given such an opportunity.

The first evening, Pradyumna took the service of reading from the *Nectar of Devotion*. That was all right with me. I had to record the lecture and take care of Śrīla Prabhupāda's personal needs such as fanning him when required. The courtyard was filled with his disciples as well as many Brijbasis. Most of them did not understand English, but that did not matter. They were happy to have the association of a saintly person.

It was still light out during class. Parrots were busy getting back to their branches for the night. The monkeys were creating havoc, as usual. The atmosphere was transcendental, except for the flies. They were buzzing around Śrīla Prabhupāda while he was speaking. It was a great opportunity for me to render service. I picked up the cāmara fan and stood by my guru. I twirled the fan just like a pujari performing arati before the Deities. I felt so proud being able to perform such a service in front of my god-brothers. Up and down I waved the fan hardly noticing that the flies were still bothering Śrīla Prabhupāda. At one point, he lifted his arm and waved it across his face to chase the flies away. I was so absorbed in feelings of grandeur that it never occurred to me that I was not rendering any service. I never came close to solving the problem.

Finally, the cow dung hit the fan. My spiritual master glared at me and shouted, "Get someone up here with some intelligence." I stood motionless for what felt like a year.

Immediately a young brahmacārī named Kuñjabihārī took the fan from my sweaty hand and stood next to Śrīla Prabhupāda. He began to fan Śrīla Prabhupāda with great vigour.

I began fiddling with the tape recorder. My mind was reeling along with the reel to reel. I felt humbled, smaller than 1/10,000 part the tip of a hair! I watched Kuñjabihārī with amazement. It seemed like he could put out a forest fire with the intensity of his fanning. No fly was foolish enough to hang around as long as he was there. Seconds later, all the flies were gone. Śrīla Prabhupāda never stopped speaking to his disciples throughout this ordeal. Just as I was starting to breathe again, Śrīla Prabhupāda looked at Kuñjabihārī with a smile and nodded approvingly of his disciple's devotional service.

All I remember was getting up at the end of the lecture and walking alone toward Śrīla Prabhupāda's quarters. Before

I could get inside, a brahmacārī came up to me and said, "Śrutakīrti, you are so fortunate to get chastised like that by Śrīla Prabhupāda." I forced a strained smile and said, "Yes."

This was the first time Śrīla Prabhupāda publicly chastised me. It was difficult to accept. He was so kind to have cut down my false pride. He has blessed me with that repeatedly over the years. He must do it because I still haven't learned the simple truth that I am "fool number one." He keeps trying to teach me that service is for his pleasure, not mine.

> *Śrīla Prabhupāda, please give me another chance to fan you. No! I am still proud. Please, bless me with the desire to fan your disciple, Kuñjabihārī dāsa. He pleased you with his service. That is the way to make advancement in Kṛṣṇa Consciousness.*

27

"Just see how intelligent this monkey is..."

October 17, 1972 Rādhā Dāmodara Temple, Vṛndāvana, India

During this visit, Śrīla Prabhupāda regularly spoke in his sitting room. Local residents offered fruits and flowers by placing them at his lotus feet.

One evening in the middle of Śrīla Prabhupāda's lecture, a monkey darted into the room and lunged for the bananas. Vishaka dasi quickly threw her chaddar over the monkey and tugged at the bananas as he ran past her. She managed to get most of the bananas, but within a few seconds, the monkey was gone with a prize banana in his hand.

"Just see how intelligent this monkey is," Śrīla Prabhupāda said. "This shows that in their own respect all living entities are intelligent. How long do you think it would have taken you to do that, run in and out of here and get the bananas? This monkey is so intelligent in regards to his eating. He can do it in a few seconds. Practically no one even saw him. He just took the bananas and ran out. This is what it is like in the material world. Everyone is very expert in their own sphere. So, we have to become expert devotees, not expert like the monkeys."

The entire incident lasted about four seconds. Even though Śrīla Prabhupāda had been lecturing, he was aware of everything going on around him. Śrīla Prabhupāda was always aware of activities around him. He was expert at doing more than one thing at a time.

28

"Only Kṛṣṇa can know everything"

ISKCON Mayapur, India April 8, 1975

On a morning walk in Mayapur, a devotee asked Śrīla Prabhupāda, "Does the spiritual master know everything?"

"The spiritual master knows everything that Kṛṣṇa wants him to know," Śrīla Prabhupāda said. "Only Kṛṣṇa can know everything."

It seemed that Śrīla Prabhupāda knew everything about me. Occasionally, I tried to match wits with Śrīla Prabhupāda only to be quickly, utterly exposed and defeated. The following story is an example.

In May of 1972, I was given second initiation by Śrīla Prabhupāda at the Los Angeles temple. I had driven with Kīrtanānanda Mahārāja and a few other devotees from New Vṛndāvana to Los Angeles in an enclosed van for four days. The ride was hellish, but worth every minute.

The process of getting brahmana initiation was blissful. I went into Śrīla Prabhupāda's quarters and offered my obeisances. He held a new brahmana thread in his hands and whispered the Gāyatrī mantra in my ear. It happened very quickly. When I left his room, I was given a sheet of paper with the mantra on it. After staying for a few days, we took the long drive back to New Vṛndāvana. The return trip, however, did not seem so bad.

Then, one morning about 3:00 am, I was bathing in a muddy pond in New Vṛndāvana. The area was totally dark. I was rushing because I had to prepare the Deities plates for the mangala offering. While throwing a bucket of water over my head, I must have washed my sacred thread off my body. When I discovered it was gone, hours later, I was brought to tears. The very thread that Śrīla Prabhupāda had given me was gone forever. It was a very bad omen and I feared my connection was lost.

October 18, 1972 Rādhā Dāmodara Temple, Vṛndāvana, India

One year later, I became Śrīla Prabhupāda's personal servant. After his morning massage, I always laid fresh clothing on Śrīla Prabhupāda's bed while he bathed. Then, I went into his sitting room, opened his mirror and placed his ball of tilak beside it. I then placed his small, water-filled lota next to these items. After dressing, he sat at his desk, applied tilak and chanted the Gāyatrī mantra.

It was also my service to place a new brahmana thread on his desk every month. I did it either on the day of the full moon, or on an Ekādaśī. Śrīla Prabhupāda chanted on the new thread while holding his old one. The loss of my brahmana initiation thread etched a fault across my heart. I was eager to rectify it. This was my first month in Śrīla Prabhupāda's personal service. Therefore, I was excited to obtain His Divine Grace's prasādam thread and resume my transcendental brahmana connection.

After chanting Gāyatrī, he walked across the veranda to the kitchen where Yamunā Devī was cooking. I walked into his sitting room and picked up his discarded thread only to discover that he had pulled apart each of the threads. I could not believe it, in the two years that followed, he never did that again. I walked out of his room with the thread in my hand and sat on the veranda. I tied a knot in each of the six threads, determined to make my connection again. It did not matter to me that he had broken them. It was still HIS thread. While I contentedly sat on the veranda, Śrīla Prabhupāda walked by after finishing his lunch. I offered my obeisances and he smiled at me.

"The brahmana thread, you have disposed of it?" he asked.

"Not yet, Śrīla Prabhupāda," I said.

"You should bury it underneath the Tulasī plant in the temple courtyard," he instructed. "Put it in the dirt under the roots."

All I could say was, "All right."

I could not believe it. On other occasions, I experienced Śrīla Prabhupāda's mystic power as well. If I wanted something, he always made me ask for it. He seemed to enjoy exposing my desires. I also enjoyed it very much. I could have told him about losing my thread, but I was too ashamed. I did not like to ask Śrīla Prabhupāda for anything. I tried not to ask him questions since so many others were inquiring on a regular basis. I tried to think of what Śrīla Prabhupāda wanted, not what I wanted. However, sometimes my desire would overwhelm me.

Śrīla Prabhupāda, please forgive me for not following your instructions. I never did bury the thread as you asked. Thank you, Śrīla Prabhupāda, for tolerating me.

☙ 29 ☙

"...all he speaks will be perfect"

October 19, 1972 Rādhā Dāmodara Temple, Vṛndāvana, India

It was about 5:30 in the morning and Śrīla Prabhupāda called me into his sitting room wanting to know why Śyāmasundara and Pradyumna were still sleeping.

"I do not know," I replied.

Śrīla Prabhupāda told me to bring them to his room. When we returned, he told us we must conquer over sleep. "Rising early and taking a cold shower is not austerity, but just common sense and good hygiene," Śrīla Prabhupāda said.

Then, revealing a wonderful truth, His Divine Grace told us, "By chanting 16 rounds, following the regulative principles, rising early, reducing one's eating and sleeping, one gets spiritual energy. If one follows these guidelines for 12 years, all he speaks will be perfect!"

You have given us the opportunity to become perfect. You always showed great faith in us and unflinching faith in the Holy Name and your spiritual master's orders. You treated us as Kṛṣṇa's devotees and it made our desire to become a stronger devotee. You came from the Spiritual world and walked among us to deliver the message of Śrī Caitanya Mahāprabhu.

All glories to Śrīla Prabhupāda.

30

"In the sky"

October 21, 1972 Rādhā Dāmodara Temple, Vṛndāvana, India

Brahmacārī: "Śrīla Prabhupāda, it says in one of the Kṛṣṇa book stories that Kṛṣṇa and Balarāma jumped off a mountain eighty-eight miles high. Where is this mountain located?"

Śrīla Prabhupāda: "In the sky."

You answered in an instant. It was a sweet answer that brought smiles to our faces. You always had the right answer. Your disciples were eager to ask questions, just to have the chance to share an intimate moment and you were happy to satisfy their desires.

31

"I'm always moving"

October 21, 1972 Rādhā Dāmodara Temple, Vṛndāvana, India

Brahmacārī: "Śrīla Prabhupāda, I always want to sit by your holy lotus feet!"

Śrīla Prabhupāda: "That will be very difficult because I am always moving."

Śrīla Prabhupāda, one of the qualities I relished most about you was your sense of humour. I was happy to know that one could be a devotee of Kṛṣṇa and also be funny. Once a devotee asked if it was true Mahatma

Gandhi chanted the Holy name of "Rama" when he was shot. You looked at him with a straight face and replied, "I do not know. I was not there." I did not always know how you would respond to your disciples' questions but I always enjoyed your wit.

32

"You should take sannyasa"

October 22, 1972 Rādhā Dāmodara Temple, Vṛndāvana, India

While Śrīla Prabhupāda stayed in Vṛndāvana for the month of Kārtika in 1972, there were many transcendental events. His return to Vṛndāvana was glorious. He left his home at Rādhā Dāmodara temple in 1965 and now he was back with dozens of his initiated disciples from Europe and America. Everyone in Vṛndāvana could see that Śrīla Prabhupāda was successful in preaching Kṛṣṇa Consciousness in the West.

In the evening, he would give class from his Nectar of Devotion, in the courtyard by the Samādhi of ŚrīlaRupa Gosvāmī. This is the same auspicious place that, years before, Śrīla Prabhupāda viewed from his kitchen window, praying to ŚrīlaRupa Gosvāmī as he did his translating. Now, devotees from all over the world were coming to this place to learn the science of Kṛṣṇa Consciousness, the very centre of the spiritual world.

There were about 100 devotees attending the classes morning and evening. They were staying at different ashrams near Rādhā Dāmodara temple. In 1972, there was no ISKCON facility. Living in Vṛndāvana at this time was not so easy for Westerners. For many it was their first trip to India and they were not used to the climate, food and facilities. During the day, the devotees would try to take care of their bodily necessities. Illnesses like malaria, jaundice and dysentery were common.

It was quiet during the day at Rādhā Dāmodara temple and it was unusual to see any of Śrīla Prabhupāda's disciples around this sacred place. One morning however, there was one young brahmacārī that was walking in the temple area, chanting his rounds. Śrīla Prabhupāda could see him from his sitting place and rang his bell. I went into his room and he told me to bring the boy in to see him.

We entered the room together and offered obeisances to Śrīla Prabhupāda. He asked the eighteen year old what his service was. He told Śrīla Prabhupāda that he and Parivrajakācārya , had been travelling around India by themselves, doing some preaching. Śrīla Prabhupāda then asked him what his plans were after leaving Vṛndāvana. He said they planned on going to Vietnam to preach there and distribute books. Śrīla Prabhupāda's eyes became wide and he exclaimed, "Accha!" In 1972, Vietnam was still in the midst of a great war and was a very dangerous place. Śrīla Prabhupāda was impressed with their desire to preach the glories of Lord Caitanya in this war torn country.

He looked at Paramahaṁsa very seriously and said, "Perhaps you should take sannyasa". Paramahaṁsa was visibly surprised by Śrīla Prabhupāda's offer. Śrīla Prabhupāda saw this and advised him by saying, "You go chant your japa by the Samādhi of ŚrīlaRupa Gosvāmī. Pray to him and then you will know what to do."

Paramahaṁsa described to me how he went before the Samādhi and began chanting. The more he chanted the more he began to think sannyasa was a great idea. He returned to Śrīla Prabhupāda the next day and told him they decided they would take sannyasa. Śrīla Prabhupāda told him to go to his secretary, Śyāmasundara and inform him that they would be added to the list of sannyasa candidates. He said Śyāmasundara should take them to Loi Bazaar to get new cloth and bamboo to make their daṇḍas.

When Paramahaṁsa informed Śyāmasundara of Śrīla Prabhupāda's decision he laughed, and told him that he hadn't heard anything about it from Śrīla Prabhupāda, and he was not about to take his word for it. Paramahaṁsa had to convince him to ask Śrīla Prabhupāda so that he would help him get ready.

When other devotees found out about it, some of them could not believe that these two young brahmacārīs, who weren't very well known or experienced, were getting to take sannyasa. They tried to convince Śrīla Prabhupāda that they weren't qualified. They said the boys hadn't been around long enough, did not know the philosophy very well and hadn't even memorized any Sanskrit slokas. It did not matter what anyone said. Śrīla Prabhupāda had made up his mind.

The initiation ceremony took place on the full moon night of Rasa Yatra, the night that Lord Kṛṣṇa dances with the gopīs. It was in the courtyard of Rādhā Dāmodara temple, by the Samādhi of ŚrīlaRupa Gosvāmī. Śrīla Prabhupāda was allowing everyone in Vṛndāvana see how his western disciples were surrendering everything to serve their spiritual master and Kṛṣṇa. It was a transcendental ceremony and Śrīla Prabhupāda told us both ŚrīlaRupa Gosvāmī and Narada Muni were personally present at the fire sacrifice.

Śrīla Prabhupāda, this is the first memory I have written in almost ten years. Please continue to give me your causeless mercy so I can attempt to do some service. Telling this story at this time gives me a small glimpse of your unlimited compassion for all of us and gives me faith that it can extend even to someone as unworthy as me.

During Kārtika in 1972 sitting in your room you stated, "So, I came here, and eventually, by Kṛṣṇa's arrangement, stayed at this most sanctified place, Rādhā Dāmodara. It was here that I began writing. I thought, it may be published, or it may not be published—that does not matter. I will write for purification, that's all."

"Actually, it was my Guru Mahārāja speaking through me. But I was not very expert at writing, as he was. Oh, he was a most erudite man, most refined and expert, a gentleman, a Vaikuṇṭha man. Because I had never written before, there were so many grammatical discrepancies, yet I had to write. The subject matter was so important, so urgent. So I wrote those first three volumes of *Śrīmad-Bhāgavatam*, the First Canto. All of our philosophy, everything you need to know, is in those first three volumes. By Kṛṣṇa's grace, I managed to collect money to get them printed, and I took them with me on the boat to New York.

I did not go to America empty-handed. I went with the complete philosophy of Caitanya Mahāprabhu, written in these rooms, inspired by the Gosvāmīs. That's what is pushing this Kṛṣṇa Consciousness movement. If I have been successful, it's because I have delivered my Guru Mahārāja's message intact, without change or deletion. That is paramparā. The bona fide guru is like the postman delivering a message. He doesn't open the mail and write his own opinion. You may like the message or not, take it up or not—I have done my duty. I have delivered it. And it all began here. Therefore these Rādhā Dāmodara rooms are the hub of the wheel of the spiritual universe."

Excerpt from Vṛndāvana Days by Hayagrīva dāsa.

In this year 2005, I can see your mercy more and more. Your movement continues to spread as thousands more take shelter of you each year. In a Dallas lecture you said, "So keep this standard as you are now keeping, then things will go automatically, and one day people will understand in the [pages of] history that this movement was for saving the human society. That day will come."

By keeping to the standard you have given, everything is possible. As you said, it is very easy. Chant sixteen rounds, follow the regulative principles, and do not give our own opinion. Just deliver the mail.

What is the difficulty?

33

"This is as good as bathing in the Yamunā"

October 25, 1972 Rādhā Dāmodara Temple, Vṛndāvana, India

During a morning walk along the Yamunā River, Śrīla Prabhupāda asked one of us to get some water. Śyāmasundara prabhu brought him a handful. Śrīla Prabhupāda sprinkled a few drops on his head and told us to do the same.

"This is as good as bathing in the Yamunā ," he said.

While we were at the palace at Keshi-ghata, Śrīla Prabhupāda warned the devotees not to dive into the Yamunā because of the many large turtles in the water that could cause possible injury. He was always looking out for our welfare in every way.

34

"You have to chant and hear. That is all."

November 7, 1972 Rādhā Dāmodara Temple, Vṛndāvana, India

Devotee: "Śrīla Prabhupāda, it's very difficult to control

my mind when I chant. It wanders."

Śrīla Prabhupāda: "So what is the controlling of mind? You have to chant and hear. That is all. You have to chant with your tongue, and the sound you hear. What is the question of mind?"

> *Many times your disciples went into your room to ask you how to solve a problem. Mostly the problem evaporated as they sat before you. Being in your room, one could feel the transcendental atmosphere, and looking into your eyes, they became peaceful. You cut through our western mentality with the torchlight of knowledge and mercifully allowed us a place at your lotus feet.*

35

"The Monkey has stolen my shoe."

November 11, 1972 Rādhā Dāmodara Temple, Vṛndāvana, India

During this time, Śrīla Prabhupāda stayed in a room on the second floor of the Rādhā Dāmodara Temple. I do not remember why he did not stay in his usual two rooms on the ground floor. His rooms on the second floor opened onto a large, concrete deck, which formed the roof of his quarters on the first floor. In Vṛndāvana, most of the buildings are made of brick and concrete so the roof is usually a flat, smooth area of concrete that can be used for many purposes.

On the second floor facility, Śrīla Prabhupāda had a sitting room and a separate bedroom. His entourage shared another room. As Śrīla Prabhupāda took his massage on the patio in front of his sitting room, the sun glistened on his sparkling golden skin smeared with mustard oil. After his massage, he bathed in the same spot from a brass bucket filled with water that was naturally warmed by the sun.

Using his lota and this single bucket of warmed water, he took his bath, squatting on the patio in his gamcha. Śrīla Prabhupāda made a point of keeping the maintenance of his body very simple. After taking his bath, he returned to his bedroom and put on the fresh clothing I had laid out on his bed. On this particular day, the weather was very hot, so Śrīla Prabhupāda only wore a dhoti and no kurta.

A few minutes after he went into his room to dress, I heard him shouting. I was still outside on the patio cleaning up. As soon as I heard him shout, I raced into the room. The front door was ajar. I had no idea what was wrong and although I ran in, out of habit, I offered my obeisances. Śrīla Prabhupāda was behind his desk. As I hurriedly sat up and looked toward him, he hurled his ball of tilaka toward my head. It was the size of a golf ball and he threw it with the vigour of a baseball pitcher. It missed my head by inches. I was shocked and frightened.

"What's the matter?" I blurted out.

"That monkey has stolen my shoe," he said, pointing in my direction.

I turned around in time to see one of Vṛndāvana's furry pests run out of the room with Śrīla Prabhupāda's sandal in his grasp.

Monkeys were prolific in this part of the Dhāma and were always looking for a bead bag, glasses, or some other valuable item to steal. They used the items to barter for eatables. I was relieved knowing that my Guru Mahārāja was tossing the tilak at the monkey rather than me. It was an unusual experience to have a ball of tilak whiz by my head. Fortunately, my spiritual master was an expert marksman. The monkey vaulted to the roof of Śrīla Prabhupāda's sitting room and waited.

"This rascal, he has taken my slipper," Śrīla Prabhupāda

said. "Get some pera and come outside."

I grabbed a few milk sweets from the glass jar above Śrīla Prabhupāda's bookcase and followed my guru outside the door for the upcoming confrontation. Śrīla Prabhupāda brought his cane. The monkey sat on the edge of the roof with the sandal in his mouth and waited for negotiations to begin.

The roof was barely out of reach at about eight feet from the ground where we stood. Śrīla Prabhupāda began jumping up and down, swinging his cane over his head to intimidate the monkey. The monkey seemed to enjoy the attention. He was not threatened or concerned that Śrīla Prabhupāda might get the slipper. The furry creature began waving the shoe, taunting us. Śrīla Prabhupāda continued jumping up and down with his cane over his head. Swinging at his foe, he said, "These monkeys are such rascals."

The monkey continued taunting us. Now he was making faces at us. This was my first experience in such warfare and I have to admit, I found it very exhilarating.

"Śrīla Prabhupāda," I said. "Let me see if I can give him a sweet and get the sandal."

"Yes, see if that works," Śrīla Prabhupāda replied.

With my fearless leader beside me, I cautiously held a sweet into the air hoping the monkey would give me the magical slipper in exchange. True to the nature of a monkey, he tried to cheat me. He attempted to snatch the sweet without relinquishing Prabhupada's holy slipper. Again, I tried. I held up the sweet and motioned for the shoe. The monkey started to deliver the slipper with one hand and reach for the sweet with the other. Convinced I was successful, I let down my guard. In front of my beloved guru, I was prematurely proud of my anticipated success. I failed and gave up the sweet. Unfortunately, the menacing monkey did not surrender the slipper. To my chagrin, I managed to lose three sweets to the enemy without getting close to retrieving the lotus slipper.

At this point, the monkey began chewing on the heel of the slipper with gusto. He managed to tear some cloth from the heel and put a number of teeth marks in it. Śrīla Prabhupāda was not amused with his aggressor's demolition.

"Forget it," he said. "He has ruined the shoe."

His Divine Grace went back into his room and prepared for lunch. I started to follow him into the room. I looked up and saw the monkey drop the sandal at his feet and run away. I guess he understood it was of no use to him if it was of no use to us. I figured I might as well get the slipper, so I called for Girisha, Hayagrīva's son, and asked him to go up the stairs to the roof and get Śrīla Prabhupāda's slipper. Girisha was about ten years old and eager to help.

I watched from below as Girisha headed for the slipper. Just as he bent over to pick it up, a ruthless gang of monkeys came from nowhere and attacked him. They scared the heck out of him. One monkey started to swing at the young boy. Girisha screamed, "Śrutakīrti! Śrutakīrti!" Startled, I looked about and saw a bamboo stick. I threw it to him. As soon as he grabbed the stick and started swinging it the monkeys hastily retreated. Girisha grabbed the slipper and raced down the stairs with the beasts hot on his heels. Girisha gallantly delivered the slipper.

I brought the slipper back to Śrīla Prabhupāda because he had worn these slippers for some time and seemed to be very fond of them. He had others to choose from, but he favored these. I showed him the torn slipper.

"Ah, it doesn't look so bad," Śrīla Prabhupāda said. "Get some glue and see if you can repair it."

I took it back to my room and mended it to the best of my ability. I hurried back to Śrīla Prabhupāda's room with the saved slipper, offered my obeisances, and showed him my handy work. With a smile on his face and a nod of his head he said, "That's all right. I can still use them."

Two weeks later, we were in Hyderabad staying at the home

of Mr. Pithi, a very wealthy life member. One day Mr. Pithi noticed Śrīla Prabhupāda's slippers. I explained to him what happened.

"I would love to get Prabhupada another pair of sandals," he said.

I told him I thought it was a great idea. He sent his servant to buy a pair of sandals. When the new sandals were presented to Śrīla Prabhupāda, he accepted them graciously, but later told me, "I cannot wear these. They are made of leather."

He continued to wear his damaged sandals for weeks until we arrived at another temple. At that time, we bought some sandals to Śrīla Prabhupāda's liking and he released the others. His torn sandals now reside at the home of Kirtiraja prabhu in Alachua. They are in a glass case and are held in high esteem by their caretakers.

> *Śrīla Prabhupāda, it is very difficult to describe the immense pleasure I experienced that day as you swatted your cane at the monkey. For a few minutes, we were fighting a common foe, in the land of Kṛṣṇa. I may never again be able to take part in such transcendental pastimes. I will never forget that one special day when, for a few minutes, you allowed me to participate in a most joyful game in Vṛndāvana Dhāma. I pray that my memory of that day is never taken from me.*

36

"If they become agitated, let the brahmacārīs go to the forest."

November 31, 1972 ISKCON Mumbai

One day, I received a letter from Kulādri and was happy to hear the current news from the western world. I informed Śrīla Prabhupāda of the contents of the letter as none of the items therein were known to Śrīla Prabhupāda.

One item was especially interesting. It involved the separation of men and women in the New York temple. Śrīla Prabhupāda received a letter involving this matter at the same time as my letter arrived. When he heard that the women were only allowed in the temple at certain times because of agitated brahmacārīs, he said the brahmacārīs could go to the mountains because it was not possible to have such rules in our temples.

In a letter to Ekayani, Śrīla Prabhupāda wrote, "I do not know why these inventions are going on. We already have our Vaisnava standard. It is sufficient for all the big, big saints and ācāryas in our line. Why is it inadequate for my disciples so they must manufacture something? That is not possible. Who has introduced these things -- that women cannot chant japa in the temple, they cannot perform arati and so many things? If they become agitated, then let the brahmacārīs go to the forest. I have never introduced these things. If the brahmacārīs cannot remain in the presence of women in the temple, then they may go to the forest and not remain in New York City. In New York, there are so many women. How can they avoid seeing? The best thing is to go to the forest and not see any women if they become so easily agitated. But, then no one will see them and how our preaching work will go on?"

37

"Perhaps I Have Jaundice Also."

December 12, 1972 Ahmedabad, India

Here in Ahmedabad we were staying at a life member's house. Śrīla Prabhupāda had been in India now for over two months and I was getting my first taste of what it was like to be sick in India. He would give lecture every evening at a pandal. One evening, during Śrīla Prabhupāda's lecture I felt very weak and feverish. I could not keep my head up and I was nodding. At the time I had no idea what was wrong with me. I had never felt so ill. Śrīla Prabhupāda stopped his lecture and looked right at me. "Wake up!" he told me. "If you require sleep, go and sleep." That was all I needed. I tried hard to keep my back straight and head up for the rest of the lecture. I made it through without another incident.

I do not remember ever feeling so sick. After the lecture I went into Śrīla Prabhupāda's room and said, "I do not understand what is wrong with me. I feel very ill. I never get sick. I haven't been sick in years." Śrīla Prabhupāda looked at me with surprise. "Really, that is very wonderful," he said. "To be sick and in difficulty is the natural condition of life. You are very fortunate. In the material world one is normally diseased."

He mercifully told the lady of the house of my condition and asked if she could help take care of me. She put me in bed in the master bedroom and made me a bowl of tomato soup. Śrīla Prabhupāda came in to make sure I was okay. I felt better knowing how much he cared about me. She then called in a homeopathic doctor who gave me some small, round sugar pills from his black medical bag. The next morning I felt stronger and continued with my service.

Two weeks later we were in Bombay, staying at Kartikeya Mahadevia's flat. Just before the sun rose, we left in the Ambassador car to where Śrīla Prabhupāda often took his walk while he stayed here. We were all walking along the waterfront as the sun peeked over the horizon. Within a few minutes, Śyāmasundara prabhu looked into my eyes and started laughing aloud. Before I could ask him what was so funny he said with a smile, "Boy, are your eyes yellow. You have jaundice."

I did not know what it was, although I heard Śrīla Prabhupāda speak about it in lectures, when he used it as an analogy for our material condition. He said when you have jaundice the cure is to take sugar candy in water. It will taste bitter but as you become healthy, it will taste sweet. Śyāmasundara explained all the symptoms to me.

Finally, the weakness I had been feeling for the past few weeks made sense. Now diagnosed, I felt worse. I dragged myself along for the rest of the walk. After returning to Kartikeya's flat, I walked into Śrīla Prabhupāda's room and offered my obeisances. "Śrīla Prabhupāda, I have jaundice," I said with alarm. He looked at me with surprise and said, "Oh, what are the symptoms?"

"My urine is dark," I explained. "I have no appetite and feel very weak."

"Hmm," he said smiling. "Perhaps I have jaundice also." He had such a sense of humour, again reminding me of how being sick is the normal condition in the material world and also letting me know how the body feels when it becomes old.

Śrīla Prabhupāda knew very well the symptoms of all disease; after all he was a pharmacist for years. As far as I could tell, he knew everything. I continued, "Tamāla Kṛṣṇa Mahārāja and the other devotees suggested that perhaps I shouldn't cook for you because jaundice is highly contagious. Even touching your plates and preparing the food would be dangerous."

"No. That's all right," he said with a smile. "Do you have the strength to do your service?" I said I did. He then said, "You go ahead and do your service. There is nothing to worry about."

Due to Śrīla Prabhupāda's benediction, I continued my duties, even going on the morning walk, massaging him and cooking throughout my illness. It was sometimes difficult for me to understand Śrīla Prabhupāda's humour. Looking back, I understand that in the material world we all have 'skin disease' thinking we are this body. As long as that is our consciousness, we are diseased. Now that I am in my fifties, I see that it is rare to feel completely healthy, free from all pain and weaknesses.

When I visited Kartikeya Mahadevia's flat in November in 2005 I was told more about the mercy of my spiritual master. I was looking at Śrīla Prabhupāda's typewriter and talking with his son, Kīrtan. We were having such a nice time. Meanwhile Kartikeya's wife, Gauri, was talking with my wife about how endearing Śrīla Prabhupāda was, how he would ask her to make him puffed rice and hot milk in the evenings. Then she said that Śrīla Prabhupāda advised her not to give me more than four chapatis at lunchtime because my digestion was not good due to jaundice.

Śrīla Prabhupāda, you have always taken such good care of me and continue to do so. As time goes by, I experience your mercy more each day. It comes directly through you and your disciples. I am happy knowing you will never forget this jaundiced servant.

See also no. 103 - November 11, 1973 ISKCON Delhi

38

"In India, still there is some culture"

December 18, 1972 Mahadevīa Flat, Mumbai, India

Before Śrīla Prabhupāda's quarters were available in Juhu, he stayed at the home of a life member named Kartikeya Mahadevia. Mahadevia and his wife Gauri had two daughters named Preeti and Rādhā and a son named Kīrtan. At the time Śrīla Prabhupāda visited, Kīrtan was 13 and Preeti around 16. The facilities were first class, and Śrīla Prabhupāda was very comfortable. The Mahadevia family was very gracious and they gave Śrīla Prabhupāda the master bedroom. He was very comfortable there. A wonderful sea breeze blew in through the open door of his balcony. We had the bedroom across the hall.

Every morning Śyāmasundara would borrow Kartikeya's Ambassador car and drive Śrīla Prabhupāda and I to the waterfront area for his morning walk. The pavement was wide and not crowded. One day while walking, we passed a man lying down at the edge of the side walk. This was, unfortunately, a common sight on the streets of Bombay. "See that man lying there?" Śrīla Prabhupāda asked. "He is dead." Śrīla Prabhupāda continued walking without further comment. One hour later, we passed him again as we walked back to the car. The man hadn't moved. Śrīla Prabhupāda walked by without further comment.

After completing one morning walk, we returned to the Ambassador car and no matter how hard he tried, Śyāmasundara could not get the key to work in the ignition. He tried for several minutes. "Śrīla Prabhupāda, something is wrong with this car," he said. "This key isn't working. I'll go get a cab and I'll be right back."

He left Śrīla Prabhupāda and I sitting in the back seat of the car. We both sat there calmly chanting Japa. There were always cabs around even at this time of the morning. Since coming to India, I was getting used to situations not going as planned. After a few minutes, two well-dressed Indian men opened both front doors of the car and sat down in the front seat. I became a bit concerned. Śrīla Prabhupāda, smiling, appeared very calm and began a conversation with them in Hindi. Suddenly, they put their key in the ignition and the car immediately started. Śrīla

Prabhupāda turned to me laughing and exclaimed, "We are in their car!" They drove away. I finally realized that we had been sitting in the wrong car. This is not so hard to imagine. Thirty years later the Ambassadors still all look the same, although they have since added a few colours. The gentlemen insisted on taking Śrīla Prabhupāda back to his flat. Śrīla Prabhupāda apologised and spoke to them during the entire journey. When we arrived, he said "Please come up and take some prasadam"

"No, we have to go to work," they replied. "We have business meetings. Thank you very much, Swamiji."

"This is the difference between India and America," Śrīla Prabhupāda told me, after getting out of the car. "In America they would have said, 'Hey, what are you doing here, get out of my car!' They may possibly beat you, whereas in India, still there is some culture. In India when they see a sādhu still they have some respect. But in your country they kick you out. They say, 'Get out of my car.'"

It is interesting to note that even in this situation Śrīla Prabhupāda tried to get them to take prasādam. This is something I saw on countless occasions. Śrīla Prabhupāda wanted to see that everyone he came in contact with received prasādam.

In November of 2005, my wife and I returned to Mr. Mahadevia's flat, since it is a place of pilgrimage. I was also eager to meet his family again and see if they might remember me. Kartikeya had passed away a few years ago and his daughters were married and with their families. However, I was in for a very pleasant surprise. Again, they were very gracious and set a time when Kīrtan would be home from work, so that I could see their flat. They did not know who was coming to visit; only that it was a disciple of Śrīla Prabhupāda.

I arrived at the door at 4:30 pm, and I was greeted by Kīrtan and his mother. I immediately recognized Gauri but did not know if she would remember me. Kīrtan, who was thirteen when I was last there, asked me my name. When I told him, Śrutakīrti, they both smiled with delight. It was amazing! They were so happy to see me after thirty-two years, and remembered me with fondness. He grabbed my hand and shook it vigorously, as his mother continued to smile with surprise. They both remembered me so well. Kīrtan told me that he liked me the most out of all Śrīla Prabhupāda's disciples. His mother agreed and said I was always quiet. Then it became more exciting.

Kīrtan left the room and quickly returned with an old electric typewriter, with a great history. It was the typewriter that had been around the world several times with Śrīla Prabhupāda. Thousands of letters were typed on it and then signed by Śrīla Prabhupāda. He himself typed letters on it. What was more interesting was how they acquired it. Śrīla Prabhupāda and his entourage stayed at their flat for six weeks. They opened up their house and hearts to Śrīla Prabhupāda, his entourage and other disciples that frequented their home. They gave us shelter, fed us every day, and never asked for anything in return. Before leaving, Śrīla Prabhupāda offered to sell them the typewriter, which Kartikeya bought for about five hundred rupees.

Last year a devotee in Bombay offered to buy them a new computer system in return for the old Royal typewriter. Kīrtan laughed and said he would not trade it for a Boeing 747 Jet! I sat at the table and typed a thank you letter to them for taking such nice care of me so long ago. Kīrtan typed me an invitation letter to come and stay with them again. Amazingly, on rare occasions he still uses the machine for his business.

We sat for some time in the living room and Gauri told me how wonderful it was remembering all the happy times they had with Śrīla Prabhupāda in their house. Then, she told me to wait a minute and she left the room. She returned quickly with something in her hands that was wrapped tightly in a thick plastic bag. She handed it to me and told me to open it. I could not imagine what else they might have.

I found my way through the bag and pulled out a large, portable Uher reel-to-reel tape recorder. I immediately knew what it was. It was the same recorder I took on hundreds of morning walks, recording the transcendental words of His Divine Grace. The same recorder that I had used to record Śrīla Prabhupāda's lectures all over India, including all the lectures in Vṛndāvana in 1972 during the month of Kārtika. I could not believe it! She was so happy to show it to me. She had kept this treasure safely in her bedroom all these years. It was complete with all its cables and still in the black leather carrying case. Even though they were just a few hundred yards from the sea, the metal frame was still rust-free because of how carefully it had been kept. I was so overwhelmed I did not even ask how they managed to get this jewel.

I told them I could understand that the typewriter belonged to them, but smiling I proclaimed, "this tape recorder is mine." I thanked her for taking such good care of it and asked for it back. Both the mother and son smiled at me and ignored my request. I sat with it on my lap for several minutes recalling the vast amounts of service it had done. It was such a heavy machine. I do not know how I managed to carry it on the morning walks every day. Now, my only wish is that I get the opportunity to do it life after life.

We took some pictures of their treasures and some group photos as well before leaving that afternoon, promising to return again soon.

> *I again experienced how you touched the hearts of everyone you encountered. The room was filled with smiling faces as everyone happily remembered your activities in their flat. We all came to life as we spoke about your early efforts in Bombay, planting seeds of devotion everywhere you went. One of those seeds*

quickly took root. By your mercy, one of Kartikeya's daughters is an initiated devotee in ISKCON.

All Glories to Śrīla Prabhupāda!

39

"See this scar?"

December 27, 1972 Mahadevia Flat, Mumbai, India

One day, while massaging Śrīla Prabhupāda, he pointed to a scar on his leg.

"See this scar?" he asked. "That happened when I was young. I was in front of the house and I had matches. Somehow, I started some fire and my clothing immediately went up in flames. It was very bad. I do not know what would have happened, but out of nowhere, some man appeared and put out the flames. Then he left."

Śrīla Prabhupāda did not say anything more about the gentleman. He gave me the impression that the person who appeared "out of nowhere" was not an ordinary person. Again, I felt so privileged to hear such things from Śrīla Prabhupāda. He gave me a rare glimpse into his life, always tempered with his great humility.

I never dared to ask him to be more specific. Having been with Śrīla Prabhupāda for so long, I knew he had told me as much as he wanted me to know. In the two years I was with him, Śrīla Prabhupāda never stated in my presence that he came from the spiritual world. In the two years I was with him, every day I was more convinced that he was sent to us by the mercy of Lord Caitanya to spread His Sankīrtan movement to every town and village. Śrīla Prabhupāda, please allow me to serve you life after life.

Śrīla Prabhupāda was very merciful and always encouraged us by saying we could become Kṛṣṇa Conscious in this lifetime. He taught by example. He never asked us to do anything that he did not do himself. He rose early, chanted japa, and read Śrīmad-Bhagavatam. He never acted superior to his disciples. He allowed us to be comfortable with him by acting as if he were "practicing" Kṛṣṇa Consciousness rather than the embodiment of it.

"It is my duty to chastise because you are my disciple," he often said.

We are his children and his position was, and still is, to teach us.

40

"...maybe my father knew."

January 6, 1973 Mahadevia Flat, Mumbai, India

A morning massage with Śrīla Prabhupāda

Śrīla Prabhupāda often related his childhood pastimes. One story he told happened when he was a very young boy walking in the marketplace with his mother. Śrīla Prabhupāda saw some toy guns.

"I saw the guns and immediately I had to have them," he said.

When his mother wouldn't get him one, he started to cry.

"All right, all right, I will buy you a gun," his mother told him.

Śrīla Prabhupāda looked at the gun in one hand and then looked at his other empty hand.

"I do not have a gun for it," he said. "I must have one for each hand."

"No," his mother said.

However, even as a young child, Śrīla Prabhupāda had a great amount of determination.

When telling this story, Śrīla Prabhupāda said, "At that point I lay down in the street and started to kick my hands and feet and bang my head on the ground."

He referred to this behaviour as a tantrum. Pointing to a mark on his forehead, he said, "This scar is from that time. I was very sure that I had to have two guns. Thus, she got me the other gun. When I wanted something, I had to have it," he explained. "My mother would always get it. Otherwise, I would tell my father and he would get very upset with my mother and then she would have to do it."

In a reflective mood, Śrīla Prabhupāda said, "I do not know, maybe my father knew."

From this brief statement, I concluded that Śrīla Prabhupāda's father might have been aware of his son's exalted position as a pure devotee of the Supreme Lord.

Śrīla Prabhupāda had fulfilled the prediction of Śrīla Bhaktivinoda Thakura to spread the chanting of the mahā-mantra around the world.

I felt overwhelmed to be with him at that moment. He would never make such a statement publicly, although all of his disciples knew he was responsible for doing it. No one had done it until now and no one will ever be able to take credit for it in the future. He wrote volumes of books, describing the glories of the Supreme Lord and His devotees but always remained the humble servant of the Lord.

41

"zzzzzuuummmmm"

January 10, 1973 Mahadevia Flat, Mumbai, India

During my first tour of India in the fall and winter of 1972, Malati Devī cooked for Śrīla Prabhupāda. She was the wife of Śyāmasundara dāsa, Śrīla Prabhupāda's secretary. Their daughter, Sarasvatī, was about three years old at the time. She was the most fortunate little girl. She was the only person I knew who was able to go in and out of Śrīla Prabhupāda's quarters unannounced.

She seemed to appear out of nowhere, like a tiny Narada Muni, in different temples around the world. She always ended up in Śrīla Prabhupāda's room. Then, as quickly as she appeared, she disappeared. He enjoyed her company. Sometimes she sat on his lap. Other times, like a grandfather, he affectionately teased her. She always had prasādam in her hands or mouth. Śrīla Prabhupāda observed this and supplied her with sweets from a container on his desk.

One day, as I massaged Śrīla Prabhupāda, Sarasvatī entered his room. As usual, she was eating. Śrīla Prabhupāda laughed.

"You are always eating," he said. "You know what you remind me of, Sarasvatī?" She looked at him with a mouthful of food and shook her head.

"You remind me of New York City - the garbage trucks," he told her. "Do you know the garbage trucks in New York City? She nodded. "In New York City," Śrīla Prabhupāda continued, "they have these big garbage trucks. They go down the street and workers put the garbage in." Stretching one arm over his head and the other towards the floor, Śrīla Prabhupāda said, "They go down the street and put garbage inside the big mouth of the truck and then the truck goes zzzzzuuummmmm and it closes and the truck eats it. Then it goes iiiimmmm and opens back up. Like this."

He imitated the up and down crunching movement of the jaws of the garbage truck extending his arms in an opening and closing motion.

"Your mouth is just like that. You are always putting things in. Just like the garbage trucks in New York."

Sarasvatī was amused, but disappeared again. Perhaps she went to get more prasādam from her mataji. I continued massaging Śrīla Prabhupāda, once again amazed by his greatness. I wondered what pious activities Sarasvatī must have performed to be able to play with His Divine Grace on such an intimate level. My witnessing Śrīla Prabhupāda's līlā was certainly a sign of his causeless mercy. Śrīla Prabhupāda's playful affection continues to soften this stone heart.

42

"Kirti means expert."

January 13, 1973 Mahadevia Flat, Mumbai, India

For six weeks, Śrīla Prabhupāda stayed at the flat of Kartikeya Mahadevia. From the ground floor, there was a very small two-man elevator that was used to get to Śrīla Prabhupāda's rooms.

One morning Śrīla Prabhupāda, Tamāla Kṛṣṇa Gosvāmī and I went toward the elevator on the way to the morning walk. As Śrīla Prabhupāda's servant, I expected to get into the elevator with him, but Tamāla Kṛṣṇa Gosvāmī entered first, so there was no room for me. As the doors closed, I quickly turned and ran down two flights of stairs. I arrived at the elevator doors just in time to open them for Śrīla Prabhupāda and help him out of the elevator. As we walked away, Tamāla Kṛṣṇa Mahārāja looked at me and laughed.

"Śrīla Prabhupāda," he said. "Śrutakīrti is really expert."

"Yes," Śrīla Prabhupāda replied. "'Kirti' means expert."

He continued toward the car without commenting further on the subject.

Being Śrīla Prabhupāda's servant was filled with adventure and suspense. Whatever was going on seemed to be filled with a certain electricity. Every month I had the opportunity to shave Śrīla Prabhupāda's head with the electric clippers. Śrīla Prabhupāda was not a passive recipient during this process. He moved around and that made me more frightened. He very kindly helped me to be "Prabhupada Conscious."

"Turn the shaver off in between each stroke so it doesn't get hot," he instructed. This was easy, however, the tricky part was shaving around his ears.

I was very careful. By Kṛṣṇa's grace, there was never a mishap during this service and it helped me to be more "Prabhupada conscious". Many devotees were delighted when I distributed Śrīla Prabhupāda's hair.

43

"So, the pandal was very nice?"

January 21, 1973 Mahadevia Flat, Mumbai, India

Śrīla Prabhupāda spoke every evening for a week at a pandal programme arranged by the devotees. Thousands of people attended. Śrīla Prabhupāda sat on his vyāsāsana on the stage with his disciples gathered at his feet. Rādhā Kṛṣṇa Deities were placed on a large stage. Their Lordships were later installed at Bhaktivedanta Manor in England.

It was an eventful week. One evening, an electrical fire ignited behind the Deities' altar. The fire spread, but fortunately was put out quickly. More devotees arrived daily, so by the last day of the programme dozens of Śrīla Prabhupāda's disciples were in attendance. The western devotees could not understand the lectures because they were spoken in Hindi, but it was evident from the enthusiastic crowd that Śrīla Prabhupāda was enlivening everyone.

The last day of the programme was especially wonderful. After Śrīla Prabhupāda finished his lecture, he nodded and said, "All right, have kīrtan."

Acyutānanda Swami, sitting by a microphone with a mṛdaṅga in hand began to lead the chanting. Within a few minutes, Śrīla Prabhupāda got down from his vyāsāsana and began to circumambulate the Deities. He went around once, turned, and bowed before Śrī Śrī Rādhā Kṛṣṇa. The devotees started to follow His Divine Grace as he went around for a second time. He clapped his hands and smiled as he walked around the shaky stage for a second time. Again, he turned and bowed before Their Lordships. The kīrtan became more ecstatic. Everyone relished following Śrīla Prabhupāda as our eyes drank the nectar of his ecstasy.

He majestically walked around Their Lordships once more, completing his third time. He bowed again before the Supreme Lord and His Pleasure Potency and then faced the crowd. As he turned, he lifted his arms high in the sky. He benedicted us all with the biggest smile I had ever seen. As he danced, jumping up and down to the kīrtan, he immediately lifted us all to the transcendental realm. It was amazing how Śrīla Prabhupāda controlled us by the movement of his arms. When he raised them into the air, he picked everyone up with them and deposited us in the spiritual world. The crowd of thousands was caught up in the atmosphere. The kīrtan was out of this world.

The dancing on the wooden platform by dozens of devotees was so wild that the stage shook. Their Lordships began to move back and forth on the altar, as if They were also joining in with their pure devotee. Along with another devotee, I went behind the altar and held the Deities down by holding Their bases. Noticing the situation, Śrīla Prabhupāda stopped dancing. When the kīrtan was over, Śrīla Prabhupāda and I got into the back of an Ambassador and it started for Kartikeya Mahadevia's flat where Śrīla Prabhupāda was staying.

"So, the pandal was very nice?" he asked with a transcendental smile.

"Prabhupada, it was really wonderful," I said. "When you dance, everyone immediately goes into ecstasy."

"Yes!" he said. "Actually, I could have kept on dancing, but I saw that the Deities were endangered so I stopped. Otherwise, I would have kept on dancing."

> *Śrīla Prabhupāda, thank you for allowing me the chance to witness your spiritual potency. By our conversation in the car, it was evident that you enjoyed distributing the mercy to everyone present. I knew I was the most fortunate living entity on the planet being able to sit next to you in the car. Please raise your arms over me once again so that I may dance according to your desire.*

44

"Go get a thali and put water in it."

January 25, 1973 ISKCON Kolkata, India

Kolkata was definitely Śrīla Prabhupāda's hometown. The temple, which had a relaxed atmosphere, was situated on the second floor with a modest-sized temple room. Śrīla

Prabhupāda's room was at the end of the building. The nicest part of the facility was a marble veranda that ran the width of the building. It overlooked a pond that was across the street.

While in Kolkata, we could not stop the flow of guests entering Śrīla Prabhupāda's room. It was different from other temples where there was much more control. When Śrīla Prabhupāda rested in the afternoon, I would lie down in front of the doors of his room so no one could enter. It was one of my favourite services, getting the chance to be his guard dog. Śrīla Prabhupāda knew it was the hometown crowd so he was especially gracious. There were always a few boxes of milk sweets in his room that had been purchased at the local sweet shop. In Kolkata, this box was right next to his sitting place. The sandeśa of many varieties was the best tasting in the world. Śrīla Prabhupāda always emphasized, "All guests should be given prasādam."

One day I noticed that a box of sweets was covered with ants. I thought if I showed them to Śrīla Prabhupāda he would tell me to discard them. Then I could dust off the ants and keep them for myself. I lustfully walked into his room and offered my obeisances. I told him of the dilemma. He smiled at me, no doubt reading my mind.

"That's all right, he told me. They do not eat very much. Go get a thali (a plate with a one-inch rim around it) and put water in it. Then you can put a pot in that upside down and put the sweets on the pot. That will make a moat so the ants can't get at the sweets." I offered my obeisances, left the room and came back a few minutes later with the sweets on the plate. I put them down beside him and offered obeisances. He looked at my work and nodded with approval, not saying anything. I then left the room.

Śrīla Prabhupāda, you always bring the best out of me, even in the simplest ways. In all our dealings together, you always showed me the importance of being honest and straightforward, without making me feel guilty and ashamed of myself. You offer me protection from māyā, just as you protected those sweets from my lust. As you so often told me, "Chant sixteen rounds and follow the regulative principles and mayācan not touch you. What is the difficulty?"

45

"This Kachori has created havoc."

January 28, 1973 ISKCON Kolkata, India

One of Śrīla Prabhupāda's transcendental characteristics was he never, ever wasted anything. This quality manifested itself in many pastimes.

One afternoon while lying outside his room, I heard him moaning. I did not know what to do. A few times I looked in and saw him tossing and turning on his bed. He did not call for me, but I could not take it any more. Finally, I rushed into his room.

"Śrīla Prabhupāda, what's wrong?" I asked.

"My stomach, very painful," he said. "It must have been something I ate. It's very, very painful."

He did not ask for any assistance. I remained in the room and gently rubbed his stomach.

Later he said, "It must have been that coconut kachori my sister made me for lunch. It was not cooked. The coconut was very difficult to digest. It is causing me very much pain."

Throughout the evening different devotees took turns rubbing his body. The pain continued all night. With each breath he took, he would let out a sigh. In the morning the Kaviraja came. He confirmed what Śrīla Prabhupāda had said.

Whenever Srila Prabhupada flew, he would always sit by the window. His hand luggage would include the famous "white bag" which contained his travel documents, important papers and personal effects. Sometimes, a press reception would await him on his arrival. Even after a long journey, Srila Prabhupada was eager to speak.

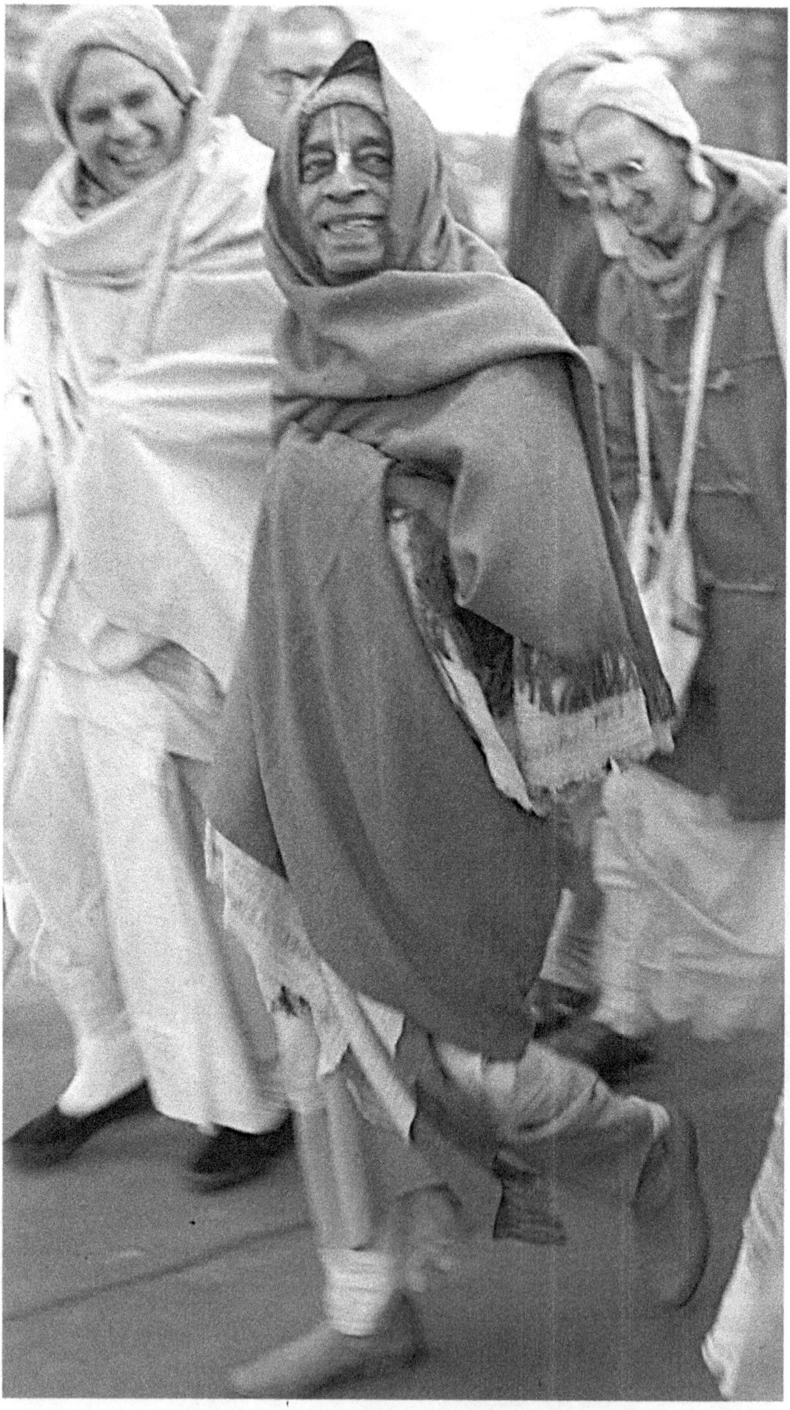

Srila Prabhupada always took his morning walk wherever he was, no matter how cold the weather. A chilly New York park; warm Juhu Beach, Mumbai; challenging the scientists with Bhakti Svarupa Damodara Maharaj at windy Venice Beach, L.A.; a moment of humour with Ambarisa dasa in Ala Moana Beach Park, Hawaii.

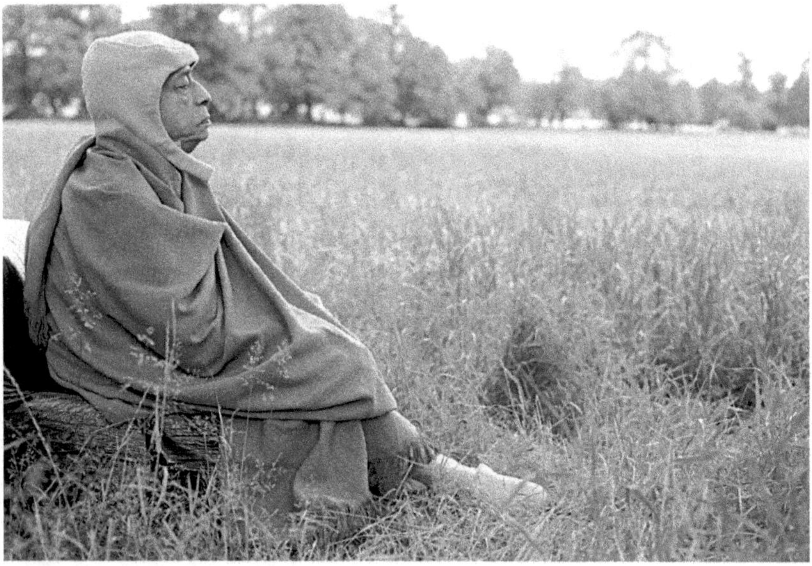

Without compromise, Srila Prabhupada displayed all the symptoms of a transcendentalist in full Krishna Consciousness. Wherever he was travelling, he continued his daily schedule of rising early, translation, japa and bhajan. He relished reading his books and he always took prasadam at a regular time, even in the middle of

a busy travel schedule. He often wrote dozens of letters a day as he attended to the personal needs of his many disciples and the management issues of a growing international movement. While his life was a whirlwind of activity, Srila Prabhupada remained peaceful and contented, fully surrendered to Krishna's desire.

I entered Śrīla Prabhupāda's room at 4:00 am

"This kachori has created havoc," he told me. "All night I have not been able to rest. It has created havoc in my life."

46

"I had to take bath, I was feeling very tired."

February 8, 1973 Bangkok Airport Transit Lounge

Śrīla Prabhupāda distributed his mercy without distinction. That was the kindness of the pure devotee. On a flight from India to the West, we had a two-hour stop over at Bangkok airport and had to wait in the transit area.

"Get my things," Śrīla Prabhupāda told me. "I am going to shower."

To accomplish this, I had first to locate our luggage, which was being changed from one aeroplane to another. I went to the baggage area, opened Śrīla Prabhupāda's bag, and grabbed his lota, towel and a fresh change of clothing. After a few minutes, I returned to His Divine Grace.

"Where is the bathroom?" he asked.

We walked together to the bathroom, but unfortunately, there was no bathing facility. Śrīla Prabhupāda was not easily discouraged. For him, there was never an obstacle.

Assessing the situation, he turned to me and said, "All right, I'll take bath from the small sink."

After covering his lower body with his gamcha, he poured water over his body again and again from his lota. He washed with soap and then rinsed again. I watched in amazement as he refreshed himself. He was transcendental to all other activities going on around him.

The local Thai attendant watched from a corner of the

bathroom. He looked disturbed at seeing the extra work that was being created for him as Prabhupada spilled water all over the floor.

I gave Śrīla Prabhupāda a towel when he was finished. He dried himself and dressed in a clean dhoti and kurta.

The attendant approached me as we were walking out of the bathroom. Although I had no idea what he was saying, I knew he was complaining. I told the attendant as nicely as I could, that I was helpless to stop Śrīla Prabhupāda.

Inside, I smiled to myself, as I realized the attendant had no idea that he was being benedicted by the grace of a Paramahaṁsa. He was, albeit unknowingly, directly serving Śrīla Prabhupāda by wiping up the spilled water.

"Śrīla Prabhupāda," I said as we walked out. "I think he is a little upset."

"Oh, well!" Śrīla Prabhupāda replied, laughing mildly "I had to take bath. I was feeling very tired."

Travelling with Śrīla Prabhupāda was always an incredible adventure. He never felt the need to conform to any social conventions. On aeroplanes, he used the restroom when the seat belt light was on. He took prasādam when we weren't allowed to have our trays down. If anyone said anything to him, he ignored them. They would then turn to me.

"I can't stop him," I would say shrugging my shoulders.

They inevitably realized they were no match for a Vaikuṇṭha person and walked away.

47

"Kṛṣṇa likes sugar very much."

Feb. 20, 1973 ISKCON Auckland, New Zealand

Before Śrīla Prabhupāda's arrival at the New Zealand temple, Siddha SvarūpaMaharaja and Tusta Kṛṣṇa Mahārāja moved the devotees out of the temple, so that Śrīla Prabhupāda would have a peaceful, quiet stay. It was an interesting and unusual thing to do, but it did allow Śrīla Prabhupāda the chance to have a relaxing visit.

One evening Śrīla Prabhupāda asked me to prepare puris and subji. As I prepared his meal, I realized I did not have any milk sweets to put on his plate. There was no Deity worship at the temple, so I was unable to get maha-prasādam for his plate. I hadn't found the time to prepare any sandeśa since our arrival the previous day. I brought the puris, subji and hot milk into Śrīla Prabhupāda's room and placed them on his table. I then offered my obeisances. Siddha Svarūpa and Tusta Kṛṣṇa were both present in the room speaking with Śrīla Prabhupāda. He allowed them to remain while he took prasādam. This was a great benediction as it was not something Śrīla Prabhupāda did often. He usually honoured prasādam in private.

I left the room and went back to the kitchen to roll and fry a few more puris. I rushed back to my spiritual master with two fresh puris, placing them on his plate before offering my humble obeisances. Śrīla Prabhupāda looked at me inquisitively.

"There is no sweet?" he asked.

"No, Prabhupada," I said. "I haven't made any yet."

"Oh, all right. Bring me some sugar," he mercifully said, realizing the situation.

I went back to the kitchen, filled a bowl with white sugar and returned to his sitting room. I placed the bowl on his plate. He took a puri, stuffed it into the bowl of sugar and took a bite.

He did this a few times. You could hear the crunching sounds as he chewed enthusiastically. He stopped for a moment, chanted, "Luci cini sarpuri laddu rasabali", and continued by saying, "This is a very good combination. It is very tasty."

As he ate, the two sannyāsīs watched in amazement. Neither of these Mahārāja disciples ate anything that contained even a trace of sugar, what to speak of eating the horrid substance in its "impure" form. This was another of Śrīla Prabhupāda's wondrous qualities. He always knew exactly how to surprise and unsettle his disciples, giving them the opportunity to understand his most transcendental position.

Once while staying in New Dvārakā, Śrīla Prabhupāda took a day trip to the Laguna Beach temple, which was a two-hour ride by car. That evening, while still in Laguna Beach, he asked for hot milk. Although this temple had Deity worship, I was unable to find sugar in the temple kitchen. I therefore, sweetened the milk with honey, because occasionally Śrīla Prabhupāda asked to have his milk sweetened with honey. However, on this evening when I brought him the hot milk, he tasted it and immediately asked, "Why it is not sweetened with sugar?"

"They do not have any sugar in this temple," I said.

"How can that be?" he asked in an angry mood.

"Some devotees think that white sugar is not healthy and that it is better to avoid it," I explained.

"That's fine," he said. "If they do not want to eat sugar, they do not have to. However, Kṛṣṇa likes sugar very much. This is nonsense. They must use sugar when they make preparations for the Deities."

Śrīla Prabhupāda, you were astonishing. Wherever you went, you quickly cut through all of the creative nonsense invented by your disciples. You did not need a network of spies to tell you what was going on. Kṛṣṇa was your spy. He gave you all the information needed, so you could set the proper path for your foolhardy children. I relished the countless opportunities when I saw you display psychic abilities. Devotees often asked if you displayed any yogic powers. I constantly saw you display them. You read the minds of your disciples and dealt with them accordingly. Often, it was to my joyful and appreciative amusement.

Please, Śrīla Prabhupāda, grant me your association always by allowing me to remember that you reside in my heart. You know I have no qualifications, but I know how merciful you are. After all, you have allowed me to personally associate with you.

48

"Oh! Thank you, Kṛṣṇa."

February 21, 1973 ISKCON Auckland, New Zealand

There was one name that never brought a smile to Śrīla Prabhupāda's face. That name was Mr. Nair. He was the "Kamsa" of ISKCON. He made the mistake of selling a piece of land in Juhu to Śrīla Prabhupāda for a small down payment. Mr. Nair's scheme was that, in the future Śrīla Prabhupāda would not be able to pay the large balloon payment, and would therefore lose possession of the land. Then, Mr. Nair would resell the property as he had done previously, several times. Mr. Nair did not realize with whom he was dealing. As soon as Śrīla Prabhupāda took possession of the land, he had his disciples build a temple on the property, install deities, and instituted full deity worship.

The history of the Juhu project is very long and I do not know all of the details, but I do know that everyone was ready to give in to Mr. Nair's antics, except for His Divine Grace.

Śrīla Prabhupāda spent many days intensely chanting japa. He was determined to acquire this particular piece of land for Their Lordships Śrī Śrī Rādhā Rasavihari. He worked to keep his disciples inspired to fight, and not give up their efforts to acquire the property. Some disciples questioned why Śrīla Prabhupāda was so attached to this property, to the point of being offensive.

One beautiful day in Auckland, during Śrīla Prabhupāda's morning massage, things became very clear. I remember it as if it were yesterday. I was sitting on the floor behind Śrīla Prabhupāda, vigorously massaging his back. Tusta Kṛṣṇa Mahārāja and Siddha SvarūpaMaharaja were also present. Tusta Kṛṣṇa went to answer a phone call. He told me to go to the phone. I spoke with the caller briefly and ran back into the room.

"Śrīla Prabhupāda," I said. "That was Bali-mardana on the phone. He wanted to tell you that Mr. Nair is dead."

Immediately, Śrīla Prabhupāda clapped his hands in prayer-like fashion and with a beaming smile, he jubilantly exclaimed, "Oh! Thank You, Kṛṣṇa!"

Confused, I sat down behind His Divine Grace to massage his back. I was surprised how happy Śrīla Prabhupāda was about someone dying. Normally, it was a time of mourning. I had expected Śrīla Prabhupāda to respond differently. I realized that I understood nothing about spiritual life or the pure devotee.

"I prayed that Kṛṣṇa would kill him," he said. "He has caused us so much difficulty. I was praying that Kṛṣṇa would do something to this demon."

He then quoted a Sanskrit sloka from Śrīmad Bhāgavatam and translated it into English.

"Prahlada Mahārāja said, 'Even the sādhu becomes pleased when a snake or scorpion is killed,'" Śrīla Prabhupāda explained. "Mr. Nair was such a serpent. Therefore, it is very good."

He read my mind and immediately corrected my bogus ideas. I felt great relief. Now armed with the proper sentiment, I asked, "Śrīla Prabhupāda, Kṛṣṇa killed him? Does that mean he has achieved liberation?"

Śrīla Prabhupāda laughed at my foolish question.

"No!" he replied. "Kṛṣṇa did not kill him personally. That only applies when Kṛṣṇa personally kills you. He was not such a great demon. Kṛṣṇa did not come personally to kill him."

As I continued to massage him, Śrīla Prabhupāda continued to clarify his attachment to the project.

"The Deities were installed on the property," he said. "Mr. Nair was making a great insult to Kṛṣṇa that I could not tolerate. He was insulting Kṛṣṇa. Kṛṣṇa was there and he tried to kick Kṛṣṇa off the land. We have money. We can buy property anywhere, but Kṛṣṇa was there at Juhu. Therefore, I was determined to have it for the Lord."

Śrīla Prabhupāda was silent for a few minutes.

"I remember when he came to visit me this last time in Mumbai," he continued. "I knew then that Kṛṣṇa was going to kill him. I noticed he was limping. Generally, he was a very robust man, very strong. He was not at all ill, but on his last visit, he was limping. Then I knew Kṛṣṇa would kill him. Actually, Kṛṣṇa has killed him."

My dear Śrīla Prabhupāda, your determination to serve the Supreme Lord is transcendental. It is apparent why you were chosen by Lord Caitanya to spread His glories to every town and village. You are fully qualified to be worshiped by all living entities on this planet for the next ten thousand years. I observed how you were resolute during the overwhelming difficulties connected with the Juhu project. You are fully surrendered to Kṛṣṇa. Please bless me with the determination to fully surrender at your lotus feet.

49

"No religion is bad"

February 21, 1973 ISKCON Auckland, New Zealand

During this trip to the Pacific Rim Śrīla Prabhupāda stayed in Auckland for six days. He stayed at the temple but the devotees stayed elsewhere so it was a very quiet, peaceful time for Śrīla Prabhupāda. Along with Śrīla Prabhupāda and his entourage, only Siddhasvarūpaand Tusta Kṛṣṇa Maharajas were present. By 1975, Siddha already had a splinter group, the first one in ISKCON. The tendency to be separate was there from the start. When Siddha came, he already had a following. Śrīla Prabhupāda always tried to get them to cooperate with the GBC but knew they wouldn't. Therefore, he gave them sufficient opportunity to get his personal association and instruction so that they could understand the philosophy well, and know how to present it "as it is". Just before coming here, Śrīla Prabhupāda invited them both to travel with him in India from October 15 until the end of January. Siddha joined Śrīla Prabhupāda for part of his stay in India.

While in Auckland, they both spent time with Śrīla Prabhupāda during the day and were always present for his late morning massage. They also came for darśana in the afternoon and evening. One day, in the early afternoon Siddha came to Śrīla Prabhupāda with a book called "Jesus loves Kṛṣṇa, Kṛṣṇa loves Jesus." He wanted to know what Śrīla Prabhupāda thought of it. As the title indicated, it showed what Christianity had in common with Kṛṣṇa Consciousness and was positive in nature. After looking through it Śrīla Prabhupāda said, "You say nothing in here about meat eating. They are killing the cow to eat her. Why you are not mentioning it in here? Christ says 'Thou shalt not kill.' So why you have not mentioned this point in your book? This is the most important point. Christ says 'Thou shall not kill and here they are killing." Śrīla

Prabhupāda was not pleased and explained, "If one truly loves Jesus they can not take part in the killing of animals. I ask the Christians that Lord Christ says that 'Thou shall not kill.' Why you are killing? They give some vague explanation. Actually, a real Christian is as good as a real Hindu, as a real Muslim. If he follows. No religion is bad." Siddha said he would make the necessary changes to the book.

At another darśana while sitting before Śrīla Prabhupāda, Siddha explained about the Chinese process of acupuncture. I sat to one side as he talked for about half an hour about it. I kept looking at Śrīla Prabhupāda as he sat there patiently listening. After about fifteen minutes Śrīla Prabhupāda put his head back on the pillow of his asana and closed his eyes. He was resting. It did not seem to matter. Siddha went on for a while more. Every now and then Śrīla Prabhupāda would open his eyes and give a nod. He did not comment on anything Siddha was saying, but allowed him to talk to his full satisfaction.

Śrīla Prabhupāda sat there patiently until he finished speaking never interrupting him. By his kindness and compassion, he encouraged them both for almost a week. He wanted them to be fixed up in Kṛṣṇa Consciousness so that they could help spread Lord Caitanya's movement, even if they were going to do it independently.

50

"The sandalwood oil cooled my body too much."

February 22, 1973 ISKCON Auckland, New Zealand

From the beginning, Siddha Svarūpa had a unique relationship with the International Society for Kṛṣṇa Consciousness. Before meeting Śrīla Prabhupāda, he had been a "guru" who surrendered to His Divine Grace, bringing with him some of his own disciples. Many ISKCON devotees had difficulty accepting the distinction awarded to Siddha Svarupa. Consequently, some members of ISKCON did not get along with him and, apparently, the feeling was mutual.

Siddha Svarūpa did have a great deal of association with Śrīla Prabhupāda, however, and His Divine Grace encouraged him to spread Lord Caitanya's sankīrtana movement.

"Work under the direction of the GBC," Śrīla Prabhupāda told him. "But, if you cannot do that, then work directly under me."

It was clear to me that Siddha Svarūpahad a great deal of love for Śrīla Prabhupāda and His Divine Grace reciprocated.

One morning in Auckland, Siddha presented Śrīla Prabhupāda with a large, aluminium bottle of Mysore sandalwood oil just before Śrīla Prabhupāda was to take his massage.

"Please use this sandalwood oil for massaging your entire body," Siddha said.

"No," Śrīla Prabhupāda replied. "Sandalwood oil is for cooling the head only and mustard oil is for the rest of the body."

Siddha Svarūpa did not understand the Ayurvedic significance of what Śrīla Prabhupāda was saying. Out of love, he wanted the best possible oil used to massage Śrīla Prabhupāda.

"Please, Śrīla Prabhupāda, just this once!" Siddha insisted.

Seeing Siddha Svarupa's determination to please him, Śrīla Prabhupāda reluctantly consented. That day I massaged Śrīla Prabhupāda's entire body with sandalwood oil as Siddha joyfully watched.

As usual, Śrīla Prabhupāda took bath after his massage, honoured lunch prasādam and took a nap. After his nap, he called for me. I hurried to his room and offered my obeisances.

"I am not feeling well," he said, looking very serious. "I

think it is because of the massage. The sandalwood oil cooled the body too much."

I was overwhelmed with disappointment because I had not taken proper care of my Gurudeva. The natural warming property of mustard oil was always used on Śrīla Prabhupāda's golden body. I understood the healthy effect of keeping His Divine Grace warm. Generally, Śrīla Prabhupāda did not let health problems interrupt his devotional service. He rarely went to bed when he was not feeling well unless his illness continued for weeks. He never took aspirin for headaches.

During an episode of illness, the only changes I saw in Śrīla Prabhupāda's daily schedule were dietary adjustments. If Śrīla Prabhupāda were not well enough to take a bath, he would ask me to massage him without oil. On a few occasions when he had a cold, he told me to put a little camphor into the mustard oil and then heat the oil.

"Make the oil as hot as you can and still be able to touch it," he instructed.

It was remarkable how much difficulty Śrīla Prabhupāda accepted for the pleasure of his disciples. He knew that using the sandalwood oil could cause difficulty. However, just to satisfy his disciple, he accepted it. Clearly, Śrīla Prabhupāda underwent hardships to satisfy his Guru Mahārāja, but he was also willing to accept difficulties for the pleasure of his devotees. He was eager to encourage us in our devotional service even if we put him into difficulty.

Śrīla Prabhupāda, I pray that I may someday understand your instructions, so I can serve you according to your desire and not according to my whim. Please forgive me for failing to protect you. I knew it was not a good idea to use the sandalwood oil. I should have explained it to Siddha Svarupa. He would have understood because his only desire was to please you.

51

"If you want to build a Temple, it is all right"

February 28, 1973 Jakarta, Indonesia

While staying at a life member's house, a few Indian guests came to visit Śrīla Prabhupāda. While there, one of them said, "Swamiji, we want you to ask us to build a temple. We want to build a temple for you, but we want your blessings. We want you to ask us."

"No, no," Śrīla Prabhupāda said laughing. "If you want to build a temple, it is all right. Build a temple. We will man it for you."

"Swamiji," the gentleman continued. "We want you to give us your blessings, to ask us to make the temple. We want the benediction."

Śrīla Prabhupāda still smiling and laughing said, "No, no. If I ask you to do it and you do not do it, then it will be offensive. If you do not comply, that will be your fall down. That is very bad. If you do it on your own that is good, but if you do not do it there is no harm done because I haven't told you to do it."

Śrīla Prabhupāda, you showed us what it means to be a leader and how to give instructions without false ego. I was always amazed how you would call me into your room and after I offered my obeisances, you would look at me and innocently say, "Can you give me massage now?"

With disbelief I could only say, "Prabhupada that is why I am here. I am waiting to serve you."

You made it very easy to want to serve you. Please let the memories of being with you flow from my heart.

52

"You can never see your wife after you have taken sannyasa."

March 14, 1973 ISKCON Kolkata, India

Once, a sannyāsī confided to Śrīla Prabhupāda that he was having difficulty because of attachment to his wife.

"Even last night," Śrīla Prabhupāda told him, "I had a dream about my wife. The attachment is that strong, even I have been away for so many years. Still, last night I had some dream about my wife. Therefore, the injunction is there. You can never see your wife after you have taken sannyasa. You can never even see her, because just by seeing her, so many thoughts can be brought to the mind."

Later, during his stay in Kolkata, he spoke humourously about attachment between men and women.

"Women are compared to fire, and men, they are like butter," he said. "Therefore, our sannyāsīs, they should have stamped on their forehead, 'keep in a cool place.' Just like on the butter package, it says that. So, our sannyāsīs, they also should have that stamped onto their forehead. That will keep them safe from danger."

Our Gurudeva mercifully engages us in Kṛṣṇa's service. In spite of our degraded condition, he heroically rescued us and is leading us "Back to Godhead."

53

"Māyāpur is your home"

March 16, 1973 Kolkata to Mayapur, India

Śrīla Prabhupāda and his entourage left the Philippines on October 14, 1972 and arrived in Delhi the same day. For the next five months, he travelled around India. On March 16, 1973, Śrīla Prabhupāda left Kolkata for Māyāpur with his devotee driver, his secretary and I. We left before sunrise with our luggage and some prasādam loaded into the standard Indian car, an Ambassador. The roads were less travelled but it turned out to be an eventful morning.

The first half of the trip was quiet. We stopped about half way between Kolkata and Māyāpur at what became a very magical place, a Prabhupada Tirtha, the mango grove. It was a small area to the side of the road with about a dozen young mango trees. It was just turning light and Śrīla Prabhupāda directed me to where he would like to sit. We sat on the grass next to him. After a moment, Śrīla Prabhupāda looked at me and said, "You can lead us in chanting the prayers to the spiritual master."

I had been with his party now for six months but had never led a kīrtan. There were always so many more qualified devotees around when Śrīla Prabhupāda was at a temple. I have the voice of a frog. I did not mind playing the mṛdaṅga or kartals for him but never considered leading a kīrtan. Now in this beautiful, intimate spot he gave me this wonderful opportunity to chant prayers to him. We all chanted together and then took prasādam. After a short time, we were back in the car and on the road to Mayapur.

By now, the sun was shining brightly and the road was active. Construction work was being done on the road as well. A few dozen Bengali men and boys were working on the small road swinging picks and digging with shovels, repairing holes in the road. Up to this point, we were making good progress. Once, Śrīla Prabhupāda even chastised his driver, saying he was going too fast.

Suddenly progress came to an abrupt halt. While driving along the work area the driver hit one of the workers. He did not knock him down as he hit him with the side of the car, but it spun the man around. Our devotee driver immediately slowed down to almost a stop. Śrīla Prabhupāda, who always knew what was to be done in every situation said, "Do not stop, keep going." The Ambassador continued moving along, picking up some speed. The situation intensified. As we looked ahead some of the workers had formed a roadblock. A dozen of them stood across the road with their shovels and picks raised and blocked the road. We waited for Śrīla Prabhupāda's next instruction. It quickly came. "All right, stop the car".

As soon as we stopped, all the workers surrounded the car, their tools in hand. Śrīla Prabhupāda sat in the back behind the driver and I was next to him. I rolled down the window for him as he indicated and Śrīla Prabhupāda began to speak to them in Bengali. The workers were all yelling and screaming at us. Being from the West we were used to being surrounded by the locals whenever we stopped, but this was different. This was scary! Their eyes were glaring at us, in a way you only see when you are in West Bengal.

The talk continued for several minutes as our Divine Master tried to diffuse the situation. Finally, Śrīla Prabhupāda said, "Give him ten rupees." His driver pulled out a ten-rupee note and handed it to one of the workers. Again they began to yell and scream and raise their shovels and picks. The arguing continued for a few more minutes. Only Śrīla Prabhupāda talked to them as we sat quietly. Finally, Śrīla Prabhupāda said, "Give them ten more rupees." The driver quickly pulled out another note and handed it to the worker. Śrīla Prabhupāda said, "Okay, now we can go." I rolled up his window as the car began to drive away. The workers were still shouting and waving their tools as we left but they let us pass.

Śrīla Prabhupāda did not chastise his disciple, driving the car again, other than telling him the importance of not driving too fast. When we came to Māyāpur Dhāma, the car slowed as it passed Yoga-pitha, the birthplace of Lord Caitanya Mahāprabhu. As we passed, Śrīla Prabhupāda folded his hands in prayer but did not ask to stop. The car went on to the ISKCON land and stopped there. He stayed there for three days in the small thatched roof hut at the front of the property and gave his senior disciples instructions on developing ISKCON Māyāpur Dhāma.

I was with Śrīla Prabhupāda two and a half years later when he returned to Māyāpur for the Gaura Pūrṇimā festival in 1975. Upon his arrival, he went to his quarters in the newly erected Lotus building. Śrīla Prabhupāda sat in his room with the managers of Mayapur, Bhavānanda Mahārāja and Jayapataka Mahārāja.

Śrīla Prabhupāda said, "Bhaktivinoda Thakura has given his blessings upon you. You are fulfilling his mission. He wanted that European and Americans should come here. It is all Bhaktivinoda Thakura's blessing. Hare Kṛṣṇa! So there is no scarcity of space for keeping all the devotees?"

Bhavānanda responded, "Everyone is situated in rooms" and Jayapataka added, "Without these wall dwellings, there would have been no hope."

Śrīla Prabhupāda, who was always so concerned about the comfort of his disciples laughed and said, "You must complete, and whatever amount required, I shall pay." Jayapataka Swami realizing the depth of Śrīla Prabhupāda's mercy said, "Only by your mercy you have brought us to this Kṛṣṇa Consciousness movement. Śrīla Prabhupāda humbly replied, "Yes. I am simply messenger. Mercy is of Bhaktivinoda Thakura and Śrīla

Prabhupāda (Śrīla Bhaktisiddhānta Sarasvatī Thakura). Before your coming they predicted, "Somebody will bring". Maybe that somebody I am." He then laughed for a moment and added, "Bhaktivinoda Thakura predicted. So anyway, Kṛṣṇa has given us nice place. Stay here."

On another day, you spoke to the devotees of the Rādhā Dāmodara Sankīrtan Party. At the end of the darśana, one of them thanked you for allowing them to stay in Māyāpur Dhāma. You quickly replied, "Māyāpur is your home! The West is only meant for two purposes, preaching and sense gratification but your home is Mayapur."

> *Śrīla Prabhupāda, for a moment you described to the few of us in the room, your position, 'Maybe that somebody I am'. You quickly changed the subject not wanting to continue on the topic. I bow down to your lotus feet, who has saved us and generations more by your causeless mercy.*

54

"They can chant their 'Nitāi-Gaura, Hari-Bols'..."

March 18, 1973 ISKCON Mayapur, India

During ISKCON's first international festival in Mayapur, many devotees demonstrated how they had become influenced by the Bengali form of kīrtan. Śrīla Prabhupāda expressed some displeasure about the chanting of so many different mantras. "They can chant their 'Nitāi-Gaura, Hari- Bols', but I will chant Hare Kṛṣṇa and go back to Godhead."

If we had understood the translation of "Hari-bol," then we would have known what to do. Śrīla Prabhupāda enjoyed chanting the Mahā-mantra.

55

"... if one is being attacked, you have the right to defend yourself."

March 16, 1973 ISKCON Mayapur, India

During my first trip to Māyāpur with Śrīla Prabhupāda, the guesthouse had not been built, so our quarters were very austere. We stayed in a goshala, a thatched hut, which had been prepared for his stay. Śrīla Prabhupāda stayed in one room and the rest of us stayed on the other side of a partition. I had never seen so many mosquitoes in my life. It was so bad that by the time I had the net over Śrīla Prabhupāda's bed there were already mosquitoes inside the net.

One night, after we both climbed under the net, I started massaging his legs.

"There are so many mosquitoes," I said. "Should I kill them, Śrīla Prabhupāda?" "Yes! They are attacking," he said. "According to śāstra, if one is being attacked, you have the right to defend yourself. And, they are attacking."

So, as I massaged him, I watched. Whenever I saw a mosquito in the air, I raised my hands and clapped them together. Sometimes I gently smacked Śrīla Prabhupāda's body as one landed on his head or back. This was the most unusual service I ever did. I enjoyed it immensely. I never considered myself much of a warrior, but this enemy was no match for me. I had finally been given a service I was good at; killing insects. Śrīla Prabhupāda was very kind.

He also had the best description of these annoying insects. One morning he rang his bell very early. I walked into his room slowly, still half asleep. He looked at me with a touch of anger and said, "Some mosquito, last night, he was cutting my forehead. He created so much disturbance. He made it difficult for me to do my translating work."

It was incredible. No matter what was going on, Śrīla Prabhupāda always related it to his service to Kṛṣṇa. It was never about bodily inconvenience. He only complained about something if it interfered with his service. Of course, all I ever saw was Śrīla Prabhupāda serving his Guru Mahārāja, and Śrīla Prabhupāda in the state of bliss. The two went on simultaneously.

56

"Go on, Take Prasādam"

March 17, 1973 ISKCON Mayapur, India

While staying in the small facility at the front of the property, Śrīla Prabhupāda sometimes walked outside and observed his disciples taking prasādam behind his quarters. In the existing conditions, Śrīla Prabhupāda considered his disciples like pioneers, undergoing great austerities to help him in his mission. In most places in India, the conditions were fair, at best. Śrīla Prabhupāda was anxious to have guest facilities built so his disciples would have adequate living arrangements.

Having no permanent cooking facility, the devotees used a small kerosene stove to cook puris. They cooked outside, near the area where they took prasādam. Cooking was going on as the devotees were eating, so they were continually being brought hot puris. During that time of the year, date trees were tapped for their sap and it was cooked down into an incredibly tasty jaggery.

One day Śrīla Prabhupāda left his room to use the meagre bathroom facility. He walked outside and, of course, everyone offered their obeisances.

"Go on. Take prasādam," he told them.

The exchange between Śrīla Prabhupāda and his disciples was so sweet. He always enjoyed seeing his disciples eat prasādam. He saw the combination of hot puris and date gur and said, "Oh, very good combination."

Later in his room, he said to me, "This is not a very good practice . . . the devotees having puris made on the spot, hot like that. This is not our system. You just take prasādam. Are we so high, lofty? These devotees have to be getting hot puris, one after another. This is not good. This must be stopped."

That day I transferred the message to one of the temple administrators so that Śrīla Prabhupāda's wishes could be carried out.

In India, especially in the holy places, Śrīla Prabhupāda was always aware of how others saw us. He knew we were Vaisnavas, despite our western birth. He also knew we needed to be trained properly in Vaisnava etiquette. For the benefit of all he wanted his temples in India to be considered first class. He patiently trained us so that it would happen.

57

"Water for bath?"

March 18, 1973 ISKCON Māyāpur and Vṛndāvana in India

The simplest arrangements were often the biggest cause of anxiety, especially in India. In 1973, while in Mayapur, I put an immersion heater in a brass bucket filled with water to warm it for Śrīla Prabhupāda's bath. Naturally it did not always work. The heaters burned out or the electricity went off. Śrīla Prabhupāda would be ready for his bath with no warm water.

"Why do not I have any hot water for bath?" he shouted.

When he stayed on the second floor at the Rādhā Dāmodara

temple in Vṛndāvana he said, "You can place a bucket of water outside on the roof and the sun will heat it sufficiently for taking bath."

That usually worked, except when the monkeys decided they wanted to drink from it and proceeded to knock over the bucket.

Serving Śrīla Prabhupāda was very easy if you were Kṛṣṇa Conscious, Prabhupada Conscious. To do it expertly one only needed to think of him twenty-four hours a day, instead of thinking of ourselves. It did not require a big education. Śrīla Prabhupāda taught us how to love Kṛṣṇa by teaching us how to love him. As he told me, 'service is love.' He taught by example.

58

"Simply they are gossiping. Tell them to stop."

March 18, 1973 ISKCON Mayapur, India

Māyāpur was chilly in the evening, but Śrīla Prabhupāda never complained. He complained, though, about the unnecessary talk between his disciples. Since we all stayed in the same room, Śrīla Prabhupāda heard us talking.

"Tell them to be quiet," he told me. "All this talk is not good. Simply they are gossiping. Tell them to stop."

This was not easy for me to do since the devotees were usually my senior god-brothers. I told them Prabhupada had asked that they be quiet. This same scenario occurred months later when we stayed in the guesthouse. In 1973, Māyāpur was such a quiet place that Śrīla Prabhupāda could hear any talking. Whenever he was at any ISKCON temple, many of his disciples would gather. It was a perfect situation for devotees to exchange stories about this person and that person.

"Why must everything deteriorate into this idle talk, idle discussion," Śrīla Prabhupāda said. "This is wasting time, destroying Kṛṣṇa Consciousness."

I always "watered it down" before relaying this to my godbrothers. I did not have the nerve to tell them as Prabhupada had told me. I never heard him mention it to anyone when they were in his room, but he definitely let me know about it!

This was one of Śrīla Prabhupāda's great qualities. He was very careful not to discourage anyone through criticism. If they were capable of dealing with it then he would chastise them. Otherwise, he was the greatest transcendental diplomat. His only goal was to infect as many people as possible with love of Kṛṣṇa and if you had the chance to personally associate with him then there was a strong possibility of becoming deeply attached to him, no matter how hard you fought it.

59

"This music is very nice,"

March 25, 1973 Air India to Mumbai from Hyderabad

Śrīla Prabhupāda's actions were ever fresh. After eight months of being his personal servant, I thought I had a good understanding of how to act and what to say in response to his questions so I did not get into trouble. I considered that our relationship was strictly spiritual master and servant. Over time, though, it became apparent that Śrīla Prabhupāda wanted me to speak freely and honestly, when he asked a question. He was very kind. I never felt he "put me on trial."

One day as Śrīla Prabhupāda and I entered an aeroplane on Air India, Indian classical music was being played over the intercom. We walked to our seats. As always, Śrīla Prabhupāda took the seat by the window and I sat down beside him. The music continued.

"Do you like this music?" he asked smiling.

I stared at him with an empty glance thinking, "How can I tell him I like this music. Sure, it sounds nice, but there is no chanting of the Lord's names going on. It is only instruments playing. That can't be Kṛṣṇa Conscious." Speculating fearfully, I missed my opportunity to be intimate with my loving spiritual master and said nothing.

"This music is very nice," Śrīla Prabhupāda mercifully said.

"Yes, Śrīla Prabhupāda," I answered with relief. "It is nice."

I felt like a cheater, unable to be honest. I was so concerned about the outcome of my answer I forgot that Śrīla Prabhupāda was a person with likes and dislikes. He heard the music and remembered Kṛṣṇa. I heard the music, calculated it was māyā, and wondered how to answer in a Kṛṣṇa conscious way.

60

"I call it Saint Hellish..."

April 2, 1973 Train from Zurich to San Moritz, Switzerland

While in Mumbai, a senior disciple showed Śrīla Prabhupāda an appealing postcard of Saint Moritz with its colourful wild flowers and rolling green meadows. It was beautiful. One devotee suggested to Śrīla Prabhupāda to stop and rest there during his long trip from Mumbai to New York. Śrīla Prabhupāda had been travelling quite briskly, spending no more than six or seven days in each location. Stopping in Saint Moritz appeared to be a gallant proposal.

Another motive to disembark at Saint Moritz, however, was gold speculation. A few senior men were thinking of fortifying

ISKCON's reserves by investing in gold before the price was deregulated. Zurich was the best place to invest in gold bullion. Śrīla Prabhupāda nipped the idea in the bud.

From Zurich Airport, Śrīla Prabhupāda, a young brahmacārī named Jai Hari, and I boarded a luxury train headed for San Moritz. The train ride through the Alps was magnificent. Following the contour of the snow-covered mountains, the train circled continuously in different directions. The awe-inspiring scenery had the full attention of Jai Hari and me. Śrīla Prabhupāda quietly chanted as we pointed out the different scenic views to each other, completely oblivious to our spiritual guide sitting beside us.

"What do they call this place?" Śrīla Prabhupāda calmly asked breaking our meditation.

"San Moritz, Śrīla Prabhupāda, Saint Moritz!" I quickly said feeling delighted to answer such a simple question.

"They may call it Saint Moritz," Śrīla Prabhupāda responded. "I call it Saint Hellish. This place is hellish. Look out there. There is no life anywhere, simply branches of trees and snow. There is not a living thing for miles."

Śrīla Prabhupāda had effectively turned our illusion into an opportunity to instruct two of his fledgling disciples. Jai Hari and I spent the rest of the journey with our heads down, quietly chanting and hearing the transcendental sound vibration of the Mahā-mantra, just as Śrīla Prabhupāda desired. Being with Śrīla Prabhupāda was the most fortunate position. Just by following his example, we knew we were rightly situated.

When we asked him a question, the answer we received was the absolute truth. He regularly pacified thousands of disciples, answering their questions, alleviating their fears and engaging them in Kṛṣṇa's service.

Śrīla Prabhupāda, please free me from my attachment to the mountains of māyā so that I can hear your kind and gentle instructions.

61

"Ooohhh, this is much too cold!"

April 3, 1973 Saint Moritz, Switzerland

The San Moritz we arrived at was much different from what we saw in the postcard. The beginning of April was still wintertime here. It was clear why it was such a popular ski resort. Snow lay on the ground as far as the eye could see. The hotel had a central lobby with an elevator and our lodging was a spacious three-bedroom condominium, complete with a kitchen. The large living room had sliding glass doors leading to a veranda with a fantastic view of the snow-covered mountains. By the standards of many it was breathtaking, but not to Śrīla Prabhupāda.

Śrīla Prabhupāda was very regulated. It never mattered where we were. His life continued like clockwork and his schedule remained constant.

The first morning there, Śrīla Prabhupāda put on his warm saffron-hooded coat and prepared for his morning walk.

"We will go for a walk," he said. "Shall we see how cold it is?"

Since we were on the ground floor, His Divine Grace opened the sliding glass door to walk onto the veranda, which led to the great outdoors. Suddenly a whistling blast of ice-cold air filled the entire condominium. It was blizzard-like.

"Ooohhh, this is much too cold!" Śrīla Prabhupāda exclaimed with his eyes opened wide.

Whenever I witnessed these childlike expressions, my heart melted with joy. Śrīla Prabhupāda exuded the innocence of a child. While most disciples experienced his powerful, determined preaching, I felt fortunate to see Śrīla Prabhupāda's face light up with endearing, intimate expressions.

"We will walk in the hallway inside the building," he said.

A little arctic blast was not going to interfere with Śrīla Prabhupāda's morning walk. So, His Divine Grace, Pradyumna and I headed for the hallway. This, however presented a different set of problems. The resort was designed to operate with very little energy waste. When the hall sensors detected someone's presence, the lights would turn on for a set amount of time and quickly turn off again. As we walked up and down the corridor, we were required to push various buttons along the way to keep the lights from going out. Otherwise, we would have been walking in the dark.

Pradyumna eventually went back into the apartment. Śrīla Prabhupāda and I continued to walk up and down the hallway. I ran from button to button pushing and chanting, pushing and chanting. This went on for about half an hour.

"The cold weather has given me an appetite," Śrīla Prabhupāda then said. "You can go in and make me some halava."

"All right, Śrīla Prabhupāda," I replied, still concerned about the button pushing. "Do you want me to wait until after your walk or should I go now?"

Śrīla Prabhupāda humourously retorted, "No, I will walk. You can go make the halava."

We always loved when Śrīla Prabhupāda had an appetite. It was a joy to cook for him. When I went in, I said to the others, "Śrīla Prabhupāda is still walking in the hall. Someone needs to go out and push the buttons to keep the lights on for him."

We all peeked out the door to see Śrīla Prabhupāda chanting, walking and pushing the buttons to keep the lights on. It was

One of my many enjoyable tasks was cooking for Śrīla Prabhupāda. The more he ate, the happier we were. Our other most enjoyable activity was watching Śrīla Prabhupāda as he did anything. It was always an education for us. As it says in *Bhagavad-gītā*, how does the devotee walk, how does he act... Being with Śrīla Prabhupāda gave us first-hand experience of how a person from the spiritual world lived every moment. He never disappointed us.

Jai Śrīla Prabhupāda!

62

"So now it takes two hands to tell time..."

April 4, 1973 Zurich, Switzerland

While spending two days in a land famous for its quality timepieces, Śyāmasundara presented Śrīla Prabhupāda with a digital watch, the latest in wristwatch technology. It looked very modern. Its round face was completely black except for a few seconds when a small button was pressed and the time appeared in red. It was quite innovative. Śrīla Prabhupāda unemotionally put on the watch and his secretary showed him how to use it. He explained that to view the time, you must press the button on the side of the watch with your right hand and then you can see the time. It did not take long for Śrīla Prabhupāda to make his evaluation of the latest technology.

"So, now it takes two hands to tell the time instead of one," he said.

Śrīla Prabhupāda was always practical. He was not impressed by so-called advancement of science and technology. For instance, on occasion he would walk outside in the early morning, look up at the sky and seeing the moon say, "Today is Ekādaśī ."

He would eagerly use any innovation that helped him in his translation work. It was a term we learned soon after we moved into a temple. As he states in *Śrīmad-Bhāgavatam* [4.29.56]: "One should not be attached to material opulence, but material opulence may be accepted in the Kṛṣṇa Consciousness movement to facilitate the propagation of the movement." In other words, material opulence may be accepted as yukta-vairāgya, that is, for renunciation. Śrīla Prabhupāda was not attached to any material facility but he was completely attached to serving his spiritual master and Kṛṣṇa.

63

"Hare Kṛṣṇa, Hare Kṛṣṇa, Kṛṣṇa Kṛṣṇa..."

April 4, 1973 Zurich, Switzerland

After leaving San Moritz, we spent one day in an exclusive hotel overlooking the River Rhine in Zurich. Śrīla Prabhupāda had a room and his entourage stayed together in the room next door. They were not adjoining rooms, however. When it was time for his massage, I had to go into his room to change my clothes to avoid walking in the hallway in my gamcha. One day when I finished giving him a massage, I inadvertently left my bead bag in his room.

They were not the japa beads Śrīla Prabhupāda had chanted on at my initiation two years earlier. Unfortunately, I lost them in New Vṛndāvana. I had considered asking Śrīla Prabhupāda to chant on another set of beads for me but I did not want to admit how careless I had been. My bead bag was prasādam given to me by His Divine Grace. When I returned to Śrīla Prabhupāda's room I noticed, to my delight, his hand in my bead bag. For the next half hour, I joyfully watched as he chanted on my beads.

Again, Śrīla Prabhupāda fulfilled my desire without me asking. I waited until he put my bead bag down and took my newly sanctified beads to our quarters. Elated, I bragged to the others how a miracle had just taken place.

Śrīla Prabhupāda, you always knew my desires and showed me such kindness. I never saw you chant on any Japa beads but your own. That day you sat there peacefully chanting round after round on my beads. It brought me so much happiness. You stated that your happiness was seeing your disciples developing their love for Kṛṣṇa. I pray to one day bring you happiness.

64

"Bring me some 7-Up."

April 5, 1973 Pan American Flight, London to New York

Since Śrīla Prabhupāda was transcendental and completely free to do as he pleased, flying with him was a thrilling experience. I never knew what to expect. This particular day was no exception.

Śrīla Prabhupāda sat in a window seat near the back of the aeroplane. Śyāmasundara and I were seated next to him. As was the custom on the transcontinental flights, the flight attendants frequently offered refreshments to passengers to avoid the dehydrating effects of recycled air. A flight attendant walked up the aisle with a tray of drinks in clear plastic cups and offered them to the passengers.

"What is that?" Śrīla Prabhupāda asked me as she approached our seats.

"Oh, that's 7-Up, Śrīla Prabhupāda," I said. "Would you like some?"

"Yes. Let me try it," he replied.

I immediately requested three cups for all of us. Śyāmasundara and I waited for Śrīla Prabhupāda to take the first sip. We wanted to be certain the 7-Up would be prasādam. We watched carefully as he put the cup to his lotus-like mouth. He drank some and put the cup down on the table.

"Ah! This is very refreshing," he said.

We finished our drinks within minutes.

During that flight, we had 7-Up three or four times. Each time Śrīla Prabhupāda drank one he said, "Ah, very refreshing. This is very good."

One time the flight attendant put the can down on the table along with the cups filled with ice. Śrīla Prabhupāda picked up the can and asked, "What are the ingredients?"

"Water, sugar, citric acid, natural lemon-lime oil," he read. "Oh! This is all right. This is very good. It is all natural ingredients."

Śrīla Prabhupāda was marvellous. He could have been doing a commercial for the soda. He was very enthusiastic about his discovery. I excitedly watched him enjoy each moment.

After arriving at the temple, one of the devotees asked if there was anything Śrīla Prabhupāda needed. I could not think of anything. I could not imagine what the devotee could get for my beloved spiritual master. The devotee was determined to offer something to him.

"Well, he likes 7-Up," I finally said. "You could get that for him."

I convinced him it was a good idea. That day the devotee brought a case of 7-Up and I stored it in Śrīla Prabhupāda's kitchen.

I must confess, for the first few days, I was hesitant and never offered the 7-Up to Śrīla Prabhupāda. I began drinking it because I was afraid to offer it to him. I could not think of the right moment, finally, the occasion arose.

One evening, a temple president arrived from out of town to see Śrīla Prabhupāda. While His Divine Grace was in his sitting room speaking with this disciple, Śrīla Prabhupāda rang his bell. I started toward Śrīla Prabhupāda's sitting room when this devotee stopped me in the hall.

"Śrīla Prabhupāda wants some water," he said.

"OK," I replied, but continued to walk toward Guru Mahārāja's room.

"Śrīla Prabhupāda wants water!" the flustered temple president loudly reiterated. Annoyed, I tried to keep my composure and replied, "Please wait. I want to ask His Divine Grace something."

Apparently, this disciple was trying to have a private conversation with Śrīla Prabhupāda and I was interrupting. Lacking sensitivity and imagination I did not immediately understand his needs, so I made my way into Śrīla Prabhupāda's sitting room and offered my obeisances.

"Śrīla Prabhupāda," I said. "Would you like some 7-Up?"

"Oh yes!" he replied smiling. "Bring me some 7-Up."

I raced back to the kitchen and filled a silver goblet with 7-Up and ice. Hurrying back to his sitting room, I placed the 7-Up on his desk in front of him and offered my obeisances. Śrīla Prabhupāda sat back on his asana and sipped the drink.

"This is very refreshing," he said.

He got up from his asana and walked around the room enjoying his 7-Up. I remained in the room, blissfully watching my spiritual master enjoy the cold drink. My god-brother was surprised by the entire affair and anxious for me to leave the room. After Śrīla Prabhupāda finished his 7-Up, I took the empty cup, offered my obeisances and happily left his room. I felt I had pleased my Guru Mahārāja by this simple act, in spite of inadvertently annoying my god-brother.

Śrīla Prabhupāda, I am forever blessed by your causeless mercy. Thank you for the opportunity to witness your playful pastimes. Observing your confidential līlā allowed me a tiny glimpse of your association with the Supreme Lord. Your beloved childlike nature contrasted sharply with your lion-like ācārya profile. For pushing on Lord Caitanya's movement, you forcefully did the needful. As a pure devotee of the Lord, you have no attachment to the fame and adoration that was constantly bestowed upon you. For this reason, you are worthy of it.

65

"Drinking 7-Up is not necessary."

April 8, 1973 ISKCON Brooklyn, New York

At this time, Bali Mardan had been talking about getting a new temple facility in New York City, so he invited Śrīla Prabhupāda to look at a possible location. The sun was brightly shining as Bali Mardan, Kirtiraja and I followed Śrīla Prabhupāda into a small Toyota. Bali Mardan drove for a while until he finally stopped across the street from a large, beautiful cathedral.

"This is the possible temple I told you about, Śrīla Prabhupāda," Bali Mardan said. "We can't go in because it may not be beneficial if they know we are Hare Kṛṣṇas. We can look at it from here."

We all got out of the car and looked at this immense cathedral from across the street. The structure was stately and beautiful. Fortunately, the front doors of the church were open and we could see inside. Śrīla Prabhupāda seemed very impressed with the facility. He could see the huge marble pillars inside.

"This will make a very nice ISKCON hall," he said. "This is beautiful."

As we stood on the side walk, Śrīla Prabhupāda turned around and saw a small Italian grocery.

"Do you think they have 7-Up?" he asked Kirtiraja.

"Well, I can see if they do, Śrīla Prabhupāda," Kirtiraja said, with a shocked look. "Do you want one?"

"Yes, I would like a 7-Up," Śrīla Prabhupāda said.

Kirtiraja went into the store and quickly returned with a can of 7-Up. Śrīla Prabhupāda regally stood with cane in hand and japa bag around his neck. He looked especially transcendental.

Kirtiraja opened the can and Śrīla Prabhupāda took it with his right hand. His cane was in his left hand, securely planted on the concrete side walk. He lifted the can to his lotus-like lips and sipped the 7-Up. I was in ecstasy watching the next episode of the 7-Up saga. We could not contain our joyful smiles seeing our Guru Mahārāja's aristocratic simplicity as he drank about half the can.

"All right. Now we will go," he said.

After we all got into the car, Śrīla Prabhupāda handed the can to Bali Mardan and said, "I've had enough. You can drink."

The three of us blissfully passed around the maha-remnants until we finished the can of soda. The ride back to the temple was light-hearted and carefree.

I tried not to spread the news, realizing it could create a 7-Up frenzy. A week later, when we arrived in Los Angeles it was apparent that the news had already reached the New Dvārakā community. Karāndhara informed Śrīla Prabhupāda that 7-Up aided in relieving gastro-intestinal digestive discomfort. Śrīla Prabhupāda occasionally drank a small glass to relieve his stomach pain.

"This is not good," he said one day. "We should not be

drinking so much 7-Up. I take it for digestion. Otherwise, drinking 7-Up is not necessary."

When we returned to India, many devotees were avidly drinking soda since they had heard that Śrīla Prabhupāda condoned such beverages. One day, as Śrīla Prabhupāda left his flat in Juhu, he noticed the stairway lined with 7-Up and Limca bottles. Disapproving of the litter he declared,

"What is this? This should not be done! This is not good! This can't be done!"

He continued walking to the temple and did not mention it further.

Śrīla Prabhupāda, I never saw you do anything for your own sense gratification. It is my feeling that you engaged in these unique pastimes just to increase the love of your disciples who were fortunate enough to be with you. You were completely renounced and totally satisfied serving the Supreme Lord. The vision of you on the side walk is forever etched upon my heart Thank you for teaching us how to use everything in Kṛṣṇa's service.

66

"They are in māyā, sleeping"

April 13, 1973 New York to Los Angeles, California

During one short flight from New York, many devotees arranged for seats in the same row as Śrīla Prabhupāda. As Śrīla Prabhupāda's personal servant, I was fortunate to be seated next to him. As the flight progressed, some of his disciples began to fall asleep and do, what I called, "the devotee dive-bomb."

It was quite a sight seeing a row of shaven heads bobbing up and down. Prabhupada was not amused.

"Just see," he said. "Everyone is wide awake except for the devotees. They are in māyā, sleeping. Everyone else is awake. Why they cannot stay awake."

Usually when Śrīla Prabhupāda addressed me in this way I became silent. I was afraid of saying the wrong thing and possibly disturbing him further. I simply sat in silence and waited for him to stop. This was one such instance.

During my stay with Śrīla Prabhupāda, I learned there was no such thing as a good reason. There was not a point you could make that Prabhupada could not defeat, and I was not advanced enough to have him start chastising me on a regular basis. Therefore, I did not even try to argue that the devotees only slept a few hours compared to the non-devotees. Prabhupada spent a few more minutes making his point. One thing was certain; I did not sleep on that flight.

Śrīla Prabhupāda often talked about reducing our eating and sleeping but he was always practical. He told us to use our common sense, and never encouraged us to fast except on prescribed days such as Ekādaśī or Appearance days of the Lord and his pure devotees. He never objected to our getting sufficient sleep but he did not like to see us sleeping during the day. He wanted us to rise early in the morning and he always set the example. He showed us practically how to be a devotee.

67

"This is what love means - to do service."

April 13, 1973 ISKCON Los Angeles, California

Certain service was particularly enlivening. Walking behind His Divine Grace as he left the aeroplane and entered the terminal building was one of the most amazing experiences. At this time, it had been eight months since Śrīla Prabhupāda was in the United States. It was wonderful the way he prepared himself for his grand entrance. After the seat belt sign went on instructing the passengers to stay seated, he usually got out of his seat, went to the bathroom and put on tilak. I accompanied him, waiting outside the bathroom door. The walk to and from our seats could be exciting if the plane rocked about due to turbulence or lumbered in for a landing. If an attendant tried to stop him, he ignored her request, as if he did not hear her. As he returned to his seat, he carefully hung his bead bag around his neck. When the plane landed, he put a flower garland on. If there were other garlands, he gave one to each person in his party.

As he left the plane and entered the corridor, chanting could be heard in the background. It grew louder and louder as we entered the lounge. Śrīla Prabhupāda's smile grew larger as he approached his loving disciples. On this day, there were several hundred devotees in the airport as Śrīla Prabhupāda walked into the terminal. They were oblivious to everyone and everything going on around them, except for their glorious spiritual master. I have no qualification to describe the feelings of my god-brothers and god-sisters, as I have never been fortunate enough to have such strong loving emotions for Śrīla Prabhupāda. It was obvious to everyone in the airport that devotees were feeling transcendental bliss. The loving reciprocation between Śrīla Prabhupāda and his disciples was the easiest to see in his "airport līlā." For several minutes, it seemed that no-one's feet touched the ground. Torrents of ecstatic tears flowed freely from everyone except for one fallen soul: me.

We arrived in New Dvārakā and entered Śrīla Prabhupāda's quarters at about noon. I immediately prepared for his massage. During the massage, my mind was very disturbed. I could not free myself from the pain of thinking that everyone had such love for their guru except for me. I was a cheater, an impostor. I finally got the courage to speak while massaging Śrīla Prabhupāda's back. This way, I did not have to speak to him face to face.

"Śrīla Prabhupāda," I said. "All of your disciples have so much love for you. It makes me feel so bad. I lack this intense love. When I'm with you at the airport, I can see everyone dancing, chanting and crying. I have so much association with you, yet I do not feel this overwhelming love like they do."

I hoped he would say something to relieve my mind. He remained silent. Tormented, I finished his massage and went back to my room to finish preparing his lunch. After he chanted Gāyatrī mantra, he called me into his room. As I entered, I offered my obeisances and looked up with great concern because he had such a serious look on his face.

"So, do you like serving me?" he asked.

"Oh, yes, Prabhupada," I said. "I like serving you very much."

"Then, that is love," he explained. "Everyone can do so many things . . . singing, dancing, and jumping up and down. But you are actually doing something. Isn't this love?"

"I guess so, Śrīla Prabhupāda," I said.

"So, you just do your service," he continued. "That is all that is necessary. This is what love means - to do service."

My dear Śrīla Prabhupāda, out of compassion for this fallen soul, you have encouraged me over the years even though I have been unable to grant you residence in my heart. I see now, as I saw then, that so many of your disciples have such great love for you and I have none. Despite my shortcomings, you allow me the intimate service of describing your amazing grace upon me. It is ironic that out of all of your disciples you have selected me to describe your nectarean līlā. This is just another display of your causeless mercy. Thank you so much for your kind words. I pray that some day I will be qualified to taste a drop of love of Godhead so that I can sing, dance and chant like your devoted disciples.

68

"I want to translate books."

April 14, 1973 ISKCON Los Angeles, California

His Divine Grace spoke many times about retiring from managerial duties to concentrate on translating the scriptures for humanity at large. My first experience was as follows:

One morning at about 9:00, Śrīla Prabhupāda called me into his room and told me to call Karāndhara. This happened often while we were in New Dvārakā. Śrīla Prabhupāda had great faith in Karāndhara's abilities. He even praised Karāndhara for fixing the concrete stairs that led to Śrīla Prabhupāda's garden.

"Karāndhara can do anything," Śrīla Prabhupāda commented, pointing to the stairs.

If any problem arose while we were in Los Angeles, Śrīla Prabhupāda called for Karāndhara to solve it.

When Karāndhara arrived in Śrīla Prabhupāda's room, His Divine Grace stunned him by saying, "I do not want to be involved in management so much. I want to translate books."

"Yes," Karāndhara enthusiastically replied. "I can do all of your secretarial work from here and you can stay here to translate. We'll keep everything very nice for you. Yes! We'll do it immediately,"

Śrīla Prabhupāda said. "I want to have no business. No more business. No more management. You handle all of my affairs for me."

Karāndhara left the room, ready to organize ISKCON from his office on Watseka Avenue.

"This is amazing," I thought. "Prabhupada is going to let the Governing Body Commission (GBC) run the society."

New Dvārakā was perfect for such an arrangement. It had facilities for Śrīla Prabhupāda, including the garden, which was his favourite place. He could have stayed there for years and translated all day if he wanted.

About one hour later, Śrīla Prabhupāda again rang his bell. I entered Śrīla Prabhupāda's quarters and offered my obeisances, but before I raised my head from the floor he said, "Call Karāndhara."

Karāndhara soon entered the room and offered his obeisances. As he did, Śrīla Prabhupāda noticed a letter in Karāndhara's kurta pocket. Śrīla Prabhupāda's eyes grew large.

"What is that?" he asked.

"Oh, it is a letter for you, Śrīla Prabhupāda," Karāndhara replied.

"Open it," Śrīla Prabhupāda instructed.

Karāndhara opened the letter and read it to Śrīla Prabhupāda. It was a typical letter from a senior disciple who managed one of ISKCON's temples. Śrīla Prabhupāda intently listened and then dictated a reply.

Śrīla Prabhupāda's retirement lasted a little over an hour. It was the first retirement I had experienced, but certainly not the last. Śrīla Prabhupāda took pleasure in translating Śrīmad Bhāgavatam for us. He also relished teaching his children how to walk on the spiritual path. His patience was endless. On a daily basis, he picked us up as we stumbled, and encouraged us to try to walk again. No matter how much he dreamed of retirement, he would not leave us until we were able to walk on our own. The time has come for us to walk. It is difficult without you here, answering our letters and overseeing our big meetings.

> *The urgency of your translating books for future generations is more apparent as each year goes by. You always knew you would only be with us for such a short time but your words live with us forever. For me your leaving was much too soon. Because I am a neophyte, I sit here and long for your personal association. Please benedict me with your personal service life after life.*
>
> *Jai Śrīla Prabhupāda!*

69

"Three things keep me alive"

April 15, 1973 ISKCON Los Angeles, California

One day while I was massaging Śrīla Prabhupāda, rubbing mustard oil on his back he said, "Three things keep me alive; my morning walk, my massage and my Ayurvedic medicine." I had heard Śrīla Prabhupāda mention this on a few occasions.

He was very regular in doing all three. Wherever he was in the world, he would go on his morning walk, even the day after a twelve-hour flight. The next morning he would be walking with his followers as the sun was rising. It did not matter if it was hot, cold or raining. His walk could be from one to two hours in length and always at a brisk pace.

His morning massage was done regularly and around the same time every day, just before noon. It would last between one to two hours and it was an Ayurvedic type massage done with sandalwood oil on his head and mustard oil on the rest of his body. He said, "sandalwood oil helps keep a cool head and the mustard oil is heating." This type of massage is very good for blood circulation. He liked it done with vigour. In the evening before resting, he would take a dry massage, mainly on his feet and legs for up to one hour.

He took the same Ayurvedic medicine the entire time I was with him from September of 1972 until July of 1975. It was a tonic, called Yogendra ras. Some of the ingredients were gold powder and crushed pearl in small quantities. It was made into small balls, reddish in colour. When Śrīla Prabhupāda was away from India for some time, he would have it sent to him along with the black cardamom seeds that it was mixed with. He would only have his disciples purchase it from one Ayurvedic pharmacy saying, "It is the only one I trust because of the expensive ingredients. The others are all cheating."

He would take this mixture every other morning before his morning walk. I would prepare it while he was in the bathroom around 5:00 am I would drop the two small balls into a black marble mortar and pestle, and then add the seeds of one black cardamom and a dab of raw honey. After mixing it up thoroughly I would place the mortar and pestle on his desk. When he sat down he would take the pestle in his hand and get as much of the tonic on it as possible and place it into his mouth, licking off every bit After that he would pick up the small mortar and with his tongue, lick every bit that was left. Śrīla Prabhupāda never, ever wasted anything and his medicine was no exception.

Śrīla Prabhupāda never spoke to me about following an Ayurvedic lifestyle by name, but it is very clear that he did. Getting up before sunrise, taking cold bath and getting morning sun during his walk are basic common sense principles in Ayurveda. He ate local fruits for breakfast with his milk or yogurt and had his main meal while the sun was highest in the sky. His lunch regularly consisted of rice Dahl, chapatis and a few chaunced vegetable preparations. In the evening about two hours before rest, he would have his very hot milk, with honey and if he had good appetite some prasādam. Only occasionally did he eat deep fried foods like puris and samosa although he liked them very much.

He was very in tune with his body and as soon as he noticed some sign of ill health, he would make adjustments in his eating and massage. He often asked for kichari for lunch at this time. Kichari is well known for balancing all three doshas in Ayurveda. In simple terms out of balance doshas, are the cause of all disease in the body. Śrīla Prabhupāda said, "disease comes from three things; anxiety, uncleanliness and overeating. Overeating means eating more than you can digest. If you can digest ten chapatis eat ten chapatis but if you can only digest one then eat one."

Another Ayurvedic principle is to eat alone. Śrīla Prabhupāda always did this. He had a very sweet way that he would get everyone in the room to leave. When I would bring his meal in and place it on the small low table on the floor, he would take a piece of fruit and give one piece to each of the disciples who were in the room at the time. Then he would give his head a little tilt and say, "Now you can go." He then sat down in front of his plate, meditating on the prasādam as he ate. He did not use utensils or drink water during his meal. He always ate with only his right hand and chewed his food very well.

He once laughingly said to me, "the best thing for health is to cook for yourself, that way no matter how hellish it tastes you will like it because you made it." Although humourously said, this is an important principle of digestion. If you do not like what you are eating, you will not digest it properly.

Thank you Śrīla Prabhupāda, for showing me how to live every moment of my life. You revealed the most important of all rules; to offer all that we do and eat to the Supreme Lord Kṛṣṇa. Everything you did was perfect and your whole life was exemplary. You are the Ācārya for all of us. You instructed us, by your example how to do everything, from the time we got up until we took rest. You even showed us how to rest. As you would so often say, "Kṛṣṇa Consciousness is common sense." Thank you for bestowing us with common sense.

70

"You have no business going to maṅgala-ārati,,"

April 17, 1973 ISKCON Los Angeles, California

I made a few devotee friends while staying with Śrīla Prabhupāda in New Dvārakā. One morning, I decided to go to maṅgala-ārati, to see them. While I was there, Pradyumna came into the temple room and said, "Śrīla Prabhupāda has been ringing his bell. He wants to see you now."

I immediately left the temple room and raced into his room. I offered my obeisances and as I lifted my head I said, "Did you want me, Śrīla Prabhupāda?"

"You have no business going to maṅgala-ārati,," he said in an angry mood. "Your service is to be with me twenty-four hours a day. If I need you, you should be available."

I apologized and said I would never do it again.

Even before going to arati I knew it was not the right thing to do. I had been restless, and thought that no one could fault me for attending maṅgala-ārati,. I figured that Śrīla Prabhupāda usually did not call me so early in the morning. Of course, I should have remembered that he always knew what I was doing, so if I did go to arati he would certainly call me. I was the only person in ISKCON who had a reason not to go to maṅgala-ārati,. For me, attending arati was a sign that I was in māyā.

It felt wonderful walking into your room that early morning. I knew I was going to be chastised for attending maṅgala-ārati,. It confirmed everything I had learned from you. Kṛṣṇa Consciousness was common sense. It was practical. It was not a ritual we performed and could not explain why we did it. Everything we did had a purpose. It was a science. We weren't blindly following rules and regulations. You were teaching us how to use our intelligence, how to be honest with ourselves and honest with you. Thank you Śrīla Prabhupāda, for showing me how to perform devotional service.

71

"Just by reading this one book you can become Kṛṣṇa Conscious."

April 21, 1973 ISKCON Los Angeles, California

Entering Śrīla Prabhupāda's quarters was always an enlightening experience. Sometimes Śrīla Prabhupāda sat and read his books. Whenever he read, it seemed as if someone else had written his books because he did not read with the mind of an author looking for editing mistakes or grammatical errors.

He read them with the appreciation of a pure devotee reading the pastimes of the Supreme Lord to whom he was completely attached.

One day, I went into Śrīla Prabhupāda's room to perform my duties. He was reading *Bhagavad-gītā As It Is*. After offering my obeisances, he looked at me and said, "If you just read this one book and understand, you will become Kṛṣṇa Conscious in this very life."

A few months later when I went into his room, he was reading *Nectar of Devotion*. He looked at me and said, "This book is so nice. Just by reading this one book you can become Kṛṣṇa Conscious."

Śrīla Prabhupāda taught us by his example. He did everything that he asked of us. He requested us to read his books, and he read them, too.

72

"He deserves the $300 for taxing his brain ..."

April 26, 1973 ISKCON Los Angeles, California

Since we had come back to Los Angeles, Śrīla Prabhupāda had come into my room a few times and shown me how to cook some new preparations. The way he came in, sat down on the floor and directed the activity was very endearing.

On another occasion, Jayatīrtha gave Śrīla Prabhupāda a desk clock that tells the time in any city in the world with a turn of the dial. Prabhupada was quite pleased with it and said the man who invented it deserved the $300 it cost for taxing his brain so much.

At this moment, there is a famous designer upstairs. He is the man who designs clothes for millionaires all over the world, and he wants to outfit Prabhupada with an entire wardrobe of clothing. I can't imagine what he can do to make a kurta and dhoti different and still have Śrīla Prabhupāda wear them.

He never did make an outfit for Śrīla Prabhupāda. Of course, Śrīla Prabhupāda was not into the latest fashion. Śrīla Prabhupāda was a sannyāsī and he adhered strictly to his vows. He would not even allow his sister to be in the room alone with him, telling me that I should sit in the room with them when they talked. Thank you, Śrīla Prabhupāda, for always setting the perfect example throughout your life. You always did what was right because your desire was always to serve Kṛṣṇa.

73

"Yes, of course"

April 26, 1973 ISKCON Los Angeles, California

It was here that Brahmānanda Mahārāja and I introduced the Bengali style of dancing to Śrīla Prabhupāda's American disciples. We had learned it at the Māyāpur festival just weeks before. It started very simply. The two of us were standing on front of Śrīla Prabhupāda's vyāsāsana facing each other as the kīrtan was going on. It was the arrival kīrtan in New Dvārakā and everyone was in ecstasy. Hundreds of us were all standing in place dancing back and forth, doing the 'Swami step'. Brahmānanda and I kept looking at each other as we danced in the kīrtan. Without saying a word, we began to move towards Śrī Śrī Rukmini Dvārakādisa, moving about ten feet forward and then back towards Śrīla Prabhupāda on the vyāsāsana. It was not easy to do at first because no one else was moving with us, but there was always a space in the centre so that Śrīla Prabhupāda could see the Deities. Using that area we began dancing enthusiastically going back and forth as the kīrtan progressed.

Within minutes, everyone in the temple room followed. Hundreds of us were moving back and forth towards Śrīla Prabhupāda and then away again. He sat there watching all his children dancing wildly as he played kartals and encouraged us by the nod of his head. Many of the devotees loved it and Śrīla Prabhupāda was smiling as he watched the devotees dance before him.

Afterwards some devotees said they thought that this new kind of dancing was not bona-fide. There was some controversy about this new dance form. Some of the devotees thought it strange and out of place in the temple room. Pradyumna asked Śrīla Prabhupāda if it was all right to dance in that way. "Yes, of course!" Śrīla Prabhupāda replied. "It is very nice."

Śrīla Prabhupāda loved to see his disciples chant "Hare Kṛṣṇa" and dance in ecstasy. It was how he started the International Society for Kṛṣṇa Consciousness. Sometimes he would tell us the only thing we needed to do was chant the Hare Kṛṣṇa mantra. Then he added, "I have given you so many other engagements, because you Westerners are so restless that you can't sit in one place and chant."

Thank you, Śrīla Prabhupāda, for giving me a reason to chant and dance. Dancing before you in kīrtan was the perfection of dancing. I will always remember your smiling face as you watched your young children chanting Hare Kṛṣṇa. It gave you such pleasure to see your thousands of followers all over the world becoming first class Vaisnavas. Because you are in our lives, we will always have reason to dance.

Jai Śrīla Prabhupāda!

74

"Do you see that bug?"

April 29, 1973 ISKCON Los Angeles, California

Śrīla Prabhupāda was in New Dvārakā in the spring of 1973. Hearing His Divine Grace ring his bell, I immediately went to his room and offered my obeisances. Pointing to the floor near my legs, he looked at me with wide eyes and great concern.

"Do you see that bug?" he asked. Looking around for a few moments, I finally spotted a small insect. I nodded.

In a serious voice Śrīla Prabhupāda said, "I have been watching that bug for some time now and he has not moved. I think he is hungry. Get a prasādam flower and take him outside. Put him on a plant so he can get some nourishment."

I immediately did what my most merciful Guru Mahārāja asked and returned to the servants' quarters. Neither of us spoke of the bug again. It was another wonderful occasion in which he revealed the indiscriminate mercy of a pure devotee. His Divine Grace did not feel it was a waste of time to mitigate the suffering of even the smallest of living entities. Now, just seeing a small insect, I am forced to think of my beloved Śrīla Prabhupāda. However insignificant we may be, if we are fortunate to get the glance of the *nitya-siddha*, our life will be immensely benefited.

75

"Ah, this is Kṛṣṇa!"

April 30, 1973 ISKCON Los Angeles, California

Often, after leaving the garden, Śrīla Prabhupāda went to his room and listened to the recording of that morning's Śrīmad Bhāgavatam class. Sometimes he had me pick star jasmine flowers that grew on the bushes just outside his garden. The flower's scent was especially fragrant at night. One evening while smelling a sprig of blossoms, he said, "Ah, this is Kṛṣṇa!"

I often brought jasmine to his bedroom in the evening. He occasionally smelled them during his massage. He then kept them on his pillow (close to his nose) all night. The following morning, I would find the flowers gently lying on the pillow exactly where they had been the night before. The flowers were as fresh and fragrant as ever, looking as if they had just been picked. His Divine Grace always showed us how Kṛṣṇa is in every part of this material creation.

These are the moments I remember so dearly. The simple, amazing ways you revealed Kṛṣṇa Consciousness to us. I witnessed it every day. One can read so many books but still be unable to taste the sweetness of how you exhibited your love for Kṛṣṇa.

76

"The morning sun gives you energy…"

April May 1, 1973 ISKCON Los Angeles, California

Whenever it was sunny, Śrīla Prabhupāda would take his morning massage in the garden. He would sit with his back to the sun. Sometimes, as I was rubbing the mustard oil in his back he would say, "The morning sun gives you energy and the afternoon sun takes it away,"

It was one of many simple, practical truths he told all of us, who were listening. "Do not eat more than you can digest. Rise early and take cold bath. Be regulated". The reason we do these things is to keep the body healthy so we can perform our devotional service nicely. Śrīla Prabhupāda set such a wonderful example for all of us to follow. He will always lead us by his instructions.

77

"That's all, take him out"

May 3, 1973 ISKCON Los Angeles, California

One sunny day, Śrīla Prabhupāda decided to have his massage in his favourite place, the New Dvārakā garden. After I placed the mat on the grass with sandalwood and mustard oil alongside it, Śrīla Prabhupāda sat down cross-legged.

While massaging Śrīla Prabhupāda's back, a kitten crawled under the garden gate. Perhaps the kitten wanted to associate with a pure devotee. This little, fuzzy thing started to lick Śrīla Prabhupāda's back and affectionately rubbed his fur against His Divine Grace. Much to my surprise Śrīla Prabhupāda allowed this to go on for a few minutes.

"That's all, take him out," Śrīla Prabhupāda finally said.

Quickly, I grabbed the cat and put him over the fence. Being very small and extremely determined to get more association with Śrīla Prabhupāda, the kitten immediately crawled under the gate again. Three times, he came in and three times, I dropped him over the fence.

Finally, I found cinder blocks and placed them along the bottom of the gate so the kitten could no longer sneak in to get another taste of His Divine Grace. Being thwarted, he loudly cried outside the gate for the duration of Śrīla Prabhupāda's massage. Howling, he lamented his misfortune. I learned something from that kitten. I should be that eager for the association of the pure devotee.

A moment's association with a pure devotee can change the life of even a small animal. The kitten was obviously attracted by the transcendental nature of Śrīla Prabhupāda. He wanted to bathe in Prabhupada's nectar no matter what obstacles were placed before him. I pray that someday I will be as determined as that kitten to associate with my Guru Mahārāja through his loving service.

78

"Everything was the same except the culture."

May 4, 1973 ISKCON Los Angeles, California

Śrīla Prabhupāda often described the differences between Vedic civilization and western civilization. One day he was walking around his room chanting Japa on his beads. He looked out the window of his sitting room and saw a young couple talking to each other.

He turned to me and said, "Boys and girls. Now a man, he wants to do something. He sees some woman and says 'I'll get that woman'. He'll go up to her and say, 'What are you doing? Why do not we go out?'

"When we were young," he continued, "the same desires were there. The desires haven't changed at all. We also had desires like that. You see a girl. You become attracted. But the culture was there. The culture was so strict you could not even look at her, what to speak of talking to her or making some proposition. Everything was the same, except the culture. Now, there is no culture. You just go up and say anything you want. We had all these desires, talking like schoolchildren, but you could never approach a woman. It was unheard of. You wouldn't consider it."

Śrīla Prabhupāda left Vṛndāvana Dhāma and the Vedic culture to save us from our so-called advanced civilization. All Glories to Śrīla Prabhupāda!

He continued, "When I was young the culture was such that if my mother was going to visit a friend across the street it was required that they would send a carriage to pick her up at her door and bring her to the door of the house where she was going. The culture was so strict. A woman would not walk across the street unaccompanied."

> *Śrīla Prabhupāda you left your home at Rādhā Dāmodara temple in Vṛndāvana Dhāma, and Vedic culture to save us from our so-called advanced civilization. You came alone to a place with no culture, on the order of your spiritual master and although you repeatedly sent letters to others requesting they assist you, no one responded favourably. It is only by your endeavours that the entire world has been blessed with the chanting of the Hare Kṛṣṇa Mahā-mantra. One who remains chaste to you and follows your instructions is guaranteed success and will go 'Back home, back to Godhead.'*

79

"Clean it properly"

May 5, 1973 ISKCON Los Angeles, California

Śrīla Prabhupāda liked to travel with only what was necessary. As he travelled around the world, I kept all of his belongings in one suitcase and had one small bag for my things. His suitcase contained all that was necessary for every situation. Inside I kept his cooker, a rolling pin, a massage mat and oils, three sets of clothes, a wool chaddar and two gamchas. With all of these items, I was prepared for almost any situation as we went from city to city around the world.

Wherever he went, there were devotees eager to clean Śrīla Prabhupāda's laundry, especially in the West. They loved to wash and iron his clothing. The only things that presented any problem were his gamchas. At the time, I had two red check ones that he used. Since he took oil massage every day they could become very dark and stained over time unless they were properly cleaned. It did not clean properly in the washing machine. One time we were in New Dvārakā for several weeks. The person who was cleaning the laundry put the soiled gamcha in with the other items but it never came out very clean. Unfortunately, I did not notice. One day I handed it to Śrīla Prabhupāda just before massage. He took it into his hand, looked at me and said, "Why isn't this gamcha clean? You keep giving me this dirty gamcha every day. Clean it properly." I told him I would take care of it.

That day, after his lunch, I took his gamcha into the bathroom and put it in the sink. I filled it with hot water and a handful of detergent and started beating it in the sink, just as they would do along the Yamunā in Vṛndāvana. To my surprise after five minutes, I noticed that it was red and white instead of maroon and brown. I could not believe it. It looked brand new. I never realized it was so dirty. I rinsed it out and dried it in my room. The next morning when it was time for massage, I handed it to Śrīla Prabhupāda. He put it on and dropped his dhoti to the floor. He then looked at me with a bright smile on his face and said, "Oh! Who has cleaned this gamcha?" I smiled and said, "I did it myself, Prabhupada".

"Just see!" he said, "so many days getting washed and it was never cleaned properly, even in a big, big washing machine. You have done it once, by hand, and now it is clean. Thank you. It is very good."

I was so happy to do such a simple chore and see my spiritual master pleased. I could understand that to be successful in spiritual life was very easy. A disciple only had to please his spiritual master and Śrīla Prabhupāda was the most compassionate and merciful devotee of Lord Kṛṣṇa and was very easy to please.

It was only a few months earlier Śrīla Prabhupāda had blessed me with an opportunity to do some special service. Śrīla Prabhupāda was leaving India by way of Kolkata. He was going to Melbourne, Australia. We had only one short stop in Bangkok to change planes. This flight was special. He travelled with only his secretary, Bali-mardana Mahārāja and me. Well, there were two others in his entourage for this flight; Rādhā and Kṛṣṇa! They were sixty centimetre marble Deities that were to be installed at the Melbourne temple. Bali carried Kṛṣṇa and I carried Rādhārāṇī. They weren't light. It was a pleasurable service but it was a bit difficult managing the other items including the baggage and prasādam, as well as seeing to the comfort of His Divine Grace. We did find seats for Them during the flight and we each sat next to our Deity the entire time.

I felt benedicted to have such an opportunity and although it was difficult taking them on and off the plane and carrying them through the airport, I never felt like it was a burden. In fact, I felt blessed. Then I was given even more cause to be ecstatic. While we were on the last leg of the flight to Melbourne, I was sitting next to Śrīla Prabhupāda. He turned towards me and had a big smile on his face. He then looked at me seriously and said the most wonderful thing; "This difficult austerity is very pleasing to Kṛṣṇa. To make spiritual advancement one has to simply satisfy Kṛṣṇa. There are so many ways of satisfying Kṛṣṇa and this is one of them. Kṛṣṇa is very pleased with your endeavours."

I was speechless, smiled broadly, and finally I thanked him. It was such a pleasure to be with Śrīla Prabhupāda. As a neophyte devotee, we can go through so much speculation trying to understand how to please Kṛṣṇa and the spiritual master. In one simple statement, he had taken all of the mystery out of it. He so often said the Kṛṣṇa Consciousness is "common sense" and "What is the difficulty?" Here he gave a practical example. At that moment I felt that it was possible to go 'back home, back to Godhead'. By the mercy of Śrīla Prabhupāda, I only had to chant my rounds, follow the principles and do some simple service for the Lord, according to my abilities. It was not complicated. Śrīla Prabhupāda has given us so many ways to please him, to put a smile on his face. What is the difficulty?

80

"... I am not having difficulty."

May 6, 1973 ISKCON Los Angeles, California

One evening at about 5:00, I was lying down, half asleep, on my mat in the servants' quarters. I heard the bell ring. I walked toward Śrīla Prabhupāda's sitting room, trying to compose myself. I realized that I was still affected by the mode of ignorance. I entered Śrīla Prabhupāda's room and offered my obeisances. I sat up hoping he wouldn't notice my condition. I was in worse shape than I realized. He was more conscious of my illusion than I was. This statement may seem elementary, but I had always thought that Śrīla Prabhupāda had too many other things to be concerned with than my Kṛṣṇa Consciousness.

He looked at me with great concern.

"So, why you are not chanting?" he asked.

I was really caught off guard. Śrīla Prabhupāda was expert at confronting someone when he least expected it. I did not know what to say, so I said something stupid, but honest.

"Śrīla Prabhupāda, I am having a difficult time," I explained. "It is hard sitting in my room all day chanting and reading."

His reply was extraordinary.

"I am sitting here all day, also," he said with a serious expression. "I simply go out once a day on a walk. The rest of the day, I am just sitting here and I am not having any difficulty."

"I am not like you, Śrīla Prabhupāda," I quickly responded. "You are like Haridas Ṭhākura. I am not very transcendental. I have to keep myself busy. Maybe I could do some typing for you?"

Still looking very serious he said, "What are we going to do?"

"Śrīla Prabhupāda, I do not know."

"Call Karāndhara," he instructed.

As previously mentioned, Śrīla Prabhupāda said these words often when he was in Los Angeles because he had confidence in Karāndhara's abilities. He was a "doer," and he was also very serious. Karāndhara and I went into Śrīla Prabhupāda's room together and offered our obeisances.

"Śrutakīrti is having trouble," Śrīla Prabhupāda told Karāndhara. "He is not chanting. He says he needs something to do to keep him busy. What shall we do?" Karāndhara, looking very intense as always, said, "We have to get him some engagement, somehow."

"Yes!" Śrīla Prabhupāda said. "I have an idea. I am translating Śrīmad-Bhagavatam here in this room. So, I will start translating the Caitanya-Caritāmṛta in the study. In this room I have my Dictaphone and I will do Śrīmad Bhāgavatam and in my study you can put another Dictaphone machine and I can start translating Caitanya-Caritāmṛta."

Looking at me he said, "So, you can type it. You can prepare everything for editing. In this way, I will keep you busy and I will keep Pradyumna busy with editing. Is that all right?"

I thanked him enthusiastically.

Karāndhara and I set up the study so Śrīla Prabhupāda could begin work on the Śrī Caitanya-Caritāmṛta .

Early the next morning Śrīla Prabhupāda went into the bathroom to get ready for his morning walk. I went into his study and took the tape out of the machine. He had done some translating. That morning I enthusiastically chanted my rounds knowing that my spiritual master loved me more than I could have imagined. Later in the day, I transcribed the tape. There was not much on it, but it was understandable because he was still translating Śrīmad-Bhāgavatam in the other room.

The next day I went into his study to get the tape and saw that it hadn't been used. He did not do any further translating of Śrī Caitanya-Caritāmṛta the rest of the time we were in Los Angeles. That did not matter to me, though. He had lit a tiny spark in me by caring so much.

Six months later, we were in his study in Los Angeles, where he had previously done the first hour of translating Śrī Caitanya-Caritāmṛta.

"You should become expert in Caitanya-Caritāmṛta and give classes on it," he told me.

I nodded and smiled, not knowing how it could ever happen.

Śrīla Prabhupāda, I know that by your love anything is possible. If I could develop for you a fraction of the affection you have shown me, my life would be successful. I pray that in some far distant life I will be able to understand my relationship with you.

81

"When I was a householder..."

May 7, 1973 ISKCON Los Angeles, California

Śrīla Prabhupāda on Chanting Japa.

It was easy to understand that Śrīla Prabhupāda enjoyed chanting japa. He always stressed the importance of chanting our sixteen rounds. He once told me that as a householder, he used a simple process for completing sixteen rounds that we could apply.

"When I was a householder," he said, "I would chant four rounds before each meal and four rounds before retiring in the evening. In this way sixteen rounds could be chanted without difficulty." He laughed and said, "If you do not take prasādam before chanting your four rounds then you will be sure to get them chanted."

In New Dvārakā, he told me, "In the evening, if I get tired, I walk and chant. If you are tired, then walk and chant like I do. Sometimes, if I am tired, I pace back and forth in the room."

It was common to see Śrīla Prabhupāda walk in his quarters or sit in his rocking chair while he chanted rounds. In the evening, he sometimes chanted rounds while I massaged him in bed.

"There, I'm finished," he would say on completing his rounds.

One day I was in his sitting room in New Dvārakā cleaning around his desk. He was sitting behind his desk chanting japa. As he pulled down a counter bead, he looked at me with a beautiful smile and said humourously, "There, I have finished my sixteen rounds. Now I can do any damn thing I want."

Devotees often asked Śrīla Prabhupāda about following certain rules in regards to Ekādaśī or following cāturmāsya.

"My disciples, they cannot even chant sixteen rounds and follow the principles," he responded. "What is the use of these other rules and regulations? First, just do these things. Do the simple things that I ask you to do. Do not concern yourself with all these rituals. First, chant your sixteen rounds and follow the principles."

One day a brahmacārī entered Śrīla Prabhupāda's room and told him he had entered a relationship with a woman and thereby broken his vows. He suggested to Śrīla Prabhupāda that perhaps he should get married.

"Marriage. Why do you think marriage is going to solve your difficulties?" Śrīla Prabhupāda answered. "You should chant. Just chant Hare Kṛṣṇa. Chant your sixteen rounds."

Many times devotees went into Śrīla Prabhupāda's room with a problem they were hoping would be solved by some particular arrangement. His solution was always the same. "Chant Hare Kṛṣṇa, chant your sixteen rounds."

"If there is some difficulty, you chant loudly," he told one disciple. "If there is some agitation, chant out loud."

One time it was brought to his attention that a senior devotee was not attending maṅgala-ārati, or chanting rounds, at least with the other devotees.

"Do it to set the example for the other devotees," Śrīla Prabhupāda said. "You, yourself are very advanced. You do not need to attend maṅgala-ārati,, but you should set the example for those that require it."

Thank you, Śrīla Prabhupāda, for being the Ācārya. You chanted rounds. You said three Gāyatrī mantras a day, rose early in the morning and put tilak on your transcendental body. You never asked any disciple to do something you were not doing yourself. I have been in illusion since time immemorial, but I pray that I am never deluded into thinking that this process of devotional service is only for the neophyte.

82

"Why are you doing these things?"

May 8, 1973 ISKCON Los Angeles, California

While in New Dvārakā Śrīla Prabhupāda wanted his lunch prepared in my room, which was adjacent to his quarters. I was pleased with how I set it up. The eight feet by ten feet room had everything I needed, even though it was the room I stayed in day and night. Karāndhara arranged for a refrigerator to be installed. There was a two-burner gas stove on the floor. I had made a shelf area with two cinder blocks and a four feet long, one feet by ten feet board. There was no running water, so I kept a supply in a plastic bucket. Śrīla Prabhupāda often told me to keep things simple and efficient. This set up worked well.

Every morning after Śrīla Prabhupāda finished breakfast I brought his silver plates into my room and transferred his remnants onto a tray. I put the refuse into my trash can and happily distributed the maha-prasādam to the devotees eagerly awaiting the "mercy."

After breakfast, Śrīla Prabhupāda often walked around his

quarters chanting japa. He walked in and out of his rooms, back and forth in the hallway, and sometimes stopped for a moment in front of my room to watch me as I prepared his lunch. One morning he entered my room.

Looking into the small trash can, he shouted, "What is this? You are such a fool." Surprised by his sudden chastisement I said, "It's from your breakfast plate."

It was not a good answer. Śrīla Prabhupāda was just getting started.

"You are supposed to be a devotee," he shouted. "You have no brains. No intelligence whatsoever. You are nothing but a mleccha. You have everything here so neat and you are preparing food for the Deities amidst this eaten garbage. How could you do such a foolish thing?"

I did not know what to say. I was thinking, "These are Prabhupada's remnants. This isn't garbage." I did not say anything though. I learned my lesson months before watching Śrīla Prabhupāda chastise my predecessor, senior god-brother. So I finally simply agreed with His Divine Grace.

"Yes, Śrīla Prabhupāda, I am a fool," I said.

He was not pacified with my hollow confession and was still very angry.

"Do they do this in the temple kitchen?" he continued. "Do they have a trash can like this?"

"Well, they do have a trash can in the kitchen," I said.

"But, do they put eaten garbage in it?" he quickly said.

"No, Śrīla Prabhupāda," I said, exhausted.

Śrīla Prabhupāda never seemed to tire. He continued to chastise me, it seemed to go on for so long. Finally, he left my room with his hand in his bead bag, chanting japa.

I emptied the trash can still, considering his remnants to be most sacred. It was ironic because the first piece of Maha-Bhāgavata prasādam given to me in New Dvārakā by Nanda

Kumar was an orange peel. I felt very fortunate and ate the whole thing. When I gave peel remnants to other devotees, they nibbled off the white area, but discarded the orange rind. Having been reprimanded, I was shaken, but understood that Śrīla Prabhupāda wanted to teach me a lesson. It seemed that whenever I became puffed-up in my service and thought I was doing a good job, Śrīla Prabhupāda let me know I was far from being a brahminical Vaiṣṇava. Later he told me I had prepared a very nice lunch. He never let me feel that he maintained any anger. Whenever he corrected me, he later said something nice, or told me a pastime about his earlier years. It was a trade off that was well worth it. Śrīla Prabhupāda knew I was very sensitive to criticism and compassionately kept it to a minimum.

In retrospect, I understand that these few instances were blissful because they were the ones I remember most vividly. There were so many opportunities for Śrīla Prabhupāda to correct me. If only I could have appreciated constructive criticism, I would have so many more memories to value.

83

"I think I'll have a regular lunch."

May 11, 1973 ISKCON Los Angeles, California

Late one morning Śrīla Prabhupāda rang his bell. I entered his sitting room and offered my obeisances.

"I am not feeling well today," Śrīla Prabhupāda said softly. "So, for my lunch please make me some kichari and cuddy sauce. You can make the kichari with two parts rice, one part dahl and use a little salt, turmeric and ghee. That will be light and easy to digest."

Śrīla Prabhupāda usually did not give much information

about his health, so a dietary adjustment was the only way I knew Śrīla Prabhupāda was ill. Occasionally, he asked for kichari when he had a cold.

I went back to my quarters to prepare his cooker. I put kichari on the top level and water on the bottom. This meal was much simpler than usual. I felt relieved knowing there was no chance of anything burning during his massage, but sad that Śrīla Prabhupāda was not feeling well. Normally, I was "cooker conscious" while massaging Śrīla Prabhupāda due to my searing memory of burning Śrīla Prabhupāda's lunch twice in two years, which was unacceptable.

After setting up the cooker, I returned to his room. Śrīla Prabhupāda sat down on the mat for his massage. Normally, I massaged his head with sandalwood oil because of its cooling affect. When he had a cold, though, he sometimes instructed me to use mustard oil over his entire body. On this day, he told me to use only mustard oil. About fifteen minutes into the massage he said, "So, I've decided. I do not think I'll take any lunch."

"All right, Śrīla Prabhupāda," I said, lamenting that he must have felt quite ill.

I continued to massage his beautiful form for another half-hour.

"Actually," Śrīla Prabhupāda then said, "I think I'll have a regular lunch."

I felt, momentarily relieved that his health was improving.

He remained silent. Suddenly, I became overwhelmed with great anxiety remembering that I did not have anything prepared except for kichari. It would take a long time to prepare a full lunch. I was too frightened to say anything about my predicament.

"Prabhupada, I do not have anything ready," I finally said. "It may take a little time."

"Whatever it takes, it takes," he said. "Just do it."

When Śrīla Prabhupāda went to bathe, I darted into my quarters and put his lunch together as quickly and conscientiously as I could. I was probably in more anxiety than necessary, but that is how my feeble mind worked. I prided myself in keeping ahead of my regulated service to eliminate potential problems. Śrīla Prabhupāda graciously waited for me to complete his lunch without any complaints. He sometimes put me through changes like this to teach me to be more flexible. My service was to do whatever he wanted, not what I wanted.

Śrīla Prabhupāda, thank you for giving me the chance to focus on your contentment while performing my duties as your servant. I often forget that devotional service means to personally please you and in this way, Kṛṣṇa is pleased. Please continue to guide me daily in your personal service, teaching me unconditional love.

84

"They may say 'Prabhupada said.'"

May 14, 1973 ISKCON Los Angeles, California

At this time New Dvārakā was more than just the headquarters for ISKCON in the West, it was the world headquarters. Śrīla Prabhupāda spent much time here and wherever he travelled, he always seemed to return to LA. His quarters were very comfortable and so too was the weather.

One afternoon one of his sannyasa disciples asked to see him. He entered the sunlit room and offered obeisances. I did not know what he wanted to speak to Śrīla Prabhupāda about but he did not seem to mind that I was with him, therefore, I stayed. Śrīla Prabhupāda looked up from behind his desk and smiled.

Mahārāja said, "Prabhupada I have to ask you a question, did you say that WWIII would begin on March 24, 1974?"

Śrīla Prabhupāda, with surprise in his face, immediately responded. "I never said such a thing. Who has said this?"

I sat before Śrīla Prabhupāda with a smile on my face. I had heard 'Prabhupada said' so many times over the years. One could write volumes of misinformation of what he supposedly had said, or take out of context what he did say to one person. My amusement was soon interrupted when he responded to Prabhupada's inquiry.

"Apparently, Śrutakīrti said that you said it." Immediately Śrīla Prabhupāda turned and looked at me with eyes wide open.

"Did you say this, Śrutakīrti?'

"No Prabhupada!" I quickly exclaimed my innocence. "I have never said such a thing. I would never make up such a story." Śrīla Prabhupāda shook his head in wonder saying, "Just see!" Then looking at both of us continued, "They may say Prabhupada said this and Prabhupada said that but I haven't said anything. Unless you hear me say, I haven't said it."

The short meeting ended there. I walked out of the room amazed at how rumours can take on a life of their own. There was nothing more dangerous than a "Prabhupada said" rumour. I could understand why he stressed the importance of reading his books. Numerous times, he stressed that the answers to all our questions were in his books. It was his greatest service to his followers, to all humanity.

Even while Śrīla Prabhupāda was here so much misinformation was eagerly passed from one devotee to another to support their understanding of what Kṛṣṇa Consciousness is. How fortunate we are that Śrīla Prabhupāda gave us so many books and lectures every day. Sometimes he would say, "Kṛṣṇa Consciousness is easy for the simple but difficult for the crooked." Do not take my word for it. Read his books. What is the difficulty?

Śrīla Prabhupāda, you sometimes emphasized how important it was to 'not talk nonsense'. Once, in Mayapur, hearing your disciples talking nearby, you called me in your room and told me to tell them to be quiet, adding, "Gossip destroys Kṛṣṇa Consciousness." It was such a strong message and one that I never want to forget. In this material world, so many things help to destroy our Kṛṣṇa Consciousness. Following your instructions is the only way to strengthen it. I pray for the desire to always follow your instructions and the example you set for us.

85

"So, which is the most beautiful animal?"

May 29, 1973 Bhaktivedanta Manor, England

It was a very beautiful afternoon. The sun was shining into Śrīla Prabhupāda's sitting room through the leaded glass windows. He was walking around the room chanting japa. He stopped in front of the windows and looked out into the garden.

"So, which is the most beautiful animal?" he asked me.

"A cow?" I blurted out with little conviction in my voice.

"No," he said quickly. "A horse. The horse has a very beautiful form. The muscle structure is very nice."

I thought Kṛṣṇa's favourite animal was a cow. It had to have been a cow. As soon as Śrīla Prabhupāda told me otherwise though, it made perfect sense.

Śrīla Prabhupāda, I beg you to tell me again that my only business is to be with you twenty-four hours a day.

86

"Who is that chanting?"

June 14, 1973 ISKCON Mayapur, India

During our stay, Śrīla Prabhupāda and his entourage had rooms on half of the second floor of the guesthouse. The other rooms were available for devotee guests. There was a beautiful veranda that surrounded the entire facility. Sometimes Śrīla Prabhupāda walked on the veranda and chanted japa there. Devotees often gathered at the other end of the terrace hoping to catch a glimpse of His Divine Grace.

One morning, an elder god-brother of mine was walking back and forth chanting japa on the marble veranda. My instincts and previous experiences told me that he was chanting too loudly and that Śrīla Prabhupāda might be disturbed. Śrīla Prabhupāda valued his quiet moments.

"Prabhu, perhaps you could chant a little softer," I said. "Śrīla Prabhupāda might not like it."

He looked at me as if I was crazy. After all, who was I to tell him what to do? I think he had the idea that Śrīla Prabhupāda would be pleased by his devotion. He continued with his loud chanting.

Within a few minutes, the bell rang. I already knew what was going to happen and, I admit, I was in bliss. I was happy my instincts were correct. I hurried into Śrīla Prabhupāda's sitting room and offered my obeisances.

"Who is that chanting out there?" Śrīla Prabhupāda said in an angry mood. "If they want to chant loudly, tell them to go into the temple room and chant before the deities."

I happily exposed the culprit and rushed outside. This time I had a rather smug look on my face. After all, I was armed with the Śrīla Prabhupāda Chakra weapon. I was indestructible. Needless to say, after conveying Śrīla Prabhupāda's message he went on his way with a new attitude.

Śrīla Prabhupāda, you once told me, "The first class servant knows what his master wants and does it without being asked."

There were so many occasions when I knew from experience what you wanted, but due to my weakness of character was unable to carry it out. I always tried to be quiet. You also said, "For oneself the devotee is meek and humble, but for Kṛṣṇa and His pure devotee, he becomes like the lion."

Thank you for always showing these characteristics.

Thank you for always showing us how to be a devotee. Please forgive me for not always having the courage to serve you properly. You patiently tolerated my many weaknesses. You tolerated all of our deficiencies. I am in awe when I remember how patient you were with your thousands of young, unqualified and sometimes obstinate disciples. You encouraged us all to advance in spiritual life and still do.

All glories to Śrīla Prabhupāda!

87

"He is my god-brother. He should be allowed in right away."

June 16, 1973 ISKCON Mayapur, India

Dāmodara Mahārāja, Śrīla Prabhupāda's god-brother, frequently visited His Divine Grace. At that time, Śrīla Prabhupāda was never very anxious to see him.

"If Dāmodara Mahārāja comes," he once told me, "I do not want to see him. He simply comes and talks, 'this maṭha [temple], they are doing this and that maṭha, they are doing that and my disciples they are doing like this.' I am not interested in these things. I would be happy if he came and talked about Kṛṣṇa or talked some philosophy, but he talks all these nonsense things. I am not very interested to hear it."

I told Śrīla Prabhupāda that I would try to prevent Dāmodara Mahārāja from entering his quarters. It was not long before I was given the opportunity to do as I was told. Within a few days Dāmodara Mahārāja visited. It was not easy for me to say anything to him. It was difficult for me to advise my god-brothers when Śrīla Prabhupāda told me to, what to speak of a sannyāsī god-brother of his.

As he approached Śrīla Prabhupāda's room, I took a breath and said, "Prabhupada is taking rest. He cannot be disturbed right now." Dāmodara Mahārāja was not satisfied with my explanation.

"Prabhupada said I could come whenever I want. Why do not you let me see him?" he demanded.

Feeling a bit stronger I again explained, "I cannot disturb him while he takes his afternoon nap." Dāmodara Mahārāja angrily paced about, determined to have his way. I was sweating. Miraculously, Śrīla Prabhupāda stepped out of his room. He had just risen from his nap and was fixing his dhoti as he was walking out the door.

"Prabhupada! Swamiji!" Dāmodara Mahārāja called.

Śrīla Prabhupāda smiled broadly and exclaimed, "Come on, come on. I will be right with you," A few minutes later Śrīla Prabhupāda returned to his sitting room. Dāmodara Mahārāja and I were both sitting there quietly, waiting for him.

When Śrīla Prabhupāda returned to his sitting room, Dāmodara Mahārāja complained. "Your disciple is giving me such a difficult time. He won't let me come in to see you."

Śrīla Prabhupāda turned to me with a look of surprise on his face.

"Why are you giving him such a hard time?" Śrīla Prabhupāda asked. "I told you whenever he comes, you should let him in. He is my god-brother. He should be allowed to come in right away."

I apologised. I offered obeisances and walked out of the room with a big smile on my face. Śrīla Prabhupāda never mentioned to me what had happened and I did not bring it up to him. It was not necessary.

It was thrilling to serve Śrīla Prabhupāda in this intimate way. I felt blessed to be privy to Śrīla Prabhupāda's inner thoughts. His Divine Grace was able to endear his god-brother to him and I was given the opportunity to assist. Śrīla Prabhupāda showed me how to treat a god-brother, no matter how we feel about them. He was a 'transcendental diplomat' and I delighted being Śrīla Prabhupāda's confidant.

It was another revealing moment of Śrīla Prabhupāda's compassion. He was always on a great mission of spreading Kṛṣṇa Consciousness around the world but he had time for everyone that came before him. When he was with his god-brothers he often encouraged them to assist him in spreading the movement in the West. He would offer to bring them to America so that they could help train his western disciples, as Śrīla Bhaktisiddhānta desired. He offered them a place to stay and everything they might need. Despite his many requests, none of his god-brothers expressed any desire to help.

Śrīla Prabhupāda, you started and maintained ISKCON on your own. You accepted the service happily. Your determination to serve your spiritual master is unparalleled. Your followers are the most fortunate souls.

☙ 88 ☙

"You should eat as much as you can digest."

June 21, 1973 ISKCON Mayapur, India

One day Śrīla Prabhupāda chastised his Sanskrit editor, Pradyumna dāsa for sleeping during the morning programme. He was my favourite devotee in Śrīla Prabhupāda's entourage, he took the correction very seriously. He decided to reduce his eating by taking only hot milk, fruit and almonds. Pradyumna said that almonds were brain food. He was known for his phographic memory.

As previously mentioned, Śrīla Prabhupāda, while in Mayapur, often walked on the veranda while his disciples took prasādam. He enjoyed watching his children eat to their full satisfaction. I felt very cared for by my spiritual father. He appeared pleased by our attraction to Kṛṣṇa prasādam. He was not pleased, however, when he noticed that Pradyumna was not with us.

"Why you are not eating with the others?" Śrīla Prabhupāda asked Pradyumna after walking to his room.

"I'm not very hungry, Śrīla Prabhupāda," Pradyumna quietly replied.

"What do you mean?" Śrīla Prabhupāda said. "You should

be taking prasādam." Pradyumna knew his spiritual master was not satisfied with his explanation.

"Well, Prabhupada," he said, "If I take prasādam, then I sleep."

"What can be done?" Śrīla Prabhupāda said. "You have to take prasādam, even if you sleep ten hours a day. How can you live if you do not eat? So, take prasādam and sleep. Otherwise, how can you go on?"

Pradyumna walked out of the room, offered his obeisances and joined in the meal with the rest of us. I was happy to have his association again.

Śrīla Prabhupāda always encouraged his disciples to minimize their eating and sleeping in order to advance in Kṛṣṇa Consciousness, but he also told us to use our common sense.

"You should eat as much as you can digest," he often said. "Take as much prasādam as you want, but eat everything that you take. Not one grain of rice should be wasted."

He was also very strict about everyone attending the morning programme. If more sleep was required, it should be done at other times such as a nap after lunch or going to bed earlier at night.

In general, Śrīla Prabhupāda ate breakfast right after he lectured in the morning and ate lunch around 1:00 pm. In the evening, he drank hot milk before taking rest. Sometimes, if he felt hungry, I prepared puris, vegetable or puffed rice. When he had an appetite, he enjoyed eating as much as we enjoyed feeding him. Some of my most joyful days were spent running back and forth from the kitchen to his room with a hot chapati and putting it on his lunch plate while it was still puffed up with steam inside. I ran back and forth five or six times within ten minutes, offering my obeisances each time I entered his room. Śrīla Prabhupāda sat with his right knee straight in the air and gracefully mixed subji with his chapati.

Śrīla Prabhupāda, please give me your mercy. I would gladly give up eating and sleeping just to be able to once again roll and cook chapatis for you. There is nothing sweeter in all the three worlds than having one glimpse of your childlike innocence as you sit and honour prasādam. I do not think it is possible for anyone to watch you eat and not fall deeply in love with you. I may never taste the nectar of love of Godhead, but I pray for your mercy on my soul that I may be able to cook chapatis for you again.

89

"This is the Vedic custom"

June 24, 1973 ISKCON Mayapur, India

In Mayapur, Śrīla Prabhupāda lived in two rooms. One room was his sitting room where he translated and received guests and next-door was his bedroom. He also used it to honour prasādam, so there was a small marble prasādam table (chowki) set against the wall to the right of his bed.

June was generally very hot, so when Śrīla Prabhupāda took lunch, I sometimes fanned him with a peacock fan. It not only created a breeze, but also kept the flies away. However, when Śrīla Prabhupāda took his lunch, it immediately alerted the resident ant population. They always had scouts running along the walls and within minutes of putting his plate on the table, they called in the battalion. In Los Angeles, Śrīla Prabhupāda told me to put turmeric where they entered. It worked in Los Angeles, I suppose those ants were more materialistic. Ants in Mayapur, however, could not be stopped. Obviously, they were spiritual entities who could not be discouraged by maha-prasādam remnants from the plate of the pure devotee.

I watched as hundreds of ants ascended the leg of the chowki, circled his plate and finally descended upon his prasādam. They seemed to know when they were allowed on a certain preparation. Śrīla Prabhupāda ate in stages. First, he ate the vegetables and chapatis, then he added the rice, and finally he ate the sweets. The ants initially congregated around the plate. Gradually they worked their way onto the preparations that Śrīla Prabhupāda had finished. It seemed like the ants were a little courteous. Finally, Śrīla Prabhupāda ended his meal with a few sweets. He then got up to wash. For the ants, the moment they had been waiting for had arrived. They now knew it was time to dive into the sweets. Incredibly, Śrīla Prabhupāda never said one word about them during this daily attack on his lunch.

This was not an isolated incident. It happened with great regularity. There seemed to be an arrangement between the pure devotee and these tiny insects. He was free to take as much time as he wanted and they were allowed to eat whatever he did not finish. I tried to take away the plates as quickly as possible so there was something left to distribute to his disciples. Referring to ants in Kolkata, Śrīla Prabhupāda once said, "It's all right, they do not eat very much."

One day while I fanned him during lunch, Śrīla Prabhupāda chuckled.

"This is the Vedic custom", he said. "The wife, she would fan the husband while he ate. After he was done, whatever he would leave, she would take. In this way, she always made sure there was plenty of prasādam. Otherwise, she may not eat. But, that was strictly a custom. Actually, in the Vedic culture that was the woman's role. They served in two ways, one by cooking nice foodstuffs, and the other by providing nice sex life. This is the essence of material life. Of course the difference is in Kṛṣṇa Consciousness, we stress chastity, being chaste."

Quietly fanning Śrīla Prabhupāda as he ate, I was amused

by his candor. This was a subject that was not often discussed amongst devotees. Sex life was to be controlled, not enjoyed. As young devotees, we were trying our best to avoid it. I tried to appreciate the knowledge he was imparting. Tongue-tied, I continued to fan him.

Śrīla Prabhupāda was completely transcendental. Only he could sit and eat with legions of insects preparing to attack his remnants. Only he could speak about sex life without reservation because he had no attraction to material enjoyment. Because he was a compassionate pure devotee, he was able to understand our fallen condition, patiently train us, and give us the opportunity to perform devotional service.

90

Śrīla Prabhupāda teases his sister

July 4, 1973 ISKCON Kolkata, India

I first met Bhavatarini, Śrīla Prabhupāda's sister, during this visit to the Kolkata temple. From then on, she was always known as "Pishima" which means "aunty." She was an incredible sight. She was a few inches shorter and quite a bit heavier than Śrīla Prabhupāda was, but her face was undeniably that of a female Śrīla Prabhupāda. Whenever she came to the temple, she brought sweets and gave them to her older brother. She then distributed them to all of the devotees in the temple. She loved to associate with Śrīla Prabhupāda and spent as much time as she could in his presence.

It was impossible for me to understand their conversations, since I did not understand Bengali, but sometimes His Divine Grace described some details. It was obvious she had great love for her brother, not just on a material platform, but was able to comprehend his topmost spiritual position as well.

She cooked for him often. This was a source of great anxiety for his disciples because she always used mustard oil in her cooking. Once, when she was approached about this method she responded, "He can digest nails, if he wants."

One day, as I massaged Śrīla Prabhupāda before lunch, he said to me, "Do you know any person who is fat, without eating?"

"No, Śrīla Prabhupāda," I said. "I do not know anyone. Are you referring to your sister?"

He laughed loudly.

"Yes!" he said. "She tells me she is eating just a little bit, but she keeps on gaining weight. You do not know anyone who keeps on gaining weight without eating, do you?"

"No, Śrīla Prabhupāda," I said, chuckling. "I do not think it is possible to gain weight without eating."

Now both of us were laughing.

"Yes!" he said. "I do not think so either. I think your conclusion is correct. She has to be eating very much. She tells me she is not eating, but I know she is eating. She complains to me about her health, that she doesn't feel well. I told her, 'You are so fat. How can you be healthy?' She said, 'I do not know how. I am hardly eating at all. I do not know how I am so fat.'"

I continued massaging Śrīla Prabhupāda, understanding how comfortable he was in his hometown surrounded by his family. I was grateful to be able to associate with Śrīla Prabhupāda during such intimate moments. I could see his concern for his sister's health as he sometimes said that disease came from anxiety, uncleanliness and overeating.

That evening Śrīla Prabhupāda was giving darśana to his disciples. Pishima was also present in the room. She did not mind that she could not understand the conversation. She enjoyed being with him as much as possible because she unconditionally loved her brother. How elevated and fortunate she was to have a natural love and affection for Śrīla Prabhupāda!

"Look at her sitting there," Śrīla Prabhupāda, said smiling. "Look at her . . . how fat she is."

Everyone began laughing, including Śrīla Prabhupāda and Pishima. He continued poking fun at her in a rascal-like, boyish way.

"She is so fat," he said. "Look at her, how fat she is. She says that she doesn't eat, but still she gets fat."

The room was filled with laughter. Pishima enjoyed seeing everyone laugh and did not realize that her older brother was making fun of her. Śrīla Prabhupāda enjoyed his joke and was happy his disciples joined in. It was a rare and wonderful moment for everyone.

Śrīla Prabhupāda, seeing you in that happy, carefree līlā was joyful. I pray that in a distant lifetime I can bring a smile to your face.

91

"I am going to London for Rathayatra."

July 7-8, 1973 Rathayatra Parade, London, England

At the completion of Śrīla Prabhupāda's visit to Kolkata, he was deciding where to travel next. That was always an exciting adventure. On this occasion the senior devotees suggested Śrīla Prabhupāda go to Hawaii or Los Angeles to rest. There was an invitation, however, from the devotees in London to attend the Rathayatra festival.

Śrīla Prabhupāda was expert in engaging his disciples in such a way as to develop their love and attachment for him.

Wherever he stayed, the process of deciding where to travel to occurred again and again. He allowed his disciples to suggest places and reasons why he should go there. Hawaii was often mentioned because of the nice weather and good fruit. He listened to his disciple's opinions and then did whatever he wanted. Once I became acquainted with the process, it was a great deal of fun.

Sometimes, he travelled to cities all over the world without ever leaving his sitting room. The most important thing for his secretary to know was that until he said, "send a telegram" or "tell them to send us tickets," it was only a suggestion by Śrīla Prabhupāda. It kept his disciples around the world busy painting temples blue and white as these were considered to be Śrīla Prabhupāda's favourite colours. Sometimes I thought Śrīla Prabhupāda considered that all temples outside of India had the fragrance of a paint store.

"Śrutakīrti, what do you think?" he asked me. "Should I go to London and attend the Rathayatra festival or should I go to Hawaii and rest?"

I had been with Śrīla Prabhupāda for almost one year and I knew he would do whatever he wanted. I was thrilled that he would even ask my opinion. Just that one acknowledgment was enough to last my entire life.

"Śrīla Prabhupāda," I quickly responded. "If you go to the Rathayatra festival in London then so many people will be benefited by your association."

"Yes, I think your observation is correct," he said with a smile.

After listening to everyone Śrīla Prabhupāda said, "Thank you for the advice. I am going to London for the Rathayatra."

It was an amazing festival. Since I stayed by Śrīla Prabhupāda's side, my perspective was limited, but it was filled with adventure. Śrīla Prabhupāda was very enthusiastic. His vyāsāsana was available on the Ratha cart, but he decided to walk with the devotees. Śrīla Prabhupāda walked in front of the cart clapping his hands to the beat of the kīrtan. He raised his hands in the air encouraging everyone to dance. He looked like the supreme puppeteer. As he raised his hands, everyone leaped into the air in ecstasy. It did not require any purification. Being near him was bliss for everyone except the policemen. They wanted to calm everyone down, they were looking for someone in charge. They were keen enough to realize that if they could control Śrīla Prabhupāda, they could control the "unruly" crowd. Somehow, they thought I was an associate" of His Divine Grace.

"You'll have to tell your leader to sit down," one bobby said. "He's causing too much of a disturbance. Everyone is becoming wild and we can't control the crowd."

"All right," I told him, and then did nothing.

It was apparent that Śrīla Prabhupāda was in charge of the festival. He was visibly enlivened. The bobbies again approached me.

"You must tell him. He'll have to sit down," they firmly said.

Again, I agreed. With fear of reprisal, I tapped Śrīla Prabhupāda on his shoulder and said, "Prabhupada, the policemen want you to sit down. They say you are creating havoc here in the parade."

Śrīla Prabhupāda looked through me for a brief moment. He quickly turned away with his arms still raised in the air. Majestically, he continued walking with a bounce in his step. He allowed everyone present to enter into his world of happiness. He never stopped. He walked the length of the parade. The bobbies gave up their attack. They were no match for the pure devotee and the Lord of the Universe.

Śrīla Prabhupāda, when I told you that so many people would benefit by your association, I had no idea of your plans. Like an ocean of mercy, you distributed your waves of kindness to all who attended.

92

"Just keep chanting Hare Kṛṣṇa"

July 14, 1973 Bhaktivedanta Manor, England

Allen Ginsberg, having just returned from India, came to see Śrīla Prabhupāda. He brought his harmonium with him.

"You are chanting Hare Kṛṣṇa?" Śrīla Prabhupāda asked.

"Yes, I still chant Hare Kṛṣṇa and I am chanting some other things, too. Is it all right if I play the harmonium for you and chant?" Ginsberg asked.

"Yes, you can do," Śrīla Prabhupāda replied.

Ginsberg played the harmonium and chanted "Ooooommm." Each time he chanted "Om" his voice got deeper. Śrīla Prabhupāda leaned back behind his desk and listened. When Ginsberg finished, Śrīla Prabhupāda chuckled and said, "You can chant whatever you want to chant. Just keep chanting Hare Kṛṣṇa. As long as you are chanting Hare Kṛṣṇa, everything else is all right. You can chant whatever you want, but do not stop chanting Hare Kṛṣṇa."

By then, many devotees had entered the room. Śrīla Prabhupāda told them to have kirtan. Ginsberg began playing the harmonium and leading the chanting of the Hare Kṛṣṇa Mahā-mantra. About five minutes had passed when Śrīla Prabhupāda looked at Haṁsadūta and said, "Your turn to lead." Turning to Ginsberg he said, "He'll lead. He'll chant now." The chanting continued. The devotees in the room became uplifted as their god-brother led the kīrtan. The chanting went on for another ten minutes before Śrīla Prabhupāda stopped it to speak to his guests.

Śrīla Prabhupāda was very accomplished in dealing with everyone. He encouraged everyone in Kṛṣṇa Consciousness according to their level of realization. Knowing his desire, he allowed Alan Ginsberg to chant for some time and then he artfully arranged for his disciple to chant. There was a lesson for all of us in every one of his actions. He showed us the proper etiquette in everything he did.

His association was magical. He gave it freely to all. Everything he did and said, was done to help us become more attached to him and to the Supreme Lord. His Divine Grace always inspired us on the path back home, back to Godhead.

Jai Śrīla Prabhupāda!

93

"Just see! Kṛṣṇa is looking at me and I am looking at Kṛṣṇa."

August 9, 1973 ISKCON Paris

When Śrīla Prabhupāda first arrived at the Paris temple, the devotees anxiously waited on a veranda high above the front entrance. Like demigods, they showered flower petals onto His Divine Grace. Śrīla Prabhupāda responded with a beautiful smile, reciprocating the love and affection his disciples exhibited.

One of the highlights of Śrīla Prabhupāda's tour of France was the installation of Rādhā Kṛṣṇa Deities. The devotees were very excited to have Śrīla Prabhupāda presiding over the festivities. His Divine Grace carefully observed his Sanskrit editor, Pradyumna dāsa, as he prepared the fire sacrifice. As Pradyumna commenced, Śrīla Prabhupāda occasionally motioned to him saying, "Do it like this, not like that."

The devotees attentively watched Śrīla Prabhupāda orchestrate every nuance of the ceremony like a transcendental conductor. Śrīla Prabhupāda's attention to detail was immaculate. He wanted everything to be done in a first-class fashion. After all, his worshipable Rādhā and Kṛṣṇa were being installed. Overwhelmed with love, Śrīla Prabhupāda decided to take the situation into his own hands.

He climbed down from the vyāsāsana and took over the fire yajna. All of the disciples present were overjoyed, watching their spiritual master artfully prepare the arena for this most auspicious event. With Śrīla Prabhupāda in charge, everything was perfect. The Deities were bathed with Pañcāmṛta (five various liquids), rinsed with warm water, dried, and wrapped in lush, new towels. Upon completion, Śrī Śrī Rādhā Kṛṣṇa were brought into the Deity room and opulently dressed. Then Śrīla Prabhupāda personally offered Their Lordships' first arati. With extreme care, he offered each item to Śrī Śrī Rādhā Kṛṣṇa as the devotees chanted the Lord's Holy Names and danced in ecstasy. All the devotees' eyes were fixed on Śrīla Prabhupāda's graceful motion as he performed arati. His eyes glistening with the ointment of love of Godhead were fixed on his Deities throughout the offering.

Three months later in his room in Vṛndāvana, Śrīla Prabhupāda was given the latest copy of Back to Godhead magazine. Śrīla Prabhupāda was always excited to receive new issues of Back to Godhead. He enthusiastically poured over each page of this new issue, focusing on the large, beautiful, coloured pictures of his Rādhā Kṛṣṇa Deities, recently installed at the Paris-yatra. His concentrated vision halted as he gazed lovingly at a particular photograph. This individual photo captured a special moment as His Divine Grace performed arati. His arm was gracefully stretched overhead, offering the cāmara (Yak tail) fan to Their Lordships. Śrīla Prabhupāda looked at the picture in a meditative gaze as if entering into it for just a fraction of a second. In the next moment, he returned to us and with twinkling eyes and a broad smile, he innocently revealed, "Just see! Kṛṣṇa is looking at me and I am looking at Kṛṣṇa!"

Śrīla Prabhupāda, I have no idea what it would be like to gaze upon the Supreme Lord and have Him return that glance. I have been fortunate, however, to have you lovingly glance upon this unworthy soul. I pray to see you again, by never losing sight of your instructions. In this way, by your mercy, I may be allowed to follow in your footsteps.

94

"You are not feeling well?"

August 22, 1973 Bhaktivedanta Manor, England

Śrīla Prabhupāda's Vyāsa-pūjā

I had been a brahmacārī for two and a half years and was feeling restless. Many times, Śrīla Prabhupāda explained how one must reduce one's sleeping and eating to make spiritual advancement, so I decided to utilize the two upcoming fast days to reduce my eating. While breaking fast at midnight on Janmāṣṭamī, I ate very little. I again ate sparingly the next afternoon for Śrīla Prabhupāda's Vyasa puja celebration. The third day I also ate less. I did not feel hungry, so I assumed my stomach had shrunk.

The next day Śrīla Prabhupāda called me into his room. I offered my obeisances and sat up to see what I could do for him. He looked at me with concern and said, "Your face is looking thin. You are not feeling well?" I was surprised by his question.

"No, Śrīla Prabhupāda, I feel fine," I explained. "I was trying to cut down on my eating and have been eating less for the last few days."

"What is this?" Śrīla Prabhupāda said. "You have service to perform. You should not cut down on your eating. This is nonsense. You have to give massage every day. That requires much strength. You must do so many things. Do not cut down. You should eat whatever you can digest. That is what you should eat."

Amazingly, in our first eleven months together, this was Śrīla Prabhupāda's second conversation with me regarding my prasādam intake. Finally, I decided not to worry about how much prasādam I ate.

Śrīla Prabhupāda you mercifully looked out for me at every moment. What great fortune, to learn first hand what was important and what was mental concoction. There was so much 'Prabhupada said' that went around the society. Even I was not immune to them. Gradually I began to understand more and more that Kṛṣṇa Consciousness was common sense. I also began to see the necessity of reading your books.

Many years have gone by. It is becoming clear that reducing my eating and sleeping did not have to be done artificially. It happens automatically as old age sets in. When I was with you for a few days you told me, "I am an old man. I can't sleep too long at one time." I now understand that.

You always advised me what to do when necessary. You could even tell when I lost a few pounds. Thank you for taking such good care of me. It is clear that although I was the servant, you did much more for me than I ever did for you. So many of us were busy concocting our own means to advance spiritually, but you carefully guided us and cared for us on every level.

Jai Śrīla Prabhupāda!

ও 95 ও

"Yes, I have my own style of chanting."

August 23, 1973 Bhaktivedanta Manor, England

After one year of being with Śrīla Prabhupāda, I became accustomed to his way of singing. At times, I sat in my quarters and heard the sweet sound of the harmonium coming from his room. I knew I could invite any nearby devotees into Śrīla Prabhupāda's room while His Divine Grace sang, but no one was around on this particular day. I went into his room alone, and offered my humble obeisances. As I sat up, my consciousness was filled with the nectar of Śrīla Prabhupāda's melodious bhajan. Just by hearing him play the harmonium and listening to the sound of his voice, my stone heart was softened. Without moving, I quietly sat and listened, not wanting to distract him while he was in this mood. It amazed me how he had so many responsibilities, but always found time to chant rounds, sing bhajans and read his books.

After a minute, he looked up from the harmonium and nodded at me. I knew that meant to accompany him with his kartals. He continued singing for some time.

"Śrīla Prabhupāda," I said when he was finished. "Your kīrtan and bhajans are so different from any others I have heard."

He started laughing and replied, "Yes, I have my own style of chanting." I put his kartals back on the shelf, offered my obeisances and went back to the servants' quarters.

My dear Śrīla Prabhupāda, your words that day were so simple but true. You do have such style, grace, humility and devotion. You did so much each day to serve your guru; the endless letters, classes, translating and management. Still you had time to sit in your room alone, play harmonium, and sing beautiful bhajans for Kṛṣṇa's pleasure. No one had to be there to witness it, but anyone could come in. You are the topmost yogi, a Paramahaṁsa, who kindly made yourself available to all.

Your style was sometimes imitated, but never duplicated. After all, who else could create an international society by chanting under a tree?

96

"... you will be intelligent when you are eighty!"

August 28, 1973 Bhaktivedanta Manor, England

After one year of massaging Śrīla Prabhupāda every day, I thought I had become quite efficient.

"The Manor is wonderful," Śrīla Prabhupāda said, "and when the sun is shining there is no place better."

As he did every day, Śrīla Prabhupāda sat on a straw mat on the highly polished hardwood floor. Two bottles were next to him. The large bottle was filled with mustard seed oil and the small bottle contained sandalwood oil. The sun's brilliant rays filtered through a series of windows and Śrīla Prabhupāda's golden complexion was effulgently sun-drenched. I sat behind His Divine Grace and rubbed his head with sandalwood oil for a cooling effect. After massaging his head for about fifteen minutes, I moved onto Śrīla Prabhupāda's back.

Śrīla Prabhupāda told me many times, "You can massage my back as hard as you are able." He really meant it. It was truly amazing! I put all of my weight and strength into massaging his back and continued that way for a half hour or more. He never said it was too much. Sometimes I deliberately used extra force, thinking there must be a limit. to how hard he liked it. I never found a limit. Śrīla Prabhupāda sat perfectly relaxed during this "passive wrestling" as he called it. He never braced himself to accept my strength. He always enjoyed his massage and this day was no different. Then I stood up and changed positions.

As I took a step to the right to massage Śrīla Prabhupāda's chest, I knocked over the bottle of mustard seed oil. His Divine Grace had warned me many times always to keep the lid on the bottle.

"You fool," he immediately yelled. "You will be intelligent when you are eighty. Go get a katori and bring it here." I ran out of the room and brought back a stainless steel katori. "All right, Śrīla Prabhupāda said sternly. "Do like I am doing. Scrap the oil off your hand and into the cup." The two of us sat there until all of the oil from the floor was in the metal cup. It was about 3 ounces. "Now use that oil to massage me," he said, looking towards the cup.

I was already quite aware that Śrīla Prabhupāda never wasted anything. As I continued to massage Śrīla Prabhupāda, the atmosphere seemed almost too quiet. I felt he was angry with me because of my foolishness. I began to think, "What can I say to mitigate my offence?" I mulled it over again and again. Finally, I got up the courage.

Hoping to change the mood I thought was there I blurted out, "Thank you very much, Śrīla Prabhupāda. I thought it would take much longer for me to become intelligent." I could not have imagined a happier response from my loving father. He laughed aloud.

"Yes," he said laughing loudly and slapping his knee. "That is an old phrase we would say when we were young boys when someone did something foolish. 'You'll be intelligent when you are eighty.' I have used it with you." He continued to chuckle for the next minute or so and I very happily continued the massage, relieved of all my anxiety.

It was another opportunity for me to see just how wonderful Śrīla Prabhupāda was. I was foolishly thinking that he was so angry with me. I still did not understand that he had no other desire then to see everyone engaged joyfully in the serve of the Supreme Lord. It was another opportunity for me to love Śrīla Prabhupāda more.

Śrīla Prabhupāda you are the most pure devotee of the Supreme Lord and Kṛṣṇa is obliged to keep the word of His devotee. I have no chance of becoming Kṛṣṇa conscious, but if I can just live to be eighty, I am sure I will finally become intelligent. Real intelligence is to be Kṛṣṇa Conscious. I pray that I can live to be eighty so I can live up to the expectations of my beloved Śrīla Prabhupāda. Over thirty years have gone by since I spilled the oil. I am no more Kṛṣṇa Conscious but I am much closer to eighty years old. I am happy you are still with me, never abandoning me, but I feel so alone. I am still addicted to personally serving you, your beautifully golden, form.

∽ 97 ∽

"...as long as he is in charge, you should follow..."

August 29, 1973 Bhaktivedanta Manor, England

Once, during Śrīla Prabhupāda's afternoon massage, a sannyāsī entered the room with a problem he thought only his spiritual master could solve.

"Śrīla Prabhupāda, my GBC is making all these decisions. I want to accept his authority, but I had to come to you because he is not chanting his rounds. I know this for a fact! He doesn't chant any rounds. In addition, many of the devotees in the temple find it difficult to follow his authority. I want to know how we should handle this."

Śrīla Prabhupāda was silent for a moment and then replied, "Your GBC is very busy. Arjuna, when he was fighting the battle of Kurukṣetra, he did not chant his sixteen rounds. When you are fighting a battle, where is the time to chant your rounds? So, perhaps your GBC is also too busy. Anyway, you should see it like that. As long as he is in charge, you should follow, and encourage him to chant if he is not chanting."

Another time during an afternoon massage in Kolkata, a devotee entered the room and asked what should be done because Gargamuni Mahārāja, the temple administrator, was not chanting his rounds.

"He should not be in office," Śrīla Prabhupāda responded. "He may be materially qualified in so many ways, but it is not enough. In management, one has to have his transcendental aspect. One has to be following the regulative principles and chanting. Otherwise, it is simply useless just to have some management knowledge."

Śrīla Prabhupāda did not remove Gargamuni Mahārāja from office at that time.

He was the ācārya and was able to make adjustments

according to time, place and circumstance. This can be understood by reading his letters and listening to recorded conversations. Sometimes Śrīla Prabhupāda wrote instructions in a letter that were meant only for the person receiving the letter. It was not meant to be a general policy. We can read his books to learn the absolute truth. He sometimes called them "law books for the next ten thousand years."

Śrīla Prabhupāda's personal presence on this planet was so potent that he could carry us all and keep us engaged in Kṛṣṇa's service, even when we were not strictly following his regulations. Since his departure, I have realized that if I want to associate with him and perform devotional service, I must strictly follow his instructions. This may seem like common sense to most devotees, but to me it is a revelation. Śrīla Prabhupāda lives eternally in his instructions and his followers live with him.

Śrīla Prabhupāda, please engage me in your service. Coming in disciplic succession from Lord Nityānanda, you are the most merciful spiritual master who came to deliver the fallen souls from the western world. Many considered it spiritual suicide to go to the West, so full of materialism. You had no such fear and were never affected by it. Instead, you infected us with the desire to follow you. You accepted whatever service we performed and offered it to your spiritual master.

98

"Devotees should get sumptuous prasādam."

August 30, 1973 Bhaktivedanta Manor, England

Indian culture was apparent while visiting Indians all over the world. While travelling, Śrīla Prabhupāda and his disciples were often invited to a life member's house for a feast. His disciples were always eager to attend such a gathering, as they would get Śrīla Prabhupāda's association as well as opulent prasādam. I do not remember Śrīla Prabhupāda ever refusing an invitation. Sometimes he gave a short lecture before prasādam was served. One such gathering took place when Śrīla Prabhupāda was staying at the manor. Several dozen devotees went to an Indian gentleman's house. The prasādam was delicious.

Śrīla Prabhupāda described prasādam in different ways. "The devotees should get sumptuous prasādam," he said. "Simple, but sumptuous. Sumptuous means very tasty. If the prasādam is tasty, you can go on eating even if you are not hungry and if it is not tasty then you'll immediately lose your appetite. Prasādam must be very nice for the devotees then everything else will be all right. Prasādam means ghee and sugar."

At the feast there was halava, sweet rice, puris and many other preparations. I watched Śrīla Prabhupāda eat. It was always special. Normally, he took prasādam alone in his room. I cannot do him justice by trying to describe the heavenly way he moved his fingers, hands and mouth as he ate prasādam, but even I could see that he was honouring Kṛṣṇa prasādam. We all ate to our full satisfaction.

When we returned to the Manor, Śrīla Prabhupāda rang his bell. I trotted to his room.

"So everyone has enjoyed prasādam?" he asked smiling. "Everyone has enjoyed the feast?"

"Well, actually, Śrīla Prabhupāda, some of the devotees, they are not feeling well," I said. "They are saying that everything was fried in oil instead of ghee."

"Well, what do you expect?" he replied. "I was watching them and I saw. Pradyumna, he ate so many puris and another devotee he ate so much of the vegetable."

I was amazed. I noticed Śrīla Prabhupāda eating, but I had no idea he had observed so much. He simultaneously did so many things without appearing to do anything at all. However, I had an observation of my own to offer.

"Yes, Śrīla Prabhupāda," I agreed, "but, I also do not feel well and I did not eat very much."

"Yes. I know this," he said. "You did not eat so much, but I do remember you ate four puris."

"Yes, Prabhupada, I guess I did," I answered in disbelief.

I offered my obeisances and left the room still trying to figure out how he knew all of this. He knew more about what I ate than I did. It was remarkable to me how he was so aware of everything that was going on around him at a simple function.

Thank you, Śrīla Prabhupāda, for paying such close attention to your disciples. I pray that I never forget all the time you spent patiently instructing me in countless situations. You performed such monumental service, but I am more impressed by all the wonderful little things you did for me and continue to do for me every day. Please, let me remember your kindness birth after birth. Separation from you is so bittersweet. It is a taste of which I can't get enough.

99

"This prasādam...did not you help?"

September 5, 1973 ISKCON Bhaktivedanta Manor, England

Being with a pure devotee of the Lord for two years was the most wonderful opportunity to learn how to act in Kṛṣṇa Consciousness. For a person like me, it was also an opportunity to make innumerable offences to a great soul. There are many activities etched in my mind that bring joy, but many others that give me sorrow.

An Indian devotee at the manor had a son who was about twelve years old. This boy wanted to cook lunch for Śrīla Prabhupāda. His Divine Grace agreed to the proposal. I, having the mentality of a twelve-year-old and no service attitude, thought it was a chance for me to take it easy that morning. I did not oversee any of the boy's activities and had no idea if he was qualified to cook Śrīla Prabhupāda's lunch. I gave Śrīla Prabhupāda his massage and then returned to my room.

Later the youngster brought Śrīla Prabhupāda his lunch. The dahl was burned. The chapatis were hard because they did not puff up. The rice was under cooked. Śrīla Prabhupāda sampled everything. While the boy returned to the kitchen to cook another chapati, I went into Śrīla Prabhupāda's room.

"This prasādam," he said, "did not you help?"

"No, Prabhupada," I answered. "I thought he was going to do it."

"Yes, but you should have been with him, to make sure everything was all right," he said. "This is very bad. How can I eat this?"

Just then, the boy came back into the room with another chapati.

"Everything is very nice," Śrīla Prabhupāda told him. "You have done very well." The boy was very happy. He had performed devotional service to the best of his ability and pleased his spiritual master. I, needless to say, had committed a great offence by my lethargy. Śrīla Prabhupāda did not even shout. It was difficult for me when he shouted, but it was more painful when he was silently angry with me.

This incident exemplifies another part of Śrīla Prabhupāda's greatness. He could have had any number of spiritually and materially qualified assistants with him to make his life easy, but he accepted service from me. He never asked me to leave him at any time. He gracefully accepted my incompetence and made me feel appreciated despite my many shortcomings. I have seen Śrīla Prabhupāda forgive his disciples for so many offences. This was certainly not the worst thing I have done to my spiritual master, but it involved serving him directly and that causes me sorrow.

> *Śrīla Prabhupāda, do not push me away. There is no safe place in this material world except at your beautifully golden lotus feet. Please give me the desire to serve you and your movement for the duration of my lives.*

100

"Prasādam is not to be heated up."

September 15, 1973 ISKCON Juhu Beach, Mumbai, India

After our arrival in the morning Śrīla Prabhupāda informed me he wanted the Deities' maha-prasādam for lunch. I was happy with this instruction since no one had arrived yet who could prepare his lunch. When the maha arrived from the temple, I started to heat it up. While in the kitchen, a devotee came in and told me that Śrīla Prabhupāda wanted his prasādam.

"I am heating it up," I told him. "I will bring it in right away."

In an instant they returned and said, "Śrīla Prabhupāda is angry, he wants it now." Trembling, I went into his room and offered my obeisances. He was shouting before I lifted my head.

"Why are you heating up the prasādam?" he asked. "Maha-prasādam is not to be heated up. I want it now. I did not want it heated up. I just wanted the prasādam. You bring it now."

Being with Śrīla Prabhupāda was never boring. Many devotees have commented that it must have been very difficult to be Śrīla Prabhupāda's personal servant. It was indeed. However, it was more difficult for Śrīla Prabhupāda to have had me as his personal servant. I still have no idea how much nonsense he tolerated because of my bad habits. He had so much patience. There were so many things to learn from him. He often said, "Kṛṣṇa Consciousness is common sense."

> *Śrīla Prabhupāda, please benedict me with common sense so I can begin to serve you according to your desires.*

101

"All right, do any damn thing you want."

September 23, 1973 ISKCON Mumbai, India

Besides getting ill whenever I travelled to India, cultural differences played a major part in my dislike of travelling to this very diverse part of the world. I was not alone in my aversion to staying in India. I witnessed many devotees coming to the holy land, only to leave a short time later. Their difficulties included poor health, lack of facility, personality conflicts with management and culture shock.

I observed two of Śrīla Prabhupāda's veteran disciples also facing their personal limitation in the holy land. Stories of fruitful preaching opportunities in the West seemed to call them back to the States. Preaching to potential life members seemed painfully slow in India. The Indians would tell us we were not telling them anything they did not already know. After all, they grew up hearing about Kṛṣṇa. Life members often said, "Oh, yes. We know Kṛṣṇa."

Many times Śrīla Prabhupāda illustrated this point by saying it was as if we Westerners were hundred miles away from Kṛṣṇa, but now under his guidance we were heading toward the Lord. The Indians were ten miles from Kṛṣṇa, but unfortunately going away from Him. Our problem was finding a way to turn them around, so they could return back to Godhead. Sometimes it was anything but enlivening.

One day a few disciples were in Śrīla Prabhupāda's quarters pleading with him to go back to the West.

"We are just like businessmen," one disciple told Śrīla Prabhupāda. "We are collecting money and making life members."

In one sense, he was correct, but the difference was we were doing it for Śrīla Prabhupāda and Kṛṣṇa and not for our personal profit.

Śrīla Prabhupāda was sympathetic to their frustrations, but in a stern voice told them, "But, I want you to stay here. It is the spiritual master's desire that you stay here, so that is better."

"Isn't it service to go to America and preach?" one sannyāsī asked. "In America the preaching is so much better."

I was sitting off to the side, amazed at the intensity of my god-brothers. It was a rare sight. Śrīla Prabhupāda's disciples seemed relentless. The more they were determined to leave India, the more Śrīla Prabhupāda was determined to have

In the summer of 1973, Srila Prabhupada spent eight weeks in the English countryside at Bhaktivedanta Manor—a kind donation from George Harrison. While there, he spoke with prominent people from all walks of life, trained and enthused his disciples, and personally installed the temple deities of Sri Sri Radha Gokulananda.

Srila Prabhupada chants japa before a painting of Gaurakisora das Babaji. Described as "renunciation personified" he had just one disciple, Srila Bhaktisiddhanta Saraswati Thakur, Srila Prabhupada's own spiritual master. In the service of his Guru Maharaja, Srila Prabhupada initiated over 5,000 disciples around the world.

Devotees offer their obeisances at the Brooklyn temple in 1973 as Srila Prabhupada prepares to give class . Throwing flower petals at his disciples during Gurupuja in Hawaii temple in 1975. Offering Srila Prabhupada his shoes as he leaves the makeshift templeroom at Juhu, Mumbai, 1975, after giving the Srimad-Bhagavatam class.

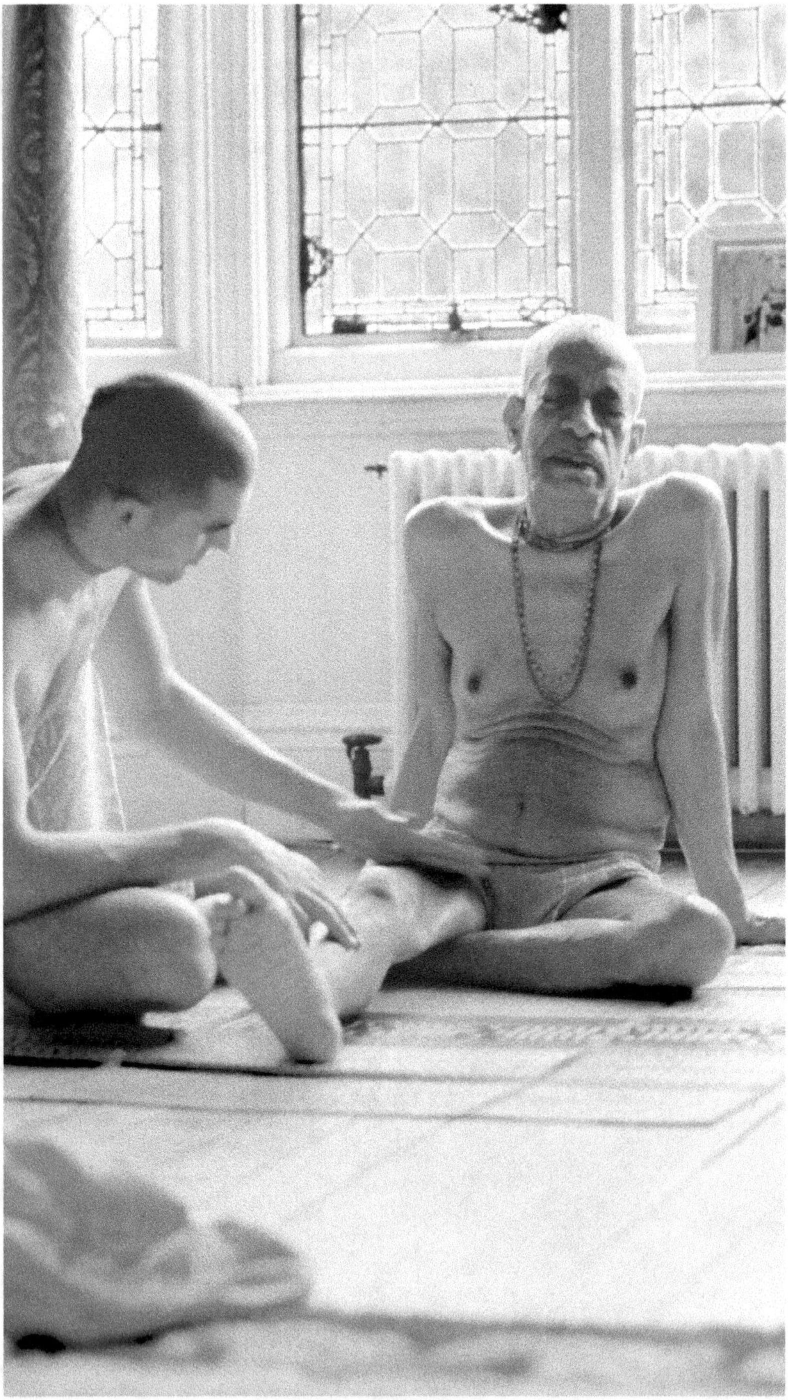

Srila Prabhupada would relax and take the morning sun during his massage while his lunch was on the flame in his famous brass "three tier cooker". When necessary, Prabhupada patiently trained his servants—here Uppendra—in the arts of cooking and massage with "mustardseed oil for the body and sandalwood oil for the head."

Srila Prabhupada returned to India with a significant number of his Western disciples in the early 1970s. He was eager to establish comfortable facilities for his followers to stay and soon established a number of temples and international guesthouses. "Vrindavan is my home, Bombay is my office, and Mayapur is my place of worship." Whether in philosophi-

cal discussion with his godbrothers—here with Sridhara Maharaja (left) and Damodara Maharaja (centre) in Navadvip—or receiving a garland of jasmine flowers, Srila Prabhupada was eager to give credit to his Western Vaishnava disciples and their efforts to serve hisi mission in India and abroad.

Srila Prabhupada takes a walk in Sevakunja, Vrindavan, accompanied by Hayagriva and Acyutananda Swami, during the month of Damodara. Here, in 1972, he gave the famous Nectar of Devotion classes in the courtyard of the Radha Damodara Temple at the samadhi of Rupa Goswami. Walking past the half-completed lotus building in Mayapur, India, 1973. Two

years later Srila Prabhupada sits on the second floor balcony outside his rooms and enlivens his disciples with words of transcendental humour and encouragement. Behind him sits Visnujana Swami. Jayapataka and Pancadravida Swamis oversee some construction work with Srila Prabhupada

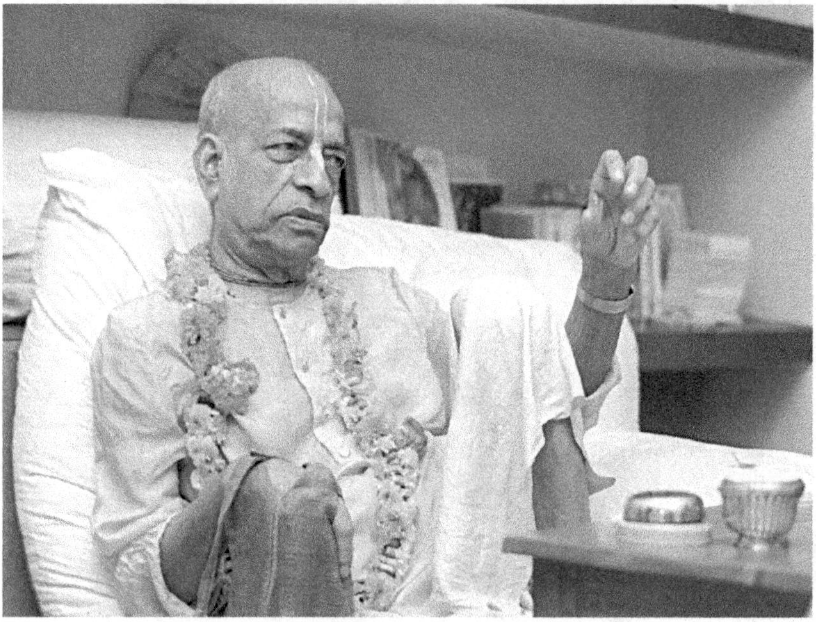

As Srila Prabhupada travelled from temple to temple, he would be sent the latest printings of his books from the Bhaktivedanta Book Trust and he saw many of them translated into other languages. The phenomenal growth of book distribution around the world gave him transcendental pleasure and he emphasised its importance, even encouraging a spirit

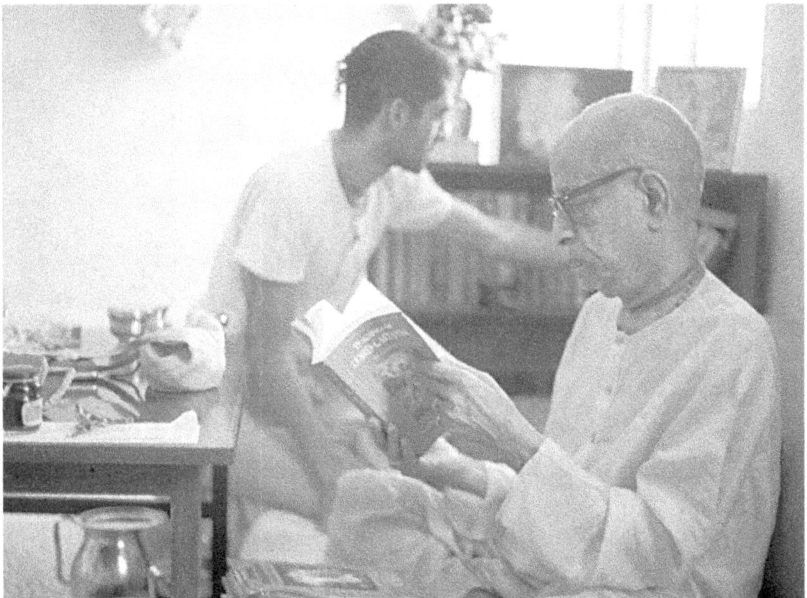

of transcendental competition between the temples. Yet the process of deity worship was just as vital he said, and he installed Radha Krishna deities in many temples around the world. Wherever he travelled, Srila Prabhupada would ask for the deities' maha prasadam and enquire after Their welfare.

With its gorgeous temple, BBT press and warehouse, art studio, translation departments, diorama workshops and extensive devotee apartments, Srila Prabhupada considered Los Angeles his western headquarters. His visits would always include a tour of the community and, as usual, he was accompanied by the temple leaders and department heads.

He was very fond of his garden there and said it was his favourite place—"non-different from Vrindavana" —because of the dozens of tulasi plants growing. Sitting there he would sometimes be quietly chant japa, receiving dignatories, talking with disciples or listening to a reading from his Krishna Book.

As a perfect sannyasa, Srila Prabhupada was expert in all activities—writing, preaching, kirtan, management and cooking—and the movement he created flourished under his guidance and by his perfect example. "Not everyone can digest the philosophy, but everyone can digest prasadam" he would sometimes say with a smile.

them stay. It was evident that Śrīla Prabhupāda considered the preaching work in India to be of the utmost importance. This was a lesson I learned on my first trip to India with my Guru Mahārāja.

Previously in January of 1973 at Kartikeya Mahadevia's flat, a heated conversation took place between Śrīla Prabhupāda and some of his disciples. The two sannyāsīs that had pleaded with Śrīla Prabhupāda before, were present for this discussion as well. It was amazing to witness Śrīla Prabhupāda's determination, as well as his mastery in managing his young disciples in devotional service.

Śrīla Prabhupāda was outraged because he had received reports that life members were paying their money, but not getting the books they had been promised. The record keeping was not being done properly. Complaints from the life members were regularly coming in the mail to Śrīla Prabhupāda.

"If you cannot manage properly then we should just pack up and leave India," Śrīla Prabhupāda told his disciples. "This is not good. Everything must be done very carefully."

Everyone could understand how important it was to Śrīla Prabhupāda that his transcendental literatures be distributed. Ultimately, we sincerely wanted to please His Divine Grace despite any obstacles placed before us.

Nine months later, Śrīla Prabhupāda was again pleading with the same two senior sannyāsīs to remain in India. It was not going well. Seeing how upset Śrīla Prabhupāda was, I was squirming in the corner of the room. I also understood how hard it was to stay in India. Śrīla Prabhupāda was depending on these men to assist him in this important work, but they just could not do it any longer. It was a fierce battle. The intensity of negotiation was what I would have expected amongst peers, rather than between spiritual master and disciple. Śrīla Prabhupāda wanted them to stay, and that was final. His disciples argued that they needed to leave India to preach. At this time, the West was a fertile preaching field. Finally, in apparent disgust, Śrīla Prabhupāda said, "All right, you just chant your sixteen rounds, follow the four regulative principles and do any damn thing you want."

That is how this rare conversation ended. Our most magnanimous leader gave them permission to serve him in whatever capacity they could. Again, it was evident that Śrīla Prabhupāda considered us all volunteers in his transcendental army. It is up to us to decide how quickly we want to get the mercy and make advancement by serving our spiritual master according to his desires. Daily, we choose what, and how much, we are willing to do in the service of our Guru Mahārāja.

Once in his quarters in New Dvārakā, Śrīla Prabhupāda said, "Ultimately, we must all fly our own aeroplane." Śrīla Prabhupāda, I am still trying to find my way back to the airport. Without you in front of me, this is very difficult. You have given us all the tools necessary to engage in devotional service, but I do not think I will ever be qualified to fly my own plane back to Kṛṣṇa. Let me serve those who are qualified to fly their own aeroplane back to Godhead. I am praying you allow me to be your flight attendant as you travel around the universe liberating conditioned souls.

ഗ 102 ഗ

"One of my favourite things..."

October 27, 1973 ISKCON Juhu Beach, Mumbai, India

My association with Śrīla Prabhupāda can be divided into three types.

The first type was sweet. These were the times I was able to witness Śrīla Prabhupāda's mercy and kindness. The second type was sweeter. These were the times I was able to massage him and cook for him on a daily basis. Massaging him was particularly sweet for me. Better still, were very special moments that can only be described as the sweetest.

One night Śrīla Prabhupāda was ready for his evening massage at about 10:00 pm in his Juhu flat, he had a separate bedroom. Juhu was especially nice because of the mosquitoes. Thanks to the mosquitoes, I had to get under the mosquito net with Śrīla Prabhupāda. This situation was very intimate. Śrīla Prabhupāda lay down and I sat on the bed by his feet. I felt like I was camping out with my spiritual master, like two youngsters in the woods. On this particular night Śrīla Prabhupāda assisted me in my fantasy.

While I was gently rubbing his body he said, "One of my favourite things, when I was young, was my shoes. Once, my father bought me a pair of shoes. They were imported from England. They had soft leather uppers and hard leather souls. At the time, perhaps they cost six rupees. That was a fortune. In India, seventy years ago, six rupees was a lot of money. I liked my shoes very much. I remember wearing them to school."

At that point, he stopped speaking for a few minutes. I was caught up in Śrīla Prabhupāda's mood. I tried to imagine him walking around in his shoes. Still massaging his beautiful form I smiled and said, "Prabhupada, when you walked to school, did you look at your shoes as you were walking?"

"Yes," he said laughing. "I would look down at my shoes. I liked them so much, these shoes."

He spoke about a few other childhood memories that night. That was a "most moving" night for me. I could have stayed there forever massaging him and listening to stories. It was like hearing Kṛṣṇa Book stories for the first time. His memory was so incredible. When he spoke about his childhood, it seemed like he was there. I could not imagine what my qualification was to be able to have shared those moments with him. Now, I can understand he was not describing these pastimes for my pleasure alone. He was telling me so I could describe them to all of his followers. I hope to relate them with at least a hint of the emotion that I felt, as he told me such sublime pastimes.

> *Thank you, Śrīla Prabhupāda, for sharing your childhood memories with me. I had no qualification yet by your special mercy, I was able to hear from Your Divine Self. I have no competency to adequately describe your glories, but somehow or other I must share whatever I have experienced of your activities. Even with my imperfect senses and limited understanding, I must share your grace.*

103

"Oh, what are the symptoms?"

November 11, 1973 ISKCON Delhi, India

One year after I had recovered from jaundice, Śrīla Prabhupāda's secretary, Brahmānanda Mahārāja, was afflicted. Being newsworthy, I decided to tell Śrīla Prabhupāda. He looked surprised. "Oh, what are the symptoms?" he asked.

I forgot that we had this same conversation the previous

year. I repeated the list of symptoms. Śrīla Prabhupāda said, once again, "Hmm, perhaps I have jaundice also."

Finally, after Śrīla Prabhupāda made this statement again, I understood. It only took me a year. Śrīla Prabhupāda was incredible. He remembered everything that happened with his disciples and mentioned it at the perfect moment. I was so dull-headed that the joke was way over my head. The yoga-māyā potency was very strong around him. I had no idea who I was with. This was fortunate. Otherwise, I would not have been able to perform my service due to awe and fear. I speculated Śrīla Prabhupāda was saying he had all the symptoms of illness that I described, but being transcendental, he went about his devotional life in spite of so many painful difficulties.

Śrīla Prabhupāda did not have jaundice, but he did experience symptoms. He showed us that when we get older, as I am beginning to experience, the body is full of aches and pains, and one's energy level decreases. Śrīla Prabhupāda explained that it was not very amazing that we feel weak, become ill or experience pain. However, it was amazing if we did not feel these things. He demonstrated how one should not be affected by the limitations of the body.

Śrīla Prabhupāda, when you were in quarantine because of not being immunized against yellow fever you said, "What do they think? I can get yellow fever? Anyone who is always engaged in Kṛṣṇa's service, there is no question of material contamination. He cannot be infected with any disease."

I pray to be infected with love for you, Śrīla Prabhupāda, so I can be cent percent engaged in your devotional service. Please give me a glimpse of your transcendental position.

See also uvacha 37 - December 12, 1972 Ahmedabad, India.

104

"I would observe Mahatma Gandhi."

November 20, 1973 ISKCON Delhi, India

Śrīla Prabhupāda lectured every evening at a pandal programme attended by thousands of residents. After the programme, he made his way back to his quarters, protected by his disciples. Surrounding Śrīla Prabhupāda, some sannyāsī disciples held their daṇḍas in such a way as to protect His Divine Grace from the hopeful admirers who tried to touch his lotus feet.

"I remember when I was young," he said one evening in his room. "I would observe Mahatma Gandhi. He had so many people around him, protecting him from the thousands of admirers. I thought, 'Someday I want to have that' and now I have it."

Śrīla Prabhupāda, it has been twenty five years since you initiated me. I have spent most of that time in illusion. On the anniversary of your disappearance, I want to take this opportunity to again serve your orders. Your first instructions to me were to chant sixteen rounds, follow the four regulative principles and become the servant of one whose activities are world-famous. It is not possible for me to serve Kṛṣṇa directly. I pray that you are kind upon me so that I may serve your lotus feet. Your activities are world-famous. I pray to spend life after life praising your glories all over the world. You are the most glorious servant of Lord Caitanya because you have fulfilled his desire and that of the previous ācārya s. Please protect me so that I do not stray from your instructions. I want you to reside forever in my heart so that I can taste the sweetness of separation from you. It is the most sublime feeling and it is only available to your faithful follower.

☙ 105 ☙

"Where is the vase? Why are they so wasteful?"

December 7, 1973 ISKCON Los Angeles, California

Once, when Śrīla Prabhupāda was in Delhi, he received a silver vase from a life member. Originally, it was to be given to Indira Gandhi and was engraved with her name. Śrīla Prabhupāda was very pleased with the gift and had me carry it in the luggage until we reached Los Angeles.

"I will keep this here," Śrīla Prabhupāda said, pointing to his desk in his quarters. I showed it to the devotees who cleaned Śrīla Prabhupāda's rooms while he went on his morning walk.

"Śrīla Prabhupāda likes this vase very much," I told them. "You should put nice flowers in it."

Every morning they made a beautiful flower arrangement in the vase. It was a good size and could hold a large amount of flowers. One day we returned from the morning walk a little earlier than usual. As soon as Śrīla Prabhupāda walked into his room, he noticed that the vase was not on his desk.

"Where is the vase?" he asked me.

"Well, they probably took it into the kitchen to put fresh flowers in it," I said.

Now he was somewhat angry, and getting angrier with each sentence.

"Why?" he asked. "The flowers in it were fine. Why do they change these flowers every day? Why are they so wasteful? Who is this person doing this? Tell them to change them only when they go bad. You should never take the flowers out of this room until they are dwindling. It is not necessary. This is just wasteful. Where is the vase? Go find it immediately!"

I quickly left his room. Actually, I was eager to leave. It was not fun for me to be around Śrīla Prabhupāda when he was yelling, even if it was not directed towards me. Fortunately, the vase was in the temple kitchen.

"You had better stop changing these flowers every day," I told the devotees. "Śrīla Prabhupāda said it is very bad. Make sure this vase is never out of his room."

Arriving in his sitting room with a beautiful new flower arrangement did not seem to appease him. I put the vase down on his desk and offered my obeisances, wishing I could just keep my head on the floor.

"Just do it when it is necessary!" he shouted. "They shouldn't be wasting so much on flowers. They shouldn't be wasting so much money, every day changing. This is your custom in America, simply wasting. In your country if you have some cloth, if there is something extra, instead of just folding it under you will cut it off and throw away. This is your process here in America. In India if there is something left, they will fold it over and sew. Whatever goes wrong, you solve it with money. In this way, it appears very good. You make some accident, and then because you have money you can cover it over very quickly. It is not that you are very capable of doing anything, but because money is there, you make everything look very good. With money you can cover over all of your deficiencies."

Śrīla Prabhupāda often said, "Kṛṣṇa has given you American boys and girls so much facility." What was not apparent to me at the time was the reason 'so much' was there was because of Śrīla Prabhupāda's potency, not anything we were doing. He saw Kṛṣṇa in everything, everywhere. Therefore, he sometimes chastised us when we were wasteful. He was so very tolerant of our spiritual and material immaturity.

Śrīla Prabhupāda, please forgive me for my wasteful habits. Most of all, forgive me for wasting so much time in the service of the illusory energy. Sometimes in a lecture, you would look at your watch and say how it was impossible to recover this moment in time ever again, no matter how much money you have. I would foolishly think, "Why is that so bad. We are eternal. What is the loss?"

Now, as I sit here with emptiness in my heart due to your absence, I have a little idea of how valuable each second was in your presence. No amount of money can bring you back to this most unfortunate soul. Again, I am feeling the bittersweet taste of separation from Your Divine Grace.

106

As he grabbed his cane, he offered me his right foot.

December 25, 1973 ISKCON Los Angeles, California

During this winter visit, we experienced extremely cold days in Los Angeles with temperatures dropping to around forty degrees. This weather, however, afforded me the opportunity to render a little more service to Śrīla Prabhupāda.

No matter how cold it was, Śrīla Prabhupāda went on his morning walk. When it was very cold, though, he wore long underwear and socks. Śrīla Prabhupāda appreciated me helping him to put them on.

First, I got his long, thermal underwear, (saffron of course), and Śrīla Prabhupāda sat on his bed already wearing his dhoti and kurta. I pulled them over his lotus feet, one foot at a time, bringing them up to his knees. While he was still sitting, I put saffron socks on those beautiful, soft lotus feet. Then Śrīla Prabhupāda stood up and pulled his long johns up to his waist while keeping his dhoti in place. He would then put on his saffron sweater without my help. Then he went to his sitting place, put on tilak and chanted Gāyatrī mantra.

If other devotees were in the room, they would also chant Gāyatrī. Usually, this was not a good idea because Śrīla Prabhupāda always finished before his disciples. Their dilemma then became trying to decide whether to stay frozen in their brahminical pose and miss their Guru Mahārāja walking out the door, or to hurriedly get up and try to keep His Divine Grace in their vision. I loved to watch this humorous scenario unfold. Even though it seemed to happen in every temple, I could never bring myself to warn my god-brothers. Being a rascal, I speculated that Śrīla Prabhupāda enjoyed seeing their desperate looks as much as I did.

After chanting the Gāyatrī mantra, Śrīla Prabhupāda stood and I helped him put on his hooded saffron overcoat. Peacock feathers hung like tassels at his neck. This favourite coat was made by Jayaśrī dasi at the Honolulu Temple in 1970 and travelled around the world with Śrīla Prabhupāda for years. I can't imagine anyone but His Divine Grace wearing such a coat. He looked glorious in it.

After buttoning his coat, Śrīla Prabhupāda headed for the front door. Generally, I had his shoes and cane waiting. As he grabbed his cane, he offered me his right foot, which I slid into his canvas shoe with the help of a shoehorn that I carried around the world. Then, with his next step, I placed his other shoe on his foot before it touched the ground. He did this all in one smooth gesture. His economy of motion was amazing. Once or twice, I allowed an eager disciple to perform this most holy service, but after seeing Śrīla Prabhupāda inconvenienced by their awe as they awkwardly fumbled, I decided to hoard the service for myself.

The gopīs pray to become Lord Kṛṣṇa's flute, always in touch with His lotus lips. I pray to become Śrīla Prabhupāda's shoehorn.

Śrīla Prabhupāda, you often told us that Kṛṣṇa Consciousness was a simple process. It doesn't require any special qualification. Whatever we know how to do, we can do that for Kṛṣṇa. I had no qualifications to do any great service. I was not qualified to distribute books or manage. Still you kindly engaged me in your service. Please allow me to continue to serve your beautiful lotus feet.

See uvacha167 for another story about this wonderful coat.

107

"This is for you and your wife."

January 3, 1974 ISKCON Los Angeles, California

Sixteen months before this visit, Śrīla Prabhupāda had warned me to stay out of the kitchen in New Dvārakā. Now his words seemed somewhat prophetic. Nanda Kumar, by getting married and leaving Śrīla Prabhupāda's personal service, had demonstrated what could happen by associating with female devotees while performing service in the kitchen. Unfortunately, I did not learn from his experience and now it was my turn to be overwhelmed with desire.

In September of 1972, Śrīla Prabhupāda instructed me to prepare his meals in the servants' quarters and stay out of the temple kitchen. Due to illusion, I gradually became careless regarding that instruction. History repeated itself and I found myself standing in front of Śrīla Prabhupāda asking if I could remain in New Dvārakā to get married. My senior god-brothers had tried to persuade me to stay with Śrīla Prabhupāda, but I was too far-gone. They also encouraged me to marry someone else, but my mind was fixated on a particular girl. I was determined in my course of action.

As easily as I became Śrīla Prabhupāda's personal servant, I quickly lost my most valued treasure due to my uncontrolled senses. Within a few days, I abandoned my Guru Mahārāja's personal service. Śrīla Prabhupāda knew me completely. He did not try to convince me to stay with him or try to stop me from getting married.

After a few days, my ever-merciful spiritual master called me to his room. I was consumed with guilt and shame as I trudged toward His Divine Grace's quarters. My senses were reeling. The intelligent part of me realized I was putting personal sense gratification before the intimate service of my spiritual master, but the lusty part of me was hopelessly unbridled. The turmoil churned within me. When I got to Śrīla Prabhupāda's lotus feet, I awkwardly offered my humble obeisances. He kindly spared my shame.

"Bring me my white bag," he instructed.

This white bag travelled with Śrīla Prabhupāda all over the world. He kept all of his important papers, bankbooks, in this bag. I walked into his bedroom, opened his metal Almirah and took out the bag.

When I returned to his sitting room, I placed the white bag on his desk and sat in front of him. I felt disoriented and out of place not having been in his quarters for a few days. I felt I was an intruder and did not belong in this hallowed place, this inner sanctum of spirituality. I had no idea what was happening. I knew I was making a very big mistake leaving him, but could not stop myself from plunging headlong.

Śrīla Prabhupāda opened the bag, took out two rings, and gave them to me.

"This is for you and your wife," he said.

To say I was shocked would be an understatement. I was feeling completely fallen, leaving my spiritual master to satisfy my desires and he was presenting me with gifts and expressing his gratitude for the service I had performed. It was not out of character for my beloved Gurudeva. It was his normal course of action. I accepted the gifts, as I had learned long ago that when Śrīla Prabhupāda wanted to give you something, it was best to accept his mercy.

A few days later, he again called for me. "So, Kīrtanānanda Mahārāja wants you to go back to New Vṛndāvana with your new wife," he said smiling.

"Citsukānanda prabhu asked me to go to Caracas temple and assist with the Deity worship," I replied.

"Kīrtanānanda is anxious for you to return to New Vṛndāvana," he continued.

"Śrīla Prabhupāda," I said. "I really do not have any interest in going back."

He smiled and nodded, understanding my determination. I offered my obeisances and left the room.

On January 7, 1974, he sent a letter to Kīrtanānanda Mahārāja that included the following:

"Regarding Śrutakīrti, I proposed to him that he go to New Vṛndāvana, but he said he did not like farm work and so he wants to go to Caracas and perform deity worship in the temple. So, I have already asked him, but I will say again, how you require him at New Vṛndāvana and how he should work nicely there with the cows, under your guidance."

Śrīla Prabhupāda did not ask me again. Knowing how stubborn I was, he did not give me the chance to commit another offence at his lotus feet. There were no long lectures. He never tried to manipulate me in any way. He never made me feel guilty. He showed compassion and appreciation for the service I had performed. Śrīla Prabhupāda's amazing grace has never been imitated.

> *Śrīla Prabhupāda, if one's level of purity is evidenced by his acceptance of a situation as the mercy of Kṛṣṇa, then it proves you are the purest devotee of the Lord. You accepted the inconvenience I created with grace and kindness. Please forgive me for leaving you. Thank you for never leaving me and allowing me to return to your sweet, ever-merciful lotus feet.*

PART THREE

Six Months in India

July 24, 1974 to December 14, 1974

☙ 108 ☙

"Yes, that's all right."

July 24, 1974 ISKCON New Vṛndāvana, West Virginia

In early January, my wife and I left New Dvārakā and went to Caracas, Venezuela. It was a wonderful experience for me. My wife and I were the only initiated brahmanas in the temple and were able to do most of the Deity worship. I gave many classes, which usually turned into "Prabhupada nectar" classes. My classes had to be translated because I could not speak Spanish and most of the devotees were non-English speaking. After being in Caracas for a few months, the temple administration changed, so I decided to leave.

We went to my hometown of Philadelphia and lived at my mother's house for a few months while I earned money to pay her back for our airline tickets. While I was there, Kulādri dāsa telephoned from New Vṛndāvana and asked me to go there with my wife. I finally agreed and arrived in New Vṛndāvana in the beginning of July.

Being a householder in New Vṛndāvana was different from the brahmacārī life I had previously experienced. I had my own room and was not doing nearly as much service as I had done two years earlier. Still, I experienced a discontent for farm life, as I had travelled the world over and experienced devotional service at temples on every continent.

Fortunately, good news arrived. Śrīla Prabhupāda was coming to stay for Janmāṣṭamī week from July 18 until July 24. When I left Śrīla Prabhupāda in December of 1973, Satsvarūpa Mahārāja had become his personal servant. Satsvarūpa Mahārāja personally served Śrīla Prabhupāda for more than seven months until His Divine Grace left New Dvārakā on July 15, 1974. When Śrīla Prabhupāda arrived in New Vṛndāvana, Brahmānanda Mahārāja was travelling with him as his secretary but he did not have a personal servant. I eagerly accepted the opportunity of cooking for Śrīla Prabhupāda and massaging him while he stayed in New Vṛndāvana.

The day before Śrīla Prabhupāda was to leave New Vṛndāvana, Brahmānanda Mahārāja asked if I wanted to resume my duties as Śrīla Prabhupāda's servant. The difficulty was His Divine Grace was returning to India. It was a difficult choice. The attraction was to serve Śrīla Prabhupāda. The aversion was living in India for six months, a place where my health had always been poor. I would also remain working on the farm in New Vṛndāvana. With my wife's blessings I decided to go with Śrīla Prabhupāda. Brahmānanda Mahārāja asked Śrīla Prabhupāda if he wanted me to be his personal servant once more.

He accepted me. Śrīla Prabhupāda never asked me what I had been doing during for the last seven months. He never asked anything about my wife. He did not tell me I had finally come to my senses. He did not say he missed me or that it was difficult without me. He said volumes to me by not saying anything at all.

Śrīla Prabhupāda's mood of renunciation and austerity were evidenced by his acceptance of whatever Kṛṣṇa did or did not provide. Whether His Divine Grace had a servant or not, it did not matter. He never asked anything for himself. Śrīla Prabhupāda once said that an attached person pretends to be detached, but a detached individual acts in a considerate, loving manner. I saw Śrīla Prabhupāda demonstrate this in his daily life. Śrīla Prabhupāda treated us all so lovingly, although he was completely detached.

I began performing my duties as Śrīla Prabhupāda's servant as if I had never stopped. He was, and will always be, my master, and I, his servant. It is an eternally sweet relationship. I understood that Śrīla Prabhupāda was allowing me to perform devotional service by his mercy. My only qualification was the desire to serve him. I pray to continue to serve him as if I had never left.

Śrīla Prabhupāda, you are an unconditionally loving personality. That is why Lord Caitanya picked you to distribute the Holy Name throughout the world, without regard for caste, creed, colour, or gender. You are the most liberal avatar of all.

109

"I will show you how to make Rasgulla."

July 24, 1974 ISKCON New Vṛndāvana, West Virginia

I rejoined Śrīla Prabhupāda after being away from him for seven months.

One day, while in New Vṛndāvana, devotees discussed the proper way to make rasgulla. "I will show you how to make rasgulla," Śrīla Prabhupāda told them. "You get everything ready."

The devotees became very excited. For some, this would be their first opportunity to see Śrīla Prabhupāda work in the kitchen. Śrīla Prabhupāda first explained how to prepare the curd and sugar water. When everything was in order Śrīla Prabhupāda entered the kitchen and began to cook. All eyes were on His Divine Grace as he artfully coaxed the balls to rotate in the syrup except for one sannyāsī who was looking at the rasgulla.

Śrīla Prabhupāda chastised him saying, "You have already half eaten these." After a while, Śrīla Prabhupāda turned to Kīrtanānanda Mahārāja and said, "Now you can take over."

The moment Śrīla Prabhupāda took his hand off the spoon the rasagullās collapsed, shrinking to half their size. Kīrtanānanda Mahārāja tried to save the offering, but it was useless. They were ruined. A few of us tasted them to be sure, but unfortunately, they tasted terrible.

ဟ 110 ဟ

"One can shave very simply with a blade,..."

August 15, 1974 ISKCON Vṛndāvana, India

During the seven months I had been away from Śrīla Prabhupāda, I had married and increased my possessions. I brought one of my new acquisitions, an electric shaver, to India.

One morning, while giving Śrīmad Bhāgavatam class, Śrīla Prabhupāda spoke about "ugra-karma."

"One can shave very simply with a blade," he said. "There is no difficulty, but now it becomes complicated. One must use electricity. Noise is there and when it breaks then you cannot shave. By trying to solve a small problem, so many other problems are made."

He never said anything to me directly, but I knew he was referring to the fact that, only an hour before, I had been shaving in my servant's quarters and this created a disturbance for him.

Śrīla Prabhupāda, on many occasions you would give me instructions in this way, with such compassion. Please forgive me for being so sensitive and unsubmissive that you could not just tell me what to do. Thank you for allowing me to serve you. There is no reason for my existence, except to serve your lotus feet.

111

"When I want to stop managing, I'll stop."

August 25, 1974 ISKCON Vṛndāvana, India

For several weeks, Śrīla Prabhupāda had been very ill. He was barely eating and required assistance to walk. After quite a long time his health improved, to the relief of all of his disciples.

Some of the GBC members who were present there at the time met to discuss relieving Śrīla Prabhupāda from his managerial duties. They hoped his health would improve if he weren't concerned with the daily management of ISKCON.

The GBC members called for a meeting in Śrīla Prabhupāda's presence.

"Śrīla Prabhupāda," one member said. "We've decided that we can handle all of the management so you can be free to do your translating work. You do not have to worry about managing the society. We are competent to do it."

Śrīla Prabhupāda was sitting behind his desk and he responded immediately in an angry tone.

"When I want you to manage," he said, "when I want to stop managing, I'll stop. Do not tell your spiritual master when to give up the management. Who do you think you are, telling your spiritual master that he doesn't have to manage any more? I'm quite fit to know when I do not want to manage. When I decide I do not want to do it, then I'll stop managing. That is up to me to decide. Not for you."

Meeting adjourned! You were our general and you were never going to leave the field of battle prematurely. It was revealing to see how little some of the leaders knew of your mood. From experience, I had a good idea what your response would be before you started speaking. It is why I felt so safe and secure in your company. You were going to do whatever you could to ensure that your ISKCON would expand purely.

Śrīla Prabhupāda, you always set the perfect example. You did what you expected and desired us to do. You never gave up your service. So often, you told your disciples to take care of the management so that you would be free to translate peacefully. Fortunately for us, you never renounced what you sometimes referred to as 'your duty'. You took, as your life and soul, the mission given to you by your spiritual master, to print books in English and preach to the westerners. You never gave up that service. All glories to you and your disciples who take your order as their life and soul.

112

"Eighty Percent Are Not Following"

August 31, 1974 ISKCON Vṛndāvana, India

Śrīla Prabhupāda arrived in Vṛndāvana, on August 2, 1974. He was hoping to have the opening of the Kṛṣṇa Balarāma Mandir at that time but the construction was not finished so the opening was postponed until the Gaura Pūrṇimā festival of 1975. He was not pleased with the delays. That was not the most difficult situation for me to deal with. Soon after arriving in Vṛndāvana Śrīla Prabhupāda became very ill. It lasted for almost six weeks.

This was not the first time I had been with Śrīla Prabhupāda during the course of an illness. While at the Sydney temple in February of 1973, he had a very painful infection on his right index finger. It caused throbbing for some days. Śrīla Prabhupāda had sandalwood paste made and applied it to his finger but it did not offer much relief. At the request of his disciples, he took some medicine for it. He said that it was specifically caused by fallen disciples not following the rules and regulations.

The illness in Vṛndāvana was much more frightening for his disciples. He had a very high fever and, having no appetite, ate almost nothing for over two weeks. His body was so weak that when he wanted to use the bathroom I would help him out of bed and walk behind him with my arms under his armpits. News spread very quickly all over the world of his condition. Some devotees feared they would never see Śrīla Prabhupāda again. He authorized a letter that was sent to all temples informing them to perform twenty-four hour kīrtan to pray for his recovery. He said, "Kīrtan is what actually gives us life." For the last two weeks of August 1974 devotees all around the world performed kīrtan vigils all day and night.

The mood was very sombre and intense. I've already described how he asked that his disciples should not touch his feet saying, "By their touching I have to suffer. They may not be trying to achieve some goal by touching my feet, still, the spiritual master has to suffer by accepting their sinful reactions." Now Śrīla Prabhupāda said things to me that I could not comprehend. It was very disturbing. These words cut through my heart. He mentioned it to me on two separate occasions during his illness saying, "One of my disciples is simply waiting 'when will the old man die so that I can become guru'". I could not believe what I was hearing. I never imagined the day that Śrīla Prabhupāda wouldn't be with us. I was young and naive and thought that Śrīla Prabhupāda would be with us until he was at least hundred years old. Thoughts of his being gone and others giving initiation had never been a subject of conversation.

He sat up in his bed and, looking at me, said, "This illness is because eighty percent of the leaders are not following the rules and regulations." He did not elaborate on his words and I certainly did not ask any questions at the time. Previously Śrīla Prabhupāda had told us that at the time of initiation, Kṛṣṇa relieves the new initiate of all karma due to past sinful acts. However, the spiritual master accepts some of his disciple's karma, and suffers the reactions and this will sometimes cause illness. We all knew the importance of strictly following his orders. Śrīla Prabhupāda knew how fallen his American and European disciples were. Still he continued to travel, preach, and make disciples all over the world. On September 14, 1974, Śrīla Prabhupāda wrote Jayatīrtha prabhu a letter and said the following:

"Regarding my retiring and resting in Hawaii, if Kṛṣṇa desires I shall do it. I like Hawaii very much. Somehow or other secure that house. I am anxious to go there. Although I am Indian, I see now that the Indian climate does not suit me very much. The sickness I had, I never had such experience in the foreign countries. I think the dangerous point is now over, and I am improving slowly. Not only that but also several members have fallen sick in this season in Vṛndāvana. I am very much anxious for all of them. Even Śrutakīrti has to return. His health is not very suitable. Similarly, Bharadrājahas also fallen sick. So kindly arrange for their dispatch to L.A."

I did not leave at that time. By Śrīla Prabhupāda's mercy, I remained with him for another three months before returning to Hawaii to regain my health. After leaving Vṛndāvana Śrīla Prabhupāda travelled to Mayapur, remained there for one month, and then went to Juhu where he stayed for three months. While there, he wrote to one GBC. "I am very much depressed by the recent incidences in Germany. It is now evident that some of our top men are very much ambitious and there have been so many fall-downs." He continued saying he wanted to meet with and rectify those having difficulties. This is always how Śrīla Prabhupāda dealt with his disciples. He never gave up on us, never rejected us. He would stop everything to try to help us when we struggled. He did all that was necessary to train his disciples, translate books, manage temples and spread the chanting of the Holy Name to every town and village of the world. He was unaffected by the three fold miseries and completely aloof to materail considerations.

> *Śrīla Prabhupāda, you always had complete faith in the order given by your spiritual master. You accepted every difficult situation that we placed before you without complaint. Your example was always of a completely surrendered soul. From the moment you started your ISKCON society you protected it from difficulties from within and without. You did all this while being so patient with us despite our creating havoc in your society.*
>
> *You have always showered your affection upon me and continue to do so. Allow me to remain in the association of your followers so that I can share your transcendental activities with them. Let me remain part of your ISKCON and never stray just as you will never leave my side.*

113

"This Upma is very first class."

September 15, 1974 ISKCON Vṛndāvana, India

One would think that being in Vṛndāvana with Śrīla Prabhupāda would have been the most blissful situation, but this seven-week period was very difficult. Śrīla Prabhupāda was extremely ill, so we were in tremendous anxiety. It appeared he might leave us at any moment. He had eaten very little for a prolonged period of time and as a result, he had very little strength.

One morning he called me into his sitting room. He was sitting up in his bed. "You can make me some upma like I have shown you," he said in a soft voice.

It seemed like a peculiar request since he hadn't been eating. It was also difficult for me to understand why he wanted me to do it, since Yamunā was present and more qualified than I to cook for Śrīla Prabhupāda. I went to the kitchen, told her his request, and asked if there were any vegetables available. Unfortunately, there were no fresh vegetables in the kitchen, but she did have some dried peas. Since time was of the essence, I made the upma with the dried peas, after re-hydrating them as quickly as possible. We were excited that Śrīla Prabhupāda had asked to eat something cooked since he had been eating only sliced oranges.

I remembered though that in the past he had asked me to prepare his favourite dishes in order to increase his appetite. He personally taught me how to make a preparation and if I was able to recreate it then he would ask me to make it every day for a week. Perhaps, on this day, he was thinking about the upma he had taught me to make. I recalled him teaching me to make a wet cauliflower and potato vegetable with fried curd at Bhaktivedanta Manor. In New Dvārakā, he came into the servant quarters and told me to get a head of cabbage and some potatoes. He instructed me in the art of finely shredding cabbage with a knife and sautīing it in a wok with cubed potatoes to create a delicious cabbage-potato subji. I felt fortunate that he had asked me to serve him.

When completed, I brought Śrīla Prabhupāda the upma. Placing it on the chowki, I placed the small table in front of him on his bed. I offered my obeisances and left the room. Along with a few devotees, I anxiously waited in the kitchen, hoping that Śrīla Prabhupāda would enjoy the offering and eat all of it. After about five minutes, Śrīla Prabhupāda rang the bell. I hurried back into his sitting room and eyed the scarcely eaten upma. I offered my obeisances and as I looked up my glorious spiritual master looked at me in a loving way.

"This upma was first-class," he said. "I could not eat very much because I have no appetite, but I want you to know that it was very good. I thought that if you prepared something I liked, I could eat, but it is not possible. I ate a little bit and it tasted very good."

"Thank you, Śrīla Prabhupāda," I replied with great appreciation.

I picked up the plate and the chowki and left the room.

Śrīla Prabhupāda, I was always amazed by the kind way you dealt with me. Throughout the world, there were thousands of devotees engaged in twenty-four hour kīrtan and praying to the Supreme Lord for you to stay with us. Still, you took the time to see that your lowly servant was not upset because you did not eat the upma. Even though you were ill, you encouraged me. You were always transcendental and thinking of others, no matter how you felt personally. I hope that one day I can care about you a fraction of the amount that you cared for me. I wanted to please you that day, and knowing this, you reciprocated by filling my heart with joy.

114

"She is my sister."

September 17, 1974 ISKCON Vṛndāvana, India

Śrīla Prabhupāda stayed in Vṛndāvana for six weeks, during which time, he was very ill. In many temples around the world, twenty-four hour kīrtan was being held. His sister, Pishima, was also staying at the temple in Vṛndāvana a lot of the time. She was concerned and wanted to see her brother as often as she could.

One of my duties was to minimize this as much as possible. It was not an easy or enjoyable service. It was no coincidence that Pishima's powerful determination was similar to that of Śrīla Prabhupāda's. She never listened to me. In fact, she would become quite upset and angry with me. She had a way of slipping into his room when no one noticed.

After one of her visits, Śrīla Prabhupāda called me into his room.

"I am a sannyāsī," he said. "It is not good that she stays in the room when no one else is present. Even she is my sister . . . Because she is my sister she cannot understand it. I cannot have a woman in the room with me, even though she is my sister."

One afternoon I walked into the servants' quarters, which was also my bedroom, and she was sleeping in my bed. I was amazed. I hurried into Śrīla Prabhupāda's room, where he was sitting at his desk. I offered my obeisances with visible anxiety.

"Prabhupada, "I said. "Your sister is sleeping in my bed. I do not know what to do."

"She cannot," he said. "You tell her! She must be told that she can't be doing these things. It is not good. They'll talk."

Śrīla Prabhupāda was referring to the local sannyāsīs, caste

Gosvāmīs and god-brothers who might criticize our beloved Gurudeva. Śrīla Prabhupāda often said that everything must be first-class while in Vṛndāvana or we would not be taken seriously. As always, him being the ācārya , he set an example for us.

"It is not good that she is spending so much time like this," he continued.

"Prabhupada, I can't say anything to her," I explained nervously. "She won't listen to me. She only listens to you."

That day he spoke to her for quite a while. I do not know what the conversation was about, but when I went to the servants' quarters the following day, I cautiously peeked into the room and there she was, sleeping in my room, quite soundly. I gave up. I left the area and found a spot on the other side of Śrīla Prabhupāda's room. She knew her brother was transcendental and it did not matter to her what anyone else thought in regards to her being a woman. She was his sister. Her resolve to be near her pure devotee brother was much greater than my ability to prevent her from doing so. She did whatever she had to do, to get Śrīla Prabhupāda's association. I later mentioned to him that she had been in my room again.

"She is my sister," he compassionately said. "She wants to be around me." At the end of 1977, Satsvarūpa Mahārāja told me that Śrīla Prabhupāda had asked her forgiveness for his offences.

I beg forgiveness from Bhavatarini for my many offences that I committed while trying to do my service. I beg that in the future my love for Śrīla Prabhupāda will develop to the degree displayed by his sister. By her determination, she was able to be Śrīla Prabhupāda's younger sister and assist him throughout their lives. I pray to have the same desire that Bhavatarini had to serve the lotus feet of Śrīla Prabhupāda life after life.

115

"I did not want to disturb you because you were resting."

September 18, 1974 ISKCON Vṛndāvana, India

During the time Śrīla Prabhupāda was ill, there was a great deal of activity going on. His living quarters were in the final stages of construction and other projects were going on just outside his room. The temple and the guesthouse were being erected, causing loud building sounds to fill the atmosphere. Śrīla Prabhupāda had been eating so little that he had become very weak. When he needed to go from one room to another, one or two disciples assisted him.

The summer air was extremely hot, so we set up his bed on his back porch because it was cooler than his sitting room. In the evening, he rested outside. Even though work was being done on the porch and garden area, there was just enough room for his bed. When it was time to take rest at night, I helped him get into his bed and then climbed under the mosquito net with him to massage his legs. After the massage, I put a straw mat under his bed for me to sleep. The mosquito net was attached to his bedposts and extended to the floor so I was also covered by the net. I spent each night sleeping directly under His Divine Grace's bed so that if he needed anything I was immediately available.

This was the first time I slept next to Śrīla Prabhupāda. He wanted me close by so that if he had to get up I could help him walk. It was a very grave situation. I thought of myself as my master's dog, lying on the ground by his bedside waiting for an opportunity to serve him. I considered this to be my actual position.

One night at about 1:00 am, I awoke to the sound of a stick falling by my head onto the brick floor. When I opened my eyes, I saw my beloved spiritual master lying on the ground beside me. Horrified, I immediately clasped my Gurudeva under his arms and lifted him back onto the bed. The sound I had heard was Śrīla Prabhupāda's cane falling to the ground as he fell over attempting to walk. I instantly became wide awake and filled with fear.

"Śrīla Prabhupāda, what are you doing?" I asked. "Why did not you call me?"

"Oh, I needed to go to the bathroom," he replied softly and apologetically. "I thought I could make it on my own and I did not want to disturb you because you were resting."

I knew Śrīla Prabhupāda was modest, but this shocked me. I was angry that he had not woken me up and I began to respectfully chastise him.

"No, Śrīla Prabhupāda," I said. "There is no disturbance! That is why I am here. You are very weak. You should have called me."

"I thought I had the strength," he said. "But, I can see I have no strength at all."

Standing behind him, I placed my hands under his arms and walked him into his bathroom. I waited outside the door. When he was finished, I helped him walk back to his bed on the porch. The next day, he did not make any fuss about what had happened, nor did he complain to any one of any injury that may have occurred. It was another day in the life of the pure devotee. He was truly unaffected by conditions that related to his body. He was concerned that everything was going on satisfactorily with the temple construction.

Śrīla Prabhupāda exhibited humility in all circumstances. Sometimes he would call me into his room. When I entered, he would say in a meek tone, "Could you prepare something for me now?" Amazed, I would reply, "Yes, Prabhupada, I have nothing else to do but serve you. That is why I am here."

Sometimes, while waiting in his room to go on his morning

walk, he would say to the devotees who were present, "Can we go now?" He was always refined and dignified. Everything he said, every move he made, allowed us to become more attracted to him.

Śrīla Prabhupāda, there is nothing I can say to properly glorify your activities. Anyone fortunate enough to have had your personal association knows that you are the total embodiment of all exemplary qualities. You have given me reason to live. When I think of your falling to the ground as I slept, it deeply saddens me. I should have been awake, watching and guarding your beautiful form. However, I am certain that you did not regard this as something lacking on my part. That is because of your great humility. It is this quality that keeps me addicted to your lotus feet. Thank you for being my divine, loving spiritual father.

116

"I have to go out and speak something."

September 19, 1974 ISKCON Vṛndāvana, India

While Śrīla Prabhupāda was ill, there was difficulty with the construction of the temple. My knowledge of what occurred is limited because I only heard bits and pieces of conversations in Śrīla Prabhupāda's room. There had been a problem procuring cement. This, of course, created major setbacks in completing the project. A politician from Mathurā was willing to supply a large quantity of cement and was due to visit the temple to observe what was being done.

Śrīla Prabhupāda was determined to attend the programme at the temple in honour of this gentleman. This caused great concern for his disciples who did not want Śrīla Prabhupāda to expend so much energy. Some were advising His Divine Grace not to attend because he was very weak and had a high fever.

"This man has come," he said. "I have to go out and speak something."

The day of the gentleman's arrival, I helped Śrīla Prabhupāda put on fresh clothing. After that, he applied tilak. When he was leaving his quarters, he asked me, "Tilaka, have I put on my tilak yet?"

I told him that he had put it on.

"Okay, let's go," he said, nodding.

I could not believe his determination. His fever was so high, yet he was still focused on his mission of spreading the Kṛṣṇa Consciousness movement. He did not consider his condition. It was an opportunity to preach the glories of the Supreme Lord. We carried Śrīla Prabhupāda to the temple where he gave a short lecture and publicly expressed his appreciation to the politician for helping to complete the construction.

Toward the end of Śrīla Prabhupāda's illness, I contracted malaria and was confined to bed for a few days. I was on my mat on the floor of the servants' quarters. Śrīla Prabhupāda's health was beginning to improve and he was walking without assistance. As he walked past the servants' quarters, he saw me lying on the floor. Some devotees were in the room taking prasādam.

"What is he doing on the floor?" Śrīla Prabhupāda asked. "He is very ill. Get him a bed."

He looked at me with a compassionate glance, just as I was in the middle of a malaria attack.

"Have you been given anything?" he asked.

"No, Prabhupada," I said.

He turned to Pālikā and said, "Make him some hot lemonade and take care of him."

I can't remember if I took any medicine, but it was not long before I was out of bed. It was a wonderful feeling to know that you cared so much about me, Śrīla Prabhupāda. You always made me feel special. A year ago, I was asked at a 26 Second Avenue reunion if you ever treated any of your disciples "special." I did not have to think long before saying, "Yes! All of them."

If there were one service I could perform for you, it would be to try to express how much love you have for all your followers and how much appreciation you have for their assisting you in your mission. If I can realize the depth of your love for me, I would never be distracted from serving your golden lotus feet, not even for one second. I beg for the intelligence to comprehend a fraction of your love for me.

117

"Tell him to stop speaking now."

September 20, 1974 ISKCON Vṛndāvana, India

To everyone's relief, Śrīla Prabhupāda began to recover from his illness. As his health improved he spent an hour every evening sitting in a chair under the Tamāla tree in the temple courtyard and listening to his disciples give class. He was not sitting with them, but observing the class from a short distance. Sometimes he enjoyed listening to his senior disciples speak and on occasion I heard him review the lecture. He was an attentive listener. I can recall while travelling with him, he would sometimes ask a disciple to speak in his presence. My heart would stop, fearing that he would ask me. I was happy when I realized that Śrīla Prabhupāda was aware of my lack of philosophical understanding. He never put me on the spot.

One evening, the temple commander gave a class. Śrīla Prabhupāda sat comfortably in his chair while I sat at his feet on the marble floor. Śrīla Prabhupāda's disciple began to speak about the importance of following the temple programme. Some of the devotees were not strictly following the schedule and the temple commander was using the class as a means to encourage the devotees to be more careful. He began to chastise a French devotee for not attending the morning class.

"It doesn't matter if you do not understand English," he said. "It is transcendental sound vibration."

He continued to speak harshly. Finally, Śrīla Prabhupāda said to me, "Tell him to stop speaking now. He has been speaking long enough." I relayed the message and the devotee stopped speaking.

A few days later, the same temple commander was lecturing in the same way.

"These lectures should only be half an hour," he told me. "Otherwise, no one is going to listen. He is talking too much. Tell him half an hour only."

I immediately went to the speaker and relayed Śrīla Prabhupāda's message. I did not ask, but it seemed that it was not so much the length of the lecture that disturbed His Divine Grace, but the fact that the speaker was giving more of an iṣṭagoṣṭhī than a class from the śāstra. Observing Śrīla Prabhupāda's opulence of renunciation, one could see that once His Divine Grace gave a personal instruction, he was done. He never belaboured a point or belittled anyone. He was interested in training his disciples so they could advance in spiritual life.

One evening, as Śrīla Prabhupāda sat in his chair in the courtyard and I sat on the marble floor next to his glorious lotus feet, I asked him to elaborate on a statement he had made earlier while in his sitting room.

"When the Indians touch my feet," he said, "They are simply looking for some material benediction. Therefore, do not let anyone touch my feet because I will have to take their sinful reaction and then I will get sick and it will cause more weakness."

"Śrīla Prabhupāda," I said during class. "When your disciples touch your lotus feet, they are trying to show respect. They are not interested in material profit."

"Yes, that may be the case," he knowingly replied. "But, still, I have to suffer. Even they may not be trying to achieve some goal by touching my feet; still, the spiritual master has to suffer by accepting their sinful reactions."

He stayed in the courtyard a while longer. I sat by him, delighted he had decided to stay with his spiritual children. He was concerned about keeping healthy and not leaving us on our own.

Śrīla Prabhupāda, my desire is to live in the past. My understanding is that your pastimes on this planet are eternal. Therefore, I can always be with you simply by remembering your beautiful lotus feet resting softly on the courtyard floor of the Kṛṣṇa Balarāma Mandir. Thank you for allowing me to touch your feet daily. Forgive me for forcing the reactions of my sinful life upon you. Please, do not thrust me away.

107

"You have kept me alive...."

September 21, 1974 ISKCON Vṛndāvana, India

As Śrīla Prabhupāda's health improved, I became more conscious of my own bodily discomfort. I hadn't been as careful as I should have been in India. As a result, I contracted malaria, had difficulty with digestion and developed colitis. Śrīla Prabhupāda noticed I had lost weight, my spirits were low. Undoubtedly, some of my weakness was due to the stress of being responsible for Śrīla Prabhupāda's well-being during his illness. Subsequently, after losing my energy and strength, I developed an aversion to living in India.

I went to Śrīla Prabhupāda's secretary, Brahmānanda Mahārāja, and discussed the possibility of my returning to Los Angeles to regain my health. I asked him to talk with Śrīla Prabhupāda. I was ashamed to speak to His Divine Grace myself because I could not reconcile the idea of leaving his personal service. I knew in my heart that it was wrong. Brahmānanda Mahārāja spoke with Śrīla Prabhupāda about my desires.

Later, Śrīla Prabhupāda called me into his room. I nervously entered his room and offered my obeisances. He was sitting behind his desk. I was so ashamed of myself that I hung my head and was unable to look at him.

"So, you are not feeling well?" he asked.

"No, Prabhupada," I said. "I have been feeling ill for some time."

"You want to go back to Los Angeles and regain your health?" he asked.

"Yes, Śrīla Prabhupāda," I timidly said. "If it is all right with you?"

"Yes, of course," he said sweetly. "You have kept me alive for the last month. If it weren't for you, I wouldn't be here now. How can I not want you to be healthy? You have done so many things. You must take care of yourself. There is no problem in getting someone. There are so many people here in India. Anyone can do your service."

I could not believe my ears. His humility was overwhelming. I offered my obeisances and walked out of his sitting room filled with emotion. I was on top of the world. Hearing Śrīla

Prabhupāda say that I had been responsible for saving his life filled me with ecstasy. I knew he was constantly protected by Lord Kṛṣṇa, but nonetheless, the recognition he bestowed upon me was undeniably sweet. Simultaneously, I felt lower than the straw in the street. How could I leave such a magnanimous personality? My mind was reeling for the rest of the day.

That evening, I accompanied Śrīla Prabhupāda to the temple courtyard where he sat down under the Tamāla tree. As I sat by his lotus feet, I began thinking how crazy I was. There was no sweeter place in the entire universe than sitting at his golden lotus feet.

"Śrīla Prabhupāda," I finally said. "I can't leave. It isn't the right thing to do. I should just remain here and depend on Kṛṣṇa."

"Yes, this is very good," he said, smiling broadly. "Because you are sincere, Kṛṣṇa will give you all facilities to perform your service."

I felt great relief knowing I was doing the right thing.

I remained in India with Śrīla Prabhupāda for three more months before leaving his personal service for the second time.

Śrīla Prabhupāda, every day, as I write, I become sad thinking of all the opportunities I missed by not having your personal association, due to my lack of Kṛṣṇa Consciousness. Today, I am happy knowing that no matter what service I render, you are pleased, provided my desire to serve you is sincere.

ᔕ 119 ᔕ

"I think we shall go to Kurukṣetra."

September 22, 1974 Kurukṣetra, India

Śrīla Prabhupāda lived his life in an exemplary manner as demonstrated by the following incident that took place on September 22, 1974.

During the previous six weeks while staying in Vṛndāvana, he had been very ill with an intermittent temperature of 103 to 105 degrees. For weeks, he ate only some pieces of orange and a few grapes. Twenty-four hour kīrtans were being performed by concerned disciples worldwide. He said his ailment could not be cured by medicine because the illness was due to 80% of the leaders in ISKCON who were not strictly following the rules and regulations. In spite of his condition, he had one overwhelming desire, to preach Kṛṣṇa Consciousness

As soon as he began to recover, he left Vṛndāvana to visit other centres in India. His first stop was Delhi where he planned to rest for one day before continuing to Kolkata and on to Mayapur. The devotees were always enthusiastic to receive him. Soon after arriving in Delhi, he was asked to speak on the *Bhagavad-gītā* in Kurukṣetra.

Śrīla Prabhupāda replied, "These meetings are useless. These people will never accept Kṛṣṇa. What is the use of going out there and talking? It would be a waste of my time." We were relieved that he did not want to take such a difficult ride in the hot summer so soon after such a serious illness.

As the conversation progressed, he said he would consider accepting the invitation and thus take the opportunity to preach. He very sweetly told us to deliberate on the matter and advise him as to what we thought was the best course of action. Taking into consideration his fragile condition, we all thought the long trip would be too stressful.

Śrīla Prabhupāda often gave us the chance to serve in this way. It was very sweet how he engaged us. He always remained independent, but allowed us to meditate on taking care of him.

His secretary discussed the matter with other GBC men and sannyāsīs. They again concluded that Śrīla Prabhupāda was still too weak to take a long automobile drive to and from Kurukṣetra. Initially, he agreed with them.

Around 2 pm, I heard his bell ring. I went into the room and offered obeisances. He instructed, "Get everyone." Disciples entered the room eager to hear from their spiritual master who said, "I think we shall go to Kurukṣetra. This is my duty. I cannot give up this opportunity to preach. It won't be so difficult. We can leave in the morning before sunrise. The ride will be about two hours." Then looking at everyone with the compassion of a pure devotee he asked rhetorically, "Is that all right?" Brahmānanda Mahārāja, his secretary said, "If that is what you want Śrīla Prabhupāda, we can arrange everything."

Śrīla Prabhupāda arrived in Kurukṣetra in the scorching heat with a few disciples. The host took the group on a short tour to visit some nearby temples and then to the guest quarters. Later Śrīla Prabhupāda was escorted to the pandal and seated in the midst of several so-called sādhus, many with beards and long hair. They were eager for him to be present for they all knew that he was famous all over the world.

They appreciated Śrīla Prabhupāda's vapu manifestation but feared his vani, so consequently they weren't eager to have him speak, knowing his reputation as a no-nonsense Kṛṣṇa bhakta. Śrīla Prabhupāda looked glorious sitting among them, like the full moon among so many twinkling stars.

As the various speakers pontificated, you sat impatiently listening to their rhetoric as they talked in Hindi and English about unity, understanding and religious tolerance. With heightened emotions, Śrīla Prabhupāda sat in a chair with his jaw clenched and foot tapping on the stage. He became angrier at each passing moment, as the speakers talked of peace and dharma. The mutual admiration society of pseudo sādhus continued praising one another with delight. They revelled in the coming together of so many holy persons, to bring about the undertaking of a new temple there.

Śrīla Prabhupāda sat still like a lion about to pounce and finally, without any introduction, he stood and began to roar in Hindi. We, the disciples, could understand some of what he was said. "*sarva-dharmān parityajya, mām ekaṁ śaraṇaṁ vraja, ahaṁ tvāṁ sarva-pāpebhyo, mokṣayiṣyāmi mā śucaḥ.*" The lecture was short, fiery and conclusive and at the end, Śrīla Prabhupāda walked back to the car with his disciples. Everyone scattered and began leaving the assembly.

After getting into the car, Śrīla Prabhupāda turned to us and said enthusiastically, "So, you could understand the lecture? I spoke in Hindi, but, you could understand some?" We all smiled broadly, feeling his pleasure and said, "We understood the purport of what you were saying."

"Yes!" he said, "This is all nonsense. These people, they will never get anywhere because they do not accept Kṛṣṇa. This is their business. This is their idea. Here in India, they try to make unity, but they never accept Kṛṣṇa. Why they speak of *Bhagavad-gītā*? You shouldn't speak of *Bhagavad-gītā* unless you are accepting Kṛṣṇa." Chuckling, he continued, "How you are in the land of Kṛṣṇa, Kurukṣetra, where Kṛṣṇa spoke on the battlefield to Arjuna, and not one person has mentioned Kṛṣṇa? You are talking about *Bhagavad-gītā*...talking about Kurukṣetra...Kṛṣṇa spoke *Bhagavad-gītā*...Kṛṣṇa was here in Kurukṣetra...and not one of you mentioned anything about Kṛṣṇa." He enthusiastically defended his dearmost Lord and we were proud to follow in his transcendental footsteps.

Śrīla Prabhupāda, you accepted so much inconvenience to

spread the glories of Kṛṣṇa. In spite of illness, advanced age and extreme heat you pushed on. Your incredible feat at Kurukṣetra was punctuated by a severe typhoon. As our car drove on, huge Eucalyptus trees fell in front of us, uprooted onto the road, I wondered how the storms were devastating the pandal back at Kurukṣetra. Kṛṣṇa guided you, Śrīla Prabhupāda safely through torrential rains and manoeuvred your car through many obstacles on the road. It was a dramatic conclusion to a successful day.

It was your pleasure to fight triumphantly for Kṛṣṇa on the battlefield of Kurukṣetra. You always relished speaking about Kṛṣṇa, your dear most friend. In this way, you are most dear to the Lord.

> *I pray that my only desire is to serve you with the same eagerness that you have served your Guru Mahārāja, for you have spread the glories of Lord Kṛṣṇa under all circumstances, up to your last breath. I pray to serve your mission birth after birth.*

120

"I believe they call it *percolating*."

September 22, 1974 ISKCON Delhi, India

Śrīla Prabhupāda's Mastery of English

Śrīla Prabhupāda often adapted the English language to suit his requirements, usually with humourous results. One day for example, while on a morning walk in Hawaii, he looked out into the ocean and momentarily watched the surfers.

"You call them surfers," he said laughing. "I call them sufferers."

Sometimes when he spoke of the democratic form of

government in the United States, he used the words "demon crazy" instead of "democracy." Both were very appropriate.

When I was first with Śrīla Prabhupāda, he sometimes rang his bell and when I entered the room he would ask, "Where is punditji?" This was an affectionate term for his Sanskrit editor. After several months, his Sanskrit editor was not always readily available. Śrīla Prabhupāda would then call me to his room and ask, "Where is banditji?"

In Delhi, Brahmānanda dāsa and I were sitting in Śrīla Prabhupāda's quarters. I began drying the floor around Śrīla Prabhupāda's clay water pot because water was seeping through and collecting on the floor.

"Śrīla Prabhupāda," Brahmānanda said. "The water is coming out of the pot a little."

"Yes, I believe they call it percolating," Śrīla Prabhupāda said. "Is that right Brahmānanda?"

"I really do not know, but I do not think so, Śrīla Prabhupāda," Brahmānanda answered.

We both thought his description was close, but not quite correct. We had been brought up hearing the term daily because our parents drank coffee that was brewed in a percolator. Brahmānanda, an English major, looked up the word in the dictionary and found Śrīla Prabhupāda's description to be most accurate.

One of my favourite memories of Śrīla Prabhupāda adapting the English language occurred during an evening massage in New Dvārakā. Śrīla Prabhupāda was lying in bed on his back. Kneeling on the floor next to his bed, I massaged his legs. Smiling, he looked at me and pointed to his feet.

"Do my fingers," he said.

I became confused and knelt motionless for a few seconds. He pointed to his toes again and began to wiggle them. He had a bigger smile on his face and said, "My fingers, massage my fingers."

I finally realized what he meant.

"Oh! Your toes," I said. "You want me to massage your toes."

Still smilingly broadly, he said, "Yes! My fingers. Do my fingers."

He gave me this same instruction three other times during his evening massage. He waited just long enough between massages so that I did not remember what he was talking about. Each time Śrīla Prabhupāda said it to me I was caught off guard and would have to stop massaging for a moment.

> *Śrīla Prabhupāda, all of your disciples are able to experience the joy of serving you in a variety of ways. In your absence, I can only experience it by telling them about your extraordinary qualities. I am spoiled and do not know how to go on without it. Spreading the Holy Name of Kṛṣṇa around the world was thought to be impossible by many. I think it is impossible to describe the magnitude of your personality. I pray never to forget you. It is all that keeps me alive.*

121

"Mustard seed oil is very tasty."

September 25, 1974 ISKCON Kolkata, India

While staying at the Kolkata Temple in 1973, I became aware of Śrīla Prabhupāda's fondness for Bengali cooking. Amazingly, during my tenure of personal service to my beloved Śrīla Prabhupāda, His Divine Grace did not eat Bengali-style prasādam very often. Even when he stayed at the Kolkata and Māyāpur temples, he regularly honoured prasādam prepared by his western disciples. The difficulty with the wonderful

Bengali preparations, although quite tasty, was that they often contained mustard oil.

"It is difficult for me to digest," Śrīla Prabhupāda would comment.

One day at the Kolkata temple, Tamāla Kṛṣṇa Mahārāja entered Śrīla Prabhupāda's room and offered his obeisances. Sitting comfortably behind his desk, Śrīla Prabhupāda looked as effulgent as ever.

"Haven't you said that mustard oil is for the outside of the body and ghee is for the inside?" Tamāla Kṛṣṇa inquired.

"Yes," Śrīla Prabhupāda said, smiling.

"Then doesn't that mean that we shouldn't use mustard oil in our cooking?" Tamāla Kṛṣṇa Mahārāja continued.

"Well, it is true," Śrīla Prabhupāda, said. "But mustard oil is very tasty. It makes the vegetables taste first-class. Therefore, in Bengal, everyone uses mustard oil in their cooking. It is very palatable."

When Śrīla Prabhupāda stayed in Bengal, his sister would sometimes come to the temple and cook for him. This was a mixed blessing. It was known by many that Śrīla Prabhupāda's sister, Pishima, would smuggle mustard oil into the temple kitchen under her sari to use in her cooking for her beloved brother. Like Śrīla Prabhupāda, Pishima had a way of listening to what we had to say and then doing whatever she wanted. Śrīla Prabhupāda ate whatever she cooked and occasionally would complain afterwards saying, "Her cooking has made me ill." Using deadpan humour, he continued, "I think she is trying to kill me."

Sometimes I would advise him like a parent saying, "Prabhupada, you are not getting sick when you eat from your cooker, but when you eat what your sister cooks then you get sick."

"Yes! Do not give me anything else," he replied with conviction. "Let me eat what you cook. If my sister gives me something, you eat it, if you like. I do not want to eat it."

I became very enlivened by his determination to follow my instructions. Of course, when it came to eating, he never followed anyone's instructions for long. He always did what he liked. Once, one of Śrīla Prabhupāda's god-nephews, a Bengali brahmacārī, visited Śrīla Prabhupāda at his Juhu flat. He was a very good chef and offered to cook sukta, a bitter vegetable stew. I watched the young devotee as he expertly deep-fried large slices of vegetable, including bitter melon. When he had finished, there was a large pot of very bitter and very oily soup. Śrīla Prabhupāda savoured every bite.

"This is the most wonderful thing," he commented. "Śrutakīrti, you should learn. Make it like this. This is very first-class."

I was never able to recreate the dish as it was made that day. come close to duplicating the wet vegetable that Śrīla Prabhupāda savoured that day. Fortunately, for me, Śrīla Prabhupāda accepted the much simpler cooking I regularly prepared. I was delighted hear him say that my cooking did not make him sick.

Śrīla Prabhupāda, I always marvel at your depth of compassion. You regularly accepted service from everyone, regardless of the consequences to you. No one knows this better than I do. You never gave up on me. I know that as long as I have a sincere desire to serve you, you will never turn your back on me. Please give me a taste for the sukta you ate and a taste for devotional service.

☙ 122 ☙

"I did not like to run around."

September 24, 1974 Kolkata, India

One day, Paramahaṁsa Swami and I accompanied Śrīla Prabhupāda on a car ride in his hometown. Passing a playground, Śrīla Prabhupāda pointed to a field, smiled and said, "I played football (soccer) there when I was young. I would be the goalie because I was lazy. I did not like to run around. That was the position I liked." We all laughed with him at his revelation. We loved to hear him tell us anything about his life, especially his childhood. We knew he was not lazy and felt so fortunate to hear him speak about himself in such intimate and casual terms.

Although we were all around the age of twenty, we could barely keep up with him on his morning walk. We also knew he did not waste any energy. Whatever he did was in full Kṛṣṇa Consciousness and for the pleasure of the Supreme Lord.

☙ 123 ☙

"...that would be a serious offence."

September 28, 1974 ISKCON Mayapur, India

Personal Mercy

As Śrīla Prabhupāda's servant, there were very few times I felt I needed to question on an instruction he gave. In fact, I only remember one time. Śrīla Prabhupāda received a letter from a devotee asking sanction to divorce his wife and permission to marry another. Being present when Śrīla Prabhupāda replied to the letter, I was shocked when he gave permission. It bothered me throughout the day. I understood our philosophy to be that no divorce was allowed. Many times, I heard him speak against divorce. I knew it happened, but I did not think Śrīla Prabhupāda would condone it. I kept thinking, "This is not what Śrīla Prabhupāda would do."

I could not hold it in any longer. I planned to ask him why and decided the best time was during his evening massage. I had massaged him for about half an hour when I blurted out, "Prabhupada, I want to ask you something. This devotee who is asking about the divorce . . ."

"Oh yes," he interjected, "I told him he can do it." I felt terrible to be bothering him with my mental difficulties but I could not help myself.

"Yes, I know," I continued. "I was wondering. You always say that divorce is against Vedic principles. There can never be any divorce."

"Yes," he said. "But in this western society these things are accepted. So we can allow this."

I was not feeling satisfied. Śrīla Prabhupāda seemed indifferent about it. It was an attitude I had never before seen him have toward such a matter.

"Yes, but in this society they accept meat-eating and intoxication," I said. "All these things are accepted. Why aren't any of these things allowed?"

My most merciful spiritual master replied with compassion in his voice, "Well, actually whether I give him permission or not, he is going to get the divorce. So if I tell him, 'No, you can't get it' and he does it that will be a serious offence. If I say, 'Yes, you can do it' because he is going to do it anyway, then the offence is not so great."

The massage went on quietly after that. I was relieved of my foolish doubts.

Śrīla Prabhupāda it is only due to your great compassion that I am able to associate with devotees. You continue to forgive me for my offences. It was not necessary for me to see how you dealt with others to understand your kindness. I only have to see how you deal with me every day. I pray that one day you will be proud I am your disciple.

124

"You can call him Māyāpur Chandra."

October 8, 1974 ISKCON Mayapur, India

On the afternoon of October 8, I received an exciting telegram. My wife had delivered a baby boy on October 6, 1974, at 4:15 am I considered it to be especially auspicious because maṅgala-ārati, started at 4:15 am in Mayapur. I immediately ran to Śrīla Prabhupāda's room and offered my obeisances.

"Śrīla Prabhupāda," I said smiling, "My wife just gave birth to a son!"

"Very nice," he said, returning my smile. "So, you can call him Māyāpurcandra. Māyāpurcandra! You will not find that name anywhere in the śāstra. I have invented it. You will find Navadvīpacandra and Nadir Nimai. But, you will not find this name anywhere. So, I will give you some money. You can get one of the local boys to go to Navadvīpa to purchase a set of silver ankle and wrist bracelets for him."

Still overcome, I did not consider refusing his generous offer.

Four months later on February 9, 1975, Śrīla Prabhupāda stopped in New Dvārakā for two days on his way to Mexico City. After his afternoon nap, he called for me.

"Go find Nanda Kumar," he instructed.

Fortunately, he was across the street. I told him Śrīla Prabhupāda wanted to see him. Nanda asked me why and I responded, "I have no idea. He just told me to get you." We both raced back to Śrīla Prabhupāda's quarters and offered our obeisances. When I looked up, Śrīla Prabhupāda handed me the keys to his metal cabinet in the bedroom and said, "Bring me my white bag." I gave him the bag and we both sat before him having no clue what was about to happen next. He took two fifty-dollar bills out of his bag and gave one to me.

"Here, you can get something for your son," he said.

Whenever Śrīla Prabhupāda showered his love upon me by giving me something, I became overwhelmed with affection for him. I could not refuse such a beautiful display of love. Overjoyed, I took the bill and heartily thanked him.

He then turned to Nanda Kumar, who had been his personal servant before me, and tried to give him the other fifty-dollar bill. Nanda Kumar refused it.

"I cannot take that from you, Śrīla Prabhupāda," he said.

"It is not for you," Śrīla Prabhupāda told him. "It is for your son."

Nanda then accepted the bill from his loving spiritual master. After giving us gifts for our sons, Śrīla Prabhupāda nodded kindly and said, "Okay, now you may go." We offered our obeisances and left his quarters, discussing how fortunate we were to have such an amazingly generous spiritual master.

Śrīla Prabhupāda, many times you gave me articles of clothing, taking care of me in every way. I never thought you owed me anything for the service I did. After all, you gave all of us the greatest gift; the opportunity to develop our love of God. The personal attention you blessed us with, however, was another one of your priceless gifts. You set such an amazing example. Although you are our spiritual master, and as such should be treated as the Lord Himself, still you served us by providing all our necessities. When will the day come when I will see my god-brothers and god-sisters as "Prabhu" and offer them my respect instead of fighting over the proper way to honour and serve you?

125

"We are not afraid of snakebite."

October 10, 1974 ISKCON Mayapur, India

Śrīla Prabhupāda benedicted the devotees in Māyāpur with his association during October (Kārtika). It was an especially pleasant time of year in India. Śrīla Prabhupāda and his entourage stayed on the second floor of the Mandir, which was furthest from the road. Śrīla Prabhupāda's quarters consisted of two rooms and his entourage stayed in another two rooms. There was a large bathroom facility at each end of the building. In each bathroom were four shower stalls and four toilet stalls.

One afternoon Śrīla Prabhupāda was giving darśana in his sitting room. I was cleaning Śrīla Prabhupāda's bathroom after His Divine Grace's shower. The entire bathroom facility was exclusively used by His Divine Grace for the duration of his visit.

As I walked past the first toilet stall, a huge six-foot long cobra quickly slithered past me into the stall. Terrified, I raced out of the bathroom as fast as my shaking body could run. I did not want to create a big scene and interrupt Śrīla Prabhupāda's darśana. In spite of my inhibition, Kṛṣṇa ordained that the first devotee I happened upon was Bhavānanda Mahārāja. My heart was racing.

"Bhavānanda, Bhavānanda," I said. "There's a snake in

Prabhupada's bathroom. It went right by my feet and just missed me!"

Of course, my plan to keep calm and not create a disturbance was obviously not what Kṛṣṇa wanted, so He engaged Bhavānanda Mahārāja in the drama. Bhavānanda loudly burst into Śrīla Prabhupāda's sitting room with his arms flailing.

"OOOHHH! Prabhupada!" he dramatically exclaimed. "There is a snake in your bathroom! We need help! Let's call Rasaparayana!" Rasaparayana was known as the big, strong, temple "ksatriya."

"Come on. Let's call Rasaparayana!" Bhavānanda yelled, as we ran out of Śrīla Prabhupāda's quarters.

We effectively terminated Śrīla Prabhupāda's tranquil darśana. Śrīla Prabhupāda and his disciples left the room and went on the veranda. A couple of devotees went into the bathroom to search for the serpent while the others stayed on the porch. Śrīla Prabhupāda was undisturbed and quietly chanted japa, walking back and forth on the veranda.

"It must have been left by someone from the Gaudiya Math," Bhavānanda speculated. "Otherwise, how could the serpent get up to the second floor?"

Others agreed, saying it was not possible for a snake to appear on an upper floor without being planted. Some theorized that perhaps it was a communist plot. Since I was a visitor to this sacred Māyāpur Dhāma, I was not knowledgeable of the local political scene. I concluded that the serpent just happened to appear in Śrīla Prabhupāda's bathroom.

Rasaparayana, with a knife in hand, stalked the bathroom to find the snake.

"They travel in pairs," he said. "So if there is one, then its mate is probably nearby."

Finally, he saw part of the huge serpent's body sticking out of the plumbing work in one of the toilet stalls. He reported the good news to the devotees on the veranda. With great excitement, Bhavānanda and others began chanting, "Kill it! Kill it!"

Śrīla Prabhupāda remained outside, chanting softly on his beads. He did not instruct us on this dilemma. Rasaparayana chopped the cobra's body in two with his sharp knife.

"We'll keep looking," he said with determination. "There must be another one."

The devotees began to realize that the snakes probably came up through the plumbing. It was not a communist plot after all. Several anxious minutes passed as we searched for the other intruder. Rasaparayana finally spotted the mate in the network of pipes behind the toilets. Having been discovered it quickly slithered down the pipes, and was never seen again.

After everyone settled down, we went back into Śrīla Prabhupāda's sitting room.

"Sometimes, the snake's mission is to kill a certain person," he told us. "They will not stop until they succeed. Particularly at the end of the snake's life, sometimes, the snake grows wings. He has a particular person he has to kill. The snake will kill that person and then it goes off to die."

One evening Śrīla Prabhupāda pointed out a particular sound in the stillness of the night.

"Hear that sound?" he asked. "That is the snakebird. It has a special sound."

All the devotees became very quiet in hopes of hearing it again. I became a little frightened wondering if I was next.

That evening in Śrīla Prabhupāda's bedroom, I gently massaged his legs. The room was quiet and dark.

"So, what shall I do if I am here and the snake comes?" he asked laughing. "Only one snake has been killed. Perhaps the other will come and get me tonight."

He enjoyed remembering everyone's anxiety during the day. I understood from his tone that he was not at all concerned about the snake. I encouraged his discussion by saying, "I do not know Śrīla Prabhupāda."

"Well, we are not afraid of snakebite," he said. "We'll not worry about it. If it comes, it comes. We will just chant Hare Kṛṣṇa."

I finished massaging my beloved spiritual master. He peacefully went to bed, his fearless mind fixed on the Supreme Lord. I, on the other hand, went back to my room concerned as to the whereabouts of the other snake.

My dear Śrīla Prabhupāda, you are my hero. You are the fearless pure devotee of the Lord. Once on a morning walk in Māyāpur when everyone was discussing their fears and concerns about nuclear war you said, "If the bomb comes we will look up in the sky and say, 'Here comes Kṛṣṇa.'"

Please, benedict me with unflinching faith so I will not fear this material world. I want to chant the Holy Names as the snakebird flies above me preparing to inflict its final bite.

126

"If Kṛṣṇa wants to protect you..."

October 10, 1974 ISKCON Māyāpur India

As the evening's veil of darkness fell upon us, my godbrothers were still buzzing about the snake incident that occurred earlier that day. Everyone worried about the whereabouts and intentions of the escaped cobra whose mate had been executed. We had all heard about a snake's ability to exact revenge, especially when someone had murdered its spouse.

Finally, I left Śrīla Prabhupāda's room and went to the servants' quarters to take rest. Nitāi prabhu and I laid our mats down on the floor. We worried about the runaway snake, but not enough to lose any sleep. Exhausted by the day's excitement, we turned out the light and were ready for nescience. The room was not very big and with the two of us on the floor, there was not much room between us. This did not prevent Pradyumna prabhu from squeezing his sleeping paraphernalia between us. His opinion was that if there was a snake around and it was out to get someone, then at least he would be safe sandwiched between us. Too tired to worry about it, Nitāi and I slept comfortably that night in spite of the crowd.

No one suffered from any snakebites and the following morning we continued with our usual activies. That evening I went into Śrīla Prabhupāda's bedroom to massage him. Māyāpur was always so quiet and peaceful in the evening. It was an excellent place for Śrīla Prabhupāda to recover from his recent illness in Vṛndāvana. I sat there intoxicated by my surroundings and viewed Śrīla Prabhupāda as the centre of the universe. I felt completely relaxed as if I was getting a massage rather than giving one. I could not help telling my glorious spiritual master about the amusing night I had.

"Śrīla Prabhupāda," I said. "Last night when we went to take rest, Pradyumna squeezed in between Nitāi and me so that he wouldn't be bitten by the snake."

Śrīla Prabhupāda started laughing.

"Yes, that is very nice," he said. "Actually there is one story my god-brother Dāmodara Mahārāja has told. It took place in a village just near here. He said there was an infant, and that child was cursed by someone to be bitten by a snake. There were five family members and when they took rest, they surrounded the infant to protect him from any potential snakes. The infant would lie in the middle of the bed surrounded by family. One night the snake came into the room and quietly slithered around each of the sleeping family members and bit the infant, killing him.

So, that is the way it is with the snake. If you are destined to be killed by a snake, it doesn't matter what kind of protection you try to arrange. The snake will kill you. But, we do not worry about such things. If Kṛṣṇa wants to protect you, no one can harm you and if He wants to kill you, then no one can save you."

"All right, you go take rest," he soon instructed.

I left his bedroom feeling completely safe. Hanging onto those two golden lotus feet, fragrant as the sandalwood tree, situated at the centre of the universe, I found shelter from all danger.

Śrīla Prabhupāda, I pray that you will always allow me to remain connected to you. This world is such a dangerous place as the cobras of doubt and temptation pass daily in front of my consciousness. You easily slay them. Please be merciful to me and shield me from the serpents constantly invading my heart. I take shelter of your lotus feet.

127

"I had to have Puris."

November 1, 1974 Flight from Mumbai to Kolkata

Śrīla Prabhupāda Remembers His Youth

Sometimes Śrīla Prabhupāda spoke about his father. When he did, it was always with great affection.

"My father would make sure that whatever I wanted I would get," he said. "Even if it was in the middle of the night and I wanted puris, my father would say to my mother, 'Make him puris if he wants puris.' Sometimes my mother would resist, but my father would make her do it. It was like that. I do not know. Maybe my father knew. He was always doing things like that. Then my mother would have to comply with him."

Once during a flight Śrīla Prabhupāda was eating puris and subji. As he ate, he began laughing aloud and said to me, "When I was young I would never eat chapatis. I was very spoiled. They were no good to me. I had to have puris. Whenever my mother cooked for me, I had to have puris. Even later when I was a businessman."

He stopped talking for a minute, but it was only to laugh again. He was very pleased and enjoyed telling me what a rascal he was.

"Sometimes it was very embarrassing because I would go to people's houses," he continued. "They would have me over for dinner and they would give me chapatis."

Śrīla Prabhupāda's eyes grew very large as he expressed his dilemma.

"I could not eat them. At the same time, I could not refuse. I did not know what to do. What could I say, 'I am sorry, I do not eat chapatis.' Then they would think, 'Oh? You are superior? 'You have to have puris?' So, it became very awkward. Sometimes, I would go out and I wouldn't eat them. It was very difficult for me to say, 'Oh! I just did not like them."

Śrīla Prabhupāda never stopped smiling and laughing as he described his mischievous activities.

"Around that time I acquired a servant," he said. "He kept trying to get me to eat chapatis. Once, he insisted, 'I want you to try them. I want you to let me make you chapatis. I'm sure you will like them.' I said, 'No!' This went on for some time. He kept asking me, 'Please let me make you chapatis. I know you are going to like them.' Finally, I said, 'All right. I'll try them.' He made me first-class chapatis. Ever since that time, I have liked chapatis. It was a very abrupt change in my life. Until that time I never took chapatis."

It is difficult for me to put into words how beautifully animated Śrīla Prabhupāda was while telling this story. He expressed the emotions of each individual as he joyfully unfolded the plot of the story. His eyes became large as he expressed their alarm with his "superiority." Whenever he talked about his youth, it felt to me that it did not happen very long ago. He took great pleasure in speaking about it with his disciples.

> *Thank you, Śrīla Prabhupāda, for allowing me to enter into your childhood pastimes. It was only due to your kindness that I witnessed such glorious activities. I needed so much from you and you kindly gave it to me. I am forever in your debt.*

128

"Why is it necessary to make such disturbance?"

November 7, 1974 ISKCON Juhu Beach, Mumbai, India

Hearing Śrīla Prabhupāda's bell, I hurried from the kitchen where I had been busy making fresh vegetable juice for myself using a juicer that Pālikā Devī had gotten me.

"What is all that noise?" Śrīla Prabhupāda said in an angry mood.

"It is a juicer, Śrīla Prabhupāda," I said nervously. "I have started to drink fresh juices because I have had a difficult time staying healthy in India. I thought drinking fresh juice would help." He did not appear very sympathetic.

"So much noise," he said. "How can I concentrate? Why is it

necessary to make such disturbance?"

I agreed that it was foolish and that I would stop using it. An hour went by when Śrīla Prabhupāda rang his bell. I headed for his sitting room with thoughts of the recent incident out of my mind. He looked at me compassionately and said, "So, if these fresh juices are helping you to stay healthy then it is all right to continue. It is important for you to be healthy so you can do your service. I do not mind."

> *Śrīla Prabhupāda, I was overcome with joy knowing how much you cared for me. It is commonly known, the way to keep healthy in India is to cook your vegetables and peel your fruits before eating to avoid all types of organisms. Śrīla Prabhupāda, thank you for tolerating my foolishness.*

129

"That is the beginning of his fall down."

November 11, 1974 ISKCON Juhu Beach, Mumbai, India

Whenever Śrīla Prabhupāda came out of his Juhu flat for his morning walk all of the assembled devotees chanted, "Jai, Śrīla Prabhupāda!" and offered obeisances. All, except for one brahmacārī who remained standing with folded hands. With his cane in hand, Śrīla Prabhupāda began walking. Looking straight ahead he said, "That is the beginning of his fall down."

Many times, he spoke of this process as "the razor's edge." That morning he demonstrated just how sharp that razor was. The devotee was not conscious of his actions. We cannot be Kṛṣṇa Conscious if we are not conscious.

Śrīla Prabhupāda, I beg for your blessings so I may always be conscious of you and your service to the Supreme Lord.

130

"I can not force you to do something."

November 15, 1974 ISKCON Juhu Beach, Mumbai, India

During this tour of India with Śrīla Prabhupāda, Paramahaṁsa Swami was his secretary and Nitāi dāsa was his Sanskrit editor. We got on well together. The three of us were part of the second wave of devotees who joined the temple around 1971. While staying at Juhu, Pālikā dasi prepared Śrīla Prabhupāda's lunch, so after completion of His Divine Grace's massage, Paramahaṁsa, Nitāi and I went to the beach about a block away to swim and sunbathe. We returned before Śrīla Prabhupāda rose from his afternoon nap, in case he needed any of us.

Within a few days, both of my god-brothers stopped going to the beach because their service was not getting finished. I continued to go, however. Upon returning one day, Paramahaṁsa Swami came to me and said, "Śrīla Prabhupāda is upset about you going to the beach by yourself. He said he wants to talk with you. He's very angry."

I waited for Śrīla Prabhupāda to finish his lunch. When he went back to his sitting room, I walked into his room and offered my obeisances. As I looked up at him, I noticed he had a contented look on his face. He did not appear angry with me at all.

"Śrīla Prabhupāda, would you rather I did not go to the beach after giving you massage?" I blurted out, quite confused.

"No," he nonchalantly replied. "It's all right. You are going by yourself?"

"Yes," I said. "It started with the three of us going swimming, but now I am the only one."

"That's all right," he said. "It's nice to go to the beach a little, get some sun and go in the water. You can go."

I thanked him and left.

Immediately I approached Paramahaṁsa Swami. Still gloating, I told him of my conversation with my loving spiritual master. Shaking his head, he reconfirmed the original story.

A situation like that was not unusual. I am sure that Śrīla Prabhupāda complained about my being at the beach. What was endearing was how tolerant he was when I appeared before him with my inquiry. He was able to sense my attachment and allowed me to make my own decision. I happily stopped going to the beach because he did not force me.

Śrīla Prabhupāda, you are so expert. You often said, "You boys and girls are voluntarily performing service. I cannot force you to do something."

You always treated me with respect, which often resulted in my own embarrassment. Due to your humility, I was overwhelmed with the desire to do anything you asked. Mercifully, your only desire was for me to "chant Hare Kṛṣṇa and be happy." When I remember you, Śrīla Prabhupāda, those instructions become very easy to follow.

131

"Daab"

December 7, 1974 ISKCON Juhu Beach, Mumbai, India

Śrīla Prabhupāda's greatest pleasure was to speak about Kṛṣṇa and His associates twenty-four hours a day. He cherished every opportunity to speak the Kṛṣṇa Consciousness philosophy. This sharply contrasted with his economic use of words when it came to his own bodily maintenance.

Everyday Śrīla Prabhupāda took a short nap after lunch. Upon rising His Divine Grace walked through my designated area to get to the bathroom. Often I rested too. As soon as I heard the sweet sound of his shuffling feet, I would rise and offer my obeisances.

"Daab," Śrīla Prabhupāda said in a deep extended voice as he walked by.

It was my duty to then go to the kitchen, open a coconut, insert a gold straw through the opening and place the sweet water on his desk. This was the daily ritual. Every time I heard the word "daab", the same opportunity availed itself.

Śrīla Prabhupāda stayed in one of the flats on the Juhu property, which have since been knocked down. It was not until after 1976 that his permanent quarters were ready. He humbly accepted whatever facility was given him wherever he travelled around the world.

Śrīla Prabhupāda, anyone who has been to Juhu knows that dabs are very sweet. Hearing you ask for one in the early afternoon was sweeter still. As each year goes by it becomes more remarkable knowing that you walked among us. Some devotees have said that when you walked it appeared that your feet did not touch the ground. I appreciate that you walked all over the globe purifying the places where you placed your lotus feet.

All glories to Śrīla Prabhupāda!

132

"Get yourself another blanket..."

December 24, 1974 ISKCON Los Angeles, California

One cold evening in New Dvārakā, I had the two-burner gas stove on in the servants' quarters to warm the room, so I could sleep that night. It was helpful because I slept on a straw mat and used my chaddar as a blanket. I tried to keep my paraphernalia to a minimum because it was easier to travel. Sometimes, I used one suitcase for His Divine Grace and a small one for myself. Most of the time, though, I managed to keep both of our belongings in one large suitcase.

Śrīla Prabhupāda observed my stove on during the night, so early the next morning he called me into his room. I offered my obeisances and looked up at my merciful guru.

"Why are you keeping the stove on at night?" he asked.

I explained that the warmth of the fire helped me get to sleep since it was so cold.

"Do not you have a blanket?" he asked.

"No, Śrīla Prabhupāda," I said. "I usually do not need one."

"All right," he said. "Go into my cabinet and pick out any blanket and sweater you like."

I enthusiastically hurried over to the metal closet in his bedroom. After looking at the four blankets folded neatly on the shelf I took the thickest, most colourful quilt I could find. Then I helped myself to one of his saffron sweaters. I returned to Śrīla Prabhupāda in his sitting room to show him my choices. He smiled with approval and nodded his head.

"All right, now you can go," he instructed.

I considered myself to be the most fortunate soul in the world. I used the blanket every night, feeling enveloped in Śrīla Prabhupāda's love. It kept me spiritually warm. One day I was talking with one of my friends, Brahmarupa dāsa. He asked if I wanted to take rest in the temple room that night with some of the other devotee men, to which I agreed. Seeing as I was usually alone, it sounded adventuresome. When I went into the temple room, I brought my beautiful bright orange quilt with me. It had a shiny silk finish on one side and a more cuddly soft finish on the other. When I walked into the temple room, Brahmarupa's eyes opened wide.

"Where did you get that?" he asked.

"Śrīla Prabhupāda gave it to me," I said. "Do you want it?" I asked, feeling guilty about owning something so priceless.

"Yes," he eagerly replied.

So, I gave it to him.

A week later while I was resting in the servant quarters, Śrīla Prabhupāda noticed I did not have my blanket over me.

"Where is the blanket I gave you?" he inquired.

Feeling ashamed, I quietly answered, "One of the devotees saw it and when I told him it was yours he became so excited I just had to give it to him."

"All right. Get yourself another blanket," he calmly said. "And this time, do not give it away," he added, with a little more emotion.

Again, I happily complied with his generous instruction and helped myself to another prasādam blanket.

On a few occasions, when we were in a cold city, Śrīla Prabhupāda gave me sweaters. However, I never managed to keep any of them. Inevitably, a devotee would find out it was one of Śrīla Prabhupāda's remnants and I would feel somewhat selfish and give it away. My god-brothers very much appreciated Śrīla Prabhupāda's prasādam. While travelling with Śrīla Prabhupāda, I kept very little for myself. I did not think it was practical to have so many belongings. It was me that was me that was not practical, but I did not realise it at the time.

Śrīla Prabhupāda, in all of your actions you exhibited complete faith in the Supreme Lord. Very often, you told us that if we were fully engaged in Kṛṣṇa's service, all our necessities would be provided. I experienced this truth countless times while performing personal service to you. There was no need to make any separate endeavour. Your simplicity was exemplary. "As great men do, common men will follow." Life is a struggle when I forget to serve your lotus feet. I pray for your favour, so I may serve you eternally without regard for my personal comfort.

133

"You go back to Los Angeles to regain your health."

December 15, 1974 ISKCON Juhu Beach, Mumbai, India

My second tour of travels with His Divine Grace began unceremoniously in the middle of July and continued until the end of December. Most of this tour took place in India, the very place that had initially frightened me away from the lotus feet of my spiritual master. Unfortunately, while in India, I was sick most of the time. I struggled through the seven-week period in Vṛndāvana while Śrīla Prabhupāda was extremely ill. After he regained his health, my health deteriorated and all I could think about was leaving in order to get better. With Śrīla Prabhupāda's mercy, I managed to overcome my lack of surrender and stay at his lotus feet. However, I once again became ill and my mind became very disturbed.

I was unable to appreciate my most fortunate position and meditated on my own bodily ailments. Śrīla Prabhupāda had already been here for one month and was preparing to return to the West by way of Hawaii. I grew much attached to the intended travel plans, contemplating my survival until the expected departure date. Unfortunately, there was a delay due to the ongoing technical difficulties plaguing the Juhu project. When I heard the news, I felt dejected. As I walked on the beautiful Juhu beach every morning with my beloved Śrīla Prabhupāda, I was only conscious of the 747s flying overhead. I imagined them to be flying to the West. I wanted so much to be seated on one of those planes. His Divine Grace would be speaking philosophy with his disciples while I wistfully meditated on each plane until it was out of sight.

On a few walks, I attempted to joke with Paramahaṁsa Mahārāja, hoping to discover that he shared my desire to leave India. Since Paramahaṁsa Mahārāja could not relate to my needs, I transferred the discussion to Brahmānanda Mahārāja, hoping for some sympathy.

At this time, there was a major problem at the Hawaii temple. I told Brahmānanda about my desire to return to the United States because of my health problems. One afternoon we approached Śrīla Prabhupāda. We walked into his sitting room with great apprehension and offered our obeisances. I realized how foolish I was to want to leave the lotus feet of my beloved Guru Mahārāja, but my uncontrolled mind compelled me to do so.

"Śrīla Prabhupāda," I said. "I have been hanging on hoping you would be leaving soon, but it appears that you aren't ready to go yet. I want to know if I can return to the West to regain my health."

"That's all right," he kindly said. "You go back to Los Angeles and regain your health. Brahmānanda, you can go to Hawaii temple to help with the situation there. I will meet up with both of you when I return to Hawaii."

The return flight to the States was not the pleasurable one I had envisioned. Brahmānanda and I looked at each other, as the plane was high in the clouds and lamented our decision to leave His Divine Grace. Śrīla Prabhupāda had allowed us to leave just as easily as he allowed me to return to him a few months before. He accepted whatever Kṛṣṇa provided and never forced anyone to do anything they could not do. I observed his gracious opulence of renunciation over and over again.

One must cry for the association of guru and Kṛṣṇa. It does not come automatically or cheaply. Śrīla Prabhupāda always said, "Devotional service is voluntarily and joyfully performed."

Brahmānanda Mahārāja stopped in Hawaii and acting as Śrīla Prabhupāda's representative, tended to the temple business. I continued on to Los Angeles (New Dvārakā) to take up residence with my wife and son, who was now almost three months old. I hid my anxiety regarding never having seen my son by acting artificially detached. By denying my natural feelings I was able to live up to the stringent expectations within. Somehow I needed to externally prove my stalwart position as a good devotee. In this way, I returned to New Dvārakā not knowing that the cause of my illness may have been denial of my emotional needs. Actually, I was anxious to return to New Dvārakā to be with my family.

I spent some time at the New Dvārakā temple and then went to Honolulu (New Navadvīpa) with my family. By the time Śrīla Prabhupāda arrived on January 29, 1975, I was fully steeped in householder life. Paramahaṁsa Mahārāja and Nitāi prabhu were working very hard taking care of all of Śrīla Prabhupāda's needs. I was so caught up in my new ashram that I did not even volunteer my services, except for giving his evening massage.

Even though Śrīla Prabhupāda kindly allowed me to

massage his sublime form every evening, he never asked why I was not more active in his personal service. He did not ask me what I was doing throughout the day or why I was so busy in my household activities. It never occurred to me that I should be fully engaged in performing personal service to Śrīla Prabhupāda. My consciousness took a definite turn toward grihasta activities. Fortunately, I was not in control of my destiny and Kṛṣṇa arranged for me to resume my personal service to His Divine Grace after only a short time.

Śrīla Prabhupāda, many times, I have heard your disciples ask, "Why doesn't Kṛṣṇa force me to serve Him?"

"If you are forced, there is no question of love. It must be voluntary," you answered.

> *You have always treated me with patience and kindness. You never force us so that we do not commit a great offence by disobeying your orders. Please create the desire in me to serve you every moment. My only happiness is when I am serving your lotus feet. Please keep those soft, golden feet on my head, so I am unable to stray from your protection.*

PART FOUR

Around the World in Five Months

February 1, 1975 to June 20, 1975

134

"Go ahead, cut a joke!"

January 29, 1975 Flight from Tokyo to Honolulu

I have said it many times; the act of travelling with Śrīla Prabhupāda was always exciting. You never knew what would happen. He was like no one else. I particularly loved his sense of humour. Flying with him was always memorable for everyone. I am sure that karmīs also found us to be quite a spectacle with our tilak, shaved heads and colourful robes. Amongst us was the swan-like devotee, Prabhupada. Sometimes he would enter the plane with five or more beautiful, fragrant garlands around him, some down to his knees. Nothing fazed him. He was so beautiful and he emanated such grace and humility despite the throngs of devotees around him. He was always engaged in Kṛṣṇa's service.

This flight was like so many others. Śrīla Prabhupāda sat

by the window. Next to him was Nitāi and Paramahaṁsa Swami was by the aisle. There were some magazines in the seat pocket in front of them one of which was Time magazine. Śrīla Prabhupāda picked it up, seeing something that interested him. The cover photograph was a group of women showing their dissatisfaction with their position in the western world. The title was "Women's Liberation". It was something Śrīla Prabhupāda spoke about at times. In the seventies it was a hot topic.

He put the magazine down. A few minutes later a female flight attendant walked by. As she was approaching, Śrīla Prabhupāda nudged Nitāi and said, "So, these women, they want to be liberated? Tell her if she wants to be liberated, she can shave her head like us. She can be liberated." Nitāi made a little smile and squirmed in his seat. Again, Śrīla Prabhupāda nudged him and said, "Go ahead, make a joke. Call her over here and tell her. Cut one joke. Tell her if she wants to be liberated she can shave her head like us." Śrīla Prabhupāda chuckled. Nitāi, flustered and uncomfortable, sat and chanted, unable to say anything.

You never knew what Śrīla Prabhupāda would do. It was similar to when a female reporter asked him, "Why do you shave your head?" He looked at her with a smile and said, "Why do you shave your legs? Better to have a cool head and warm legs." Śrīla Prabhupāda liberated all of his disciples from the stronghold of material life; men and women. His mission in coming to the West and transforming Westerners into Vaisnavas was based on the fact that we are not our bodies. One can be Kṛṣṇa Conscious regardless of any bodily designation. It does not matter if you are male or female, young or old, black or white. One only has to qualify oneself by following the instructions of a bona fide spiritual master.

Bhakti-tīrtha Mahārāja told me a story of when he first met Śrīla Prabhupāda. He thought that since he was part of a spiritual group he would not be subject to some of the racist attitudes he experienced so far in his life, being in a black body. Unfortunately, it was not always like that when dealing with his god-brothers. He questioned Śrīla Prabhupāda about why his disciples were still on the bodily platform.

He expected some mercy and comfort from him. Śrīla Prabhupāda looked at him and said; "If you are affected by it you are no better than they are." Bhakti-tīrtha Mahārāja loved the response he received from him. He saw immediately how perfect the process of Kṛṣṇa Consciousness was and how perfect his spiritual master understood him. He knew immediately he "had an opportunity to go to a higher level" to use his words.

> *Śrīla Prabhupāda you continue to give all your followers an opportunity to go to higher levels. When we fail, you give us the chance again until we get it right. You are very divine and know exactly what we need. Thank you for your continued instructions.*
>
> *He asked us all to get off the bodily platform and gave each of this instruction in many different ways. He loved all of his disciples equally and engaged everyone in service. His desire was that everyone "Chant Hare Kṛṣṇa and be happy."*

135

"... neither can they work outside."

February 5, 1975 ISKCON Honolulu, Hawaii

I feel as if I am sometimes surrounded by a bubble of illusion. The presence of this bubble is directly related to how Kṛṣṇa conscious I am at any particular time. As Śrīla

Prabhupāda's personal servant, however, I was surrounded by a bubble of protection. It was a wonderful benefit that automatically came when in the proximity of the pure devotee. I was well provided for; I did not have to worry about meals; or where to take rest. My passport, visas and airline tickets seemed to manifest themselves. I travelled around the world five times, but never worried about an aeroplane accident. After all, I sat beside the Lord of the Universe's purest devotee.

It was an enviable position and unfortunately, one I gave up voluntarily. I was now in Hawaii and one of the grhastas living outside the temple and struggling to be a "fired-up" devotee. Śrīla Prabhupāda was sympathetic. I knew this because once in Vṛndāvana, Śrīla Prabhupāda spoke about the grihasta ashram saying, "It is a great dilemma. We cannot pay them to live in the temple, but neither can they work outside."

136

"If it was not for Kṛṣṇa's mercy, you would be dead."

February 5, 1975 ISKCON Honolulu, Hawaii

One day while grocery shopping with devotee friends, the loss of my bubble of protection cost me dearly. We were in a car accident. Hamsavatar and two god-sisters, one with a small child, were driving home from the store. I was sitting in the front passenger seat when a car went through a red light and slammed into our driver's door. It turned into a four-car collision with everyone in the other three cars going through their windshields. My door flew open and out went both Hamsavatar and me. I landed on my tailbone. The two matajis and the child remained in the car as it spun around and almost ran me over. I was taken to the emergency room of a nearby hospital. My back was the source of great pain for months to follow.

Because I had been in the hospital that night, I did not give Śrīla Prabhupāda his evening massage. The next day Paramahaṁsa Mahārāja located me and said, "Śrīla Prabhupāda wanted to know where you were last night." I told him my tale of woe. He went back to Śrīla Prabhupāda and explained my situation. My compassionate spiritual master said, "Oh! Call him here."

In a great deal of pain, I made my way to Śrīla Prabhupāda's room and slowly offered my obeisances. With a strained look on my face, I sat up before my effulgent master.

"What has happened?" he asked in a gentle voice. "I heard you were in a car accident."

I told him the details of the accident as he attentively listened.

"Accha!" he said. "If it was not for Kṛṣṇa's mercy, you would be dead."

"Yes, it was very frightening," I said, with a forced smile.

Over the next few days, I had the good fortune of being in Śrīla Prabhupāda's room on different occasions. Each time I was there with other devotees Śrīla Prabhupāda brought the conversation around to me. Very dramatically, he said, "Śrutakīrti, he was in a very serious accident. If not for the mercy of Kṛṣṇa he would have died."

After hearing this for the third time, it finally sunk into my thick skull. If not for the mercy of Śrīla Prabhupāda and Kṛṣṇa I would have died. I was young and careless and death was the least of my concerns. If it were, I would have never left the lotus feet of my Gurudeva. He kept driving it home. Finally, I understood and realized that Śrīla Prabhupāda was speaking the absolute truth. It was the most wonderful experience to have my compassionate guru reaffirming how Kṛṣṇa saved me. I pray to increase my understanding and faith in every word

His Divine Grace has said and every action he has performed.

During this visit to Hawaii, Śrīla Prabhupāda was translating the fifth canto of the Śrīmad Bhāgavatam. He related the story of my accident in the following way:

Śrīmad-Bhāgavatam 5:14:1

PURPORT

"When the living entity is lost in the forest of the material world, in the struggle for existence, his first business is to find a bona fide guru who is always engaged at the lotus feet of the Supreme Personality of Godhead, Visnu. After all, if he is at all eager to be relieved of the struggle for existence, he must find a bona fide guru and take instructions at his lotus feet. In this way, he can get out of the struggle.

Since the material world is compared herein to a forest, it may be argued that in Kali-yuga modern civilization is mainly situated in the cities. A great city, however, is like a great forest. Actually, city life is more dangerous than life in the forest. If one enters an unknown city without friend or shelter, living in that city is more difficult than living in a forest. There are many big cities all over the surface of the globe, and wherever one looks he sees the struggle for existence going on twenty-four hours a day. People rush about in cars going seventy and eighty miles an hour, constantly coming and going, and this sets the scene of the great struggle for existence. One has to rise early in the morning and travel in that car at breakneck speed. There is always the danger of an accident, and one has to take great care. In his automobile, the living entity is full of anxieties, and his struggle is not at all auspicious."

My dear Śrīla Prabhupāda, the years have quickly passed. Many precarious situations have crossed my path. Still, I blunder along, not realizing that, "if not for Kṛṣṇa's mercy I would have died." Please give me the intelligence to comprehend the urgency of my surrendering to you. When death arrives, I want my mind's eye fixed on your lotus feet. I do not want to be tossed about by the material energy. It is much too painful.

137

"You massage until I become tired."

February 8, 1975 ISKCON Honolulu, Hawaii

Sometimes during his evening massage, Śrīla Prabhupāda went into samādhi. This was scary for me because once he instructed me, "You massage until I become tired, not until you become tired."

He gave me this instruction one day during a morning massage. I moved from one part of his body to the next without his instruction. He let it go on for a few days before chastising me about my laziness.

So that evening, when he went into samādhi during my massage, I became scared because it was possible to massage him for hours without him saying anything. He would close his eyes. After some time, I would begin to rub a little harder hoping that he would notice I was still there. Other times he would say to me, "Are you tired?" I always denied that I was but there were times when I dozed off while massaging him.

Sometimes Śrīla Prabhupāda would close his eyes while I massaged his feet. When this happened, I would place my head on the bottom of those two beautiful lotus feet. I was always very greedy. It was not enough that I massaged his feet every day; I needed more. The massage ended with Śrīla Prabhupāda sweetly saying, "All right, that's enough."

Then there was more magic. I watched as he sat up and grabbed his covers and in one motion placed his head on the pillow while simultaneously pulling the covers over his head. I could never do it justice by trying to describe it, but it was most endearing to watch. Other times he said, "I hate taking rest. It is a complete waste of time. I wish I did not ever have to take rest. I am simply wasting my time."

Śrīla Prabhupāda, I have finally realized what you were teaching me with your gentle lessons. If you said your toes were fingers, they were fingers. Thank you for letting me massage your twenty fingers.

138

"... better not to preach."

February 8, 1975 ISKCON Honolulu, Hawaii

After six months in India, Śrīla Prabhupāda returned to the West by way of Hawaii. He remained in New Navadvīpa for one week. It was a very eventful stay. There was a great deal of agitation at this centre because of the differences between the local authorities and that of Siddha SvarūpaĀnanda Gosvāmī. The complaint was that Siddha did not follow ISKCON's authority. Objections were brought to the attention of Śrīla Prabhupāda's secretary, Paramahaṁsa Swami, who went to Śrīla Prabhupāda and explained some of the difficulties that were taking place.

"So, bring Siddha Svarūpa and we will have a meeting," Śrīla Prabhupāda instructed.

The meeting took place in Śrīla Prabhupāda's quarters. It was attended by Śrīla Prabhupāda, Siddha Svarūpa Mahārāja, Paramahaṁsa Mahārāja, Nitāi prabhu, the temple president and myself. A pleasant breeze came through several open windows in Śrīla Prabhupāda's cheerful, sun-filled room. There was a skylight above his desk. Śrīla Prabhupāda always enjoyed his visits to New Navadvīpa, this time was no exception.

Śrīla Prabhupāda did not waste time with formalities. After everyone was seated on the floor, he unemotionally looked at Siddha and objectively stated, "So, the devotees here have some complaints against you."

"What is that, Śrīla Prabhupāda?" Siddha said smiling.

"One thing. Why you do not shave your head?"

"If I shave my head then sometimes I get a cold,"

Śrīla Prabhupāda began chuckling.

"In Hawaii, you get a cold?" he asked.

"Sometimes, Śrīla Prabhupāda," Siddha said.

"Then you can wear a hat," Śrīla Prabhupāda suggested. "Then you will not catch cold. You are a sannyāsī. Other people are watching. It is important that you set a good example.Also, you do not carry your daṇḍa?"

"Well, they do not usually let me carry it on aeroplanes, so it becomes difficult to travel around with it," Siddha said.

"We have so many sannyāsīs," Śrīla Prabhupāda said. "Everyone is carrying their daṇḍa. Paramahaṁsa, he is carrying a daṇḍa. He brings it on the plane."

"Well, I have had many problems trying to get my daṇḍa on the plane," Siddha replied.

Śrīla Prabhupāda calmly moved onto the next point of contention. Each issue became more serious.

"They say that your followers, they do not come here to see me," Śrīla Prabhupāda said. "That they only see you. They only hear from and deal with you. They won't come here?"

"If they want to come, they can come," Siddha said.

Śrīla Prabhupāda replied in a more authoritative voice.

"But, this is your business, it's all right they may worship you if they like you very much. That's all right. But your business is to bring them to me. You are my disciple. The duty of the disciple is to bring the devotees to the spiritual master. This is your business. Your preaching should be like this. If your preaching does not bring them to this point, then it is useless."

"This is probably my defect," Siddha replied. "My preaching is not so good. Therefore, they are not coming. But, what can I do but try to preach to them."

"Well, if your preaching is insufficient, then better not to preach," Śrīla Prabhupāda told him.

As things became quiet, a wave of courage washed over me. To keep the conversation moving I said, "Śrīla Prabhupāda, I have one observation."

"Yes, go on," he said nodding in approval.

"For example," I said. "This morning in the temple room, Siddha Svarūpa Mahārāja was giving the class. He was sitting along side of your vyāsāsana and one of his people came up with a fresh flower garland and placed it on Siddha Svarupa. When I saw it happen, my mind became disturbed. In my opinion, the garland should have been put on you, as there was no garland on your picture on the vyāsāsana. I would think that the garland should have been put on the vyāsāsana first."

"He has a good point," Śrīla Prabhupāda said, turning to Siddha. "That is correct. It is all right, they may have wanted to put it on you, but you should have directed them to put it on my picture."

Śrīla Prabhupāda finished the discussion and did not belabour any point. He straightforwardly addressed the issue of following the instructions of the spiritual master and the relationship between guru and disciple. This final point wrapped up the meeting. We all offered obeisances and left the room of our Divine guide and loving Gurudeva.

The next day Siddha Svarūpa Mahārāja again visited

Śrīla Prabhupāda. Siddha Svarūpa gave Śrīla Prabhupāda a $10,000 donation that one of his followers had given to him. This demonstrated his understanding of Śrīla Prabhupāda's instruction.

My dear Gurudeva, you are the perfect transparent via medium to your Guru Mahārāja. You always accept service on his behalf. You are completely qualified as the perfect spiritual master because you were the perfect disciple. You pass on the devotion and adoration of your disciples to the lotus feet of your Guru Mahārāja. Śrīla Bhaktisiddhānta Sarasvatī Mahārāja passes the fruits of your devotion to the lotus feet of his Guru Mahārāja. Therefore, it goes from guru to guru within the paramparā up to the lotus feet of Lord Śrī Kṛṣṇa.

I humbly pray to remain connected to your lotus feet, always remembering you are eternally my Lord and master. My life has no meaning. I beg that you allow me to spread your glories for eternity. I pray to swim in the ocean of bliss that is available by remembering your eternal līlā.

139

"So, you are going to stay here?"

February 8, 1975 ISKCON Honolulu, Hawaii

Since Sudama Mahārāja was no longer managing New Navadvīpa, Śrīla Prabhupāda had been discussing who should take on this responsibility. His Sanskrit editor, Nitāi prabhu, suggested me. Śrīla Prabhupāda, knowing my nature, said, "No. Śrutakīrti is too easy-going to manage a temple."

When Nitāi told me Śrīla Prabhupāda's remarks, I smiled, realising he knew me better than I knew myself. Śrīla Prabhupāda arranged for Manasvi to come from Mumbai to manage the Honolulu temple.

During Śrīla Prabhupāda's stay, both Nitāi and Paramahaṁsa Mahārāja tried to persuade me to go with them to be Śrīla Prabhupāda's personal servant as he toured the West. I told them I liked the idea of being his servant in the West, but I always wound up back in India where I did not want to be. They said it would be very helpful if I came on the western tour because there was no-one to cook for Śrīla Prabhupāda. When it came time to go back to India, they would arrange for Nanda Kumar to travel with him. I told them it sounded good in theory, but it did not seem very practical. They were unable to convince me otherwise. I was a householder with a young wife and a four-month old son. My desire to remain with them in Hawaii was strong.

The day before Śrīla Prabhupāda left New Navadvīpa, Gurukrpa Mahārāja told me Śrīla Prabhupāda wanted to see me before his departure for Los Angeles. Together we went back to Śrīla Prabhupāda's room and offered our obeisances. I did not know why he wanted to see me and was unaware that my fate was not in my own hands.

Śrīla Prabhupāda looked at me with a smile and said, "So, Śrutakīrti," he said. "You are going to stay here? Your wife is here, and child?"

"Yes, Prabhupada," I replied.

"So, now you will stay here as a householder? You will help Manasvi manage the temple?"

"Yes, Prabhupada," I replied with less conviction. "I think so."

I was thinking of how selfish I was by not going with my magnificent spiritual master. He was giving me the opportunity to say I wanted to go with him but I could not say it. It was the plan from when I left him in Juhu just six months before but I had lost all composure and did not know what to do.

"So, that is good," Śrīla Prabhupāda said, smiling warmly. "You stay here with your wife and child."

I sat before Śrīla Prabhupāda with my mind reeling unsure of what to do. Śrīla Prabhupāda was giving me the opportunity to travel with him again. He was waiting for me to open my mouth and my heart, but I was not doing it. It was truly amazing how tolerant he was. I did not know what to say next. Time seemed no longer to be an influence.

Gurukripa Mahārāja, who was sitting next to me throughout the conversation, turned to me and started to laugh. "Yes, You know what they call the wife and children? They are known as the tigress and jackal."

Then he turned to Śrīla Prabhupāda. While laughing heartily he asked, "Prabhupada, I know why the woman is compared to the tigress, but why are children compared to jackals?"

"Well," Śrīla Prabhupāda said, "The children, in so many ways, create many inconveniences for the father. They are always requiring so many things and sometimes disturbing him. He cannot sleep. In this way, it is like eating the flesh of the father. This is the business of jackals; eating the flesh of other animals."

The room again became quiet. It was clear, that it was my turn to speak. It was also clear that my guru and Kṛṣṇa were being very merciful to me. They were giving me the opportunity to make sacrifices and advance in Kṛṣṇa Consciousness. I knew my wife would be happy for me to take up this service again. I looked into the eyes of my caring, loving father and with conviction stated, "Śrīla Prabhupāda, I will come with you and be your servant."

Śrīla Prabhupāda smiled broadly and tilting his head to the right said, "All right!" It was evident to me there was nothing else that had to be said. It was always like that with my compassionate master. There was no need to talk unnecessarily about it. He was happy for me and I was happy knowing I was properly situated. I offered my obeisances and walked out of Śrīla Prabhupāda's room with a spring in my step. I knew I was doing the right thing.

I began to prepare for my next exciting tour of duty with His Divine Grace. As the word spread throughout the Hawaii devotee community of my returning to Śrīla Prabhupāda's personal service, one of my god-brothers, with a rather independent nature, challenged the decision I made and told me I was in māyā for not remaining with my wife and son. It was this type behaviour that would have given me doubts but by Śrīla Prabhupāda's mercy I was unaffected by his speculation. I flashed a smile and confidently walked away feeling properly situated. Śrīla Prabhupāda had mercifully made my options clear to me. Again, he did not tell me what to do and gave me the chance to decide for myself.

Śrīla Prabhupāda, I can never repay you for the many wonderful things you have done for me. In the sweetest way, you nudged me back to your lotus feet for five more months. You could have very easily gone without me, but you allowed me to tag along, again. I bathe in the happiness of knowing that you wanted me to come with you. It does not matter why. It is more than enough that you asked me to come in the most wonderful way. I will never understand why you are so kind upon me. Please give me the intelligence to glorify you properly. Pick me up once more and place me at your lotus feet, the only safe place for this distracted soul.

∽ 140 ∽

"Deity Worship must be first class."

February 11, 1975 ISKCON Mexico City, Mexico

Touching down in Mexico City proved to be an extraordinary experience. Śrīla Prabhupāda, a transcendental emissary from Goloka Vṛndāvana, was greeted with honour by his devotees. Śrīla Prabhupāda bypassed all the mundane customs check points and airport facilities and walked directly from the plane to a waiting limousine. The devotees had also arranged a police escort to accompany Śrīla Prabhupāda's vehicle through the city as he went to the temple. This was an extremely pleasant change from our normal grueling airport experience. We were accustomed to being treated with suspicion like potential criminals as we went through customs at other international airports.

During the drive to the temple, Śrīla Prabhupāda expressed his appreciation for the VIP treatment. Eager to continue to please His Divine Grace, Hrdayānanda Mahārāja took this opportunity to report to Śrīla Prabhupāda about all the exciting service the Spanish BBT had accomplished. Many books were being translated and distributed in the Spanish language. Śrīla Prabhupāda was delighted to hear that the glories of the Lord were being spread.

When he arrived at the temple, Śrīla Prabhupāda took darśana of Their Lordships and later asked for the Deity maha-prasādam. This was his standard practice as he travelled from temple to temple. He always took personal interest to see how the Deities were being worshiped. It was as if Śrīla Prabhupāda was Kṛṣṇa's inspector making sure the Deity worship was being maintained nicely by his children.

After sampling the maha-prasādam, Śrīla Prabhupāda said, "This prasādam is horrible. The Deity worship here is not up to standard. It is important to worship the Deities very nicely." Śrīla Prabhupāda again stressed, "It is as important to perform first-class Deity worship as it is to distribute books."

I was shocked. I had never heard Śrīla Prabhupāda criticize the Deity worship anywhere before. My heart went out to the devotees doing the cooking, but I knew it was their turn to get some merciful instruction. This would be something they would never forget. I speculated about Śrīla Prabhupāda's relationship with the Deities. Being of mundane vision, I saw the beautiful forms of the Lord, but did not understand Śrīla Prabhupāda's relationship with them. Sometimes, I tried to imagine what it might be like to take darśana of the Deities and see Kṛṣṇa as Śrīla Prabhupāda undoubtedly did. Śrīla Prabhupāda emphasized how we must understand that Kṛṣṇa is non-different from His form in the temple room. He kindly reminded us again and again.

"Kṛṣṇa is here in His Arcā-vigraha form," he would say.

During this visit, His Divine Grace let everyone know it was imperative to perform first-class Deity worship along with book distribution. After all, the purpose of Śrīla Prabhupāda's books was to understand that Kṛṣṇa is the Supreme Personality of Godhead and we are His servants. Deity worship is the application of the principles delineated in Śrīla Prabhupāda's books.

When it was time for Śrīla Prabhupāda to leave Mexico City for Caracas the devotees arranged the same police escort to the airport, hoping to alleviate the usual red tape caused by international travel. It did not work very well. When Śrīla Prabhupāda arrived at the airport, there was a delay before he could board the plane. He had to stay in the car for almost one hour. While sitting there he said, "It would have been better waiting in the lounge. I am having to wait in the car."

It was an uneasy time for all of us realizing Śrīla Prabhupāda did not have the opportunity for his disciples to see him off.

He reciprocated with his many disciples at airports all over the world. For some devotees, this constituted a large part of their personal association. Śrīla Prabhupāda felt great separation from his disciples while being denied this pleasure. He understood that a great opportunity to enliven them was being missed. I was saddened by Śrīla Prabhupāda's displeasure.

Śrīla Prabhupāda please continue to guide us to properly serve your Deities, distribute your books, and love whomever we meet by following your example to put their needs ahead of our own.

See no. 143 for a similar story.

141

"Vaisnavas like to laugh"

February 13, 1975 ISKCON Mexico, City, Mexico

It is common to hear a devotee say that being in Śrīla Prabhupāda's ISKCON is never boring, this especially applied to travelling with Śrīla Prabhupāda. I always enjoyed the association of his various secretaries, editors and personal servants. One of my favourite devotee friends while being with His Divine Grace was Paramahaṁsa Swami. He joined the entourage in the fall of 1974. His nature was similar to mine. 'Easy going' was the way Śrīla Prabhupāda described me. He was the only devotee that was younger than I and he was very likeable.

When he first became Śrīla Prabhupāda's permanent secretary, he was overjoyed. He could not believe his great fortune and expressed it every time he went into his room.

All of Śrīla Prabhupāda's disciples would offer obeisances whenever they entered his room each day. If you went in and out of his room five times you would offer pranams on entering and exiting each time. While serving him lunch I would bow down every time I brought in a hot chapati, freshly cooked, from the next room. The more I put my head on the floor the happier I was. It meant Śrīla Prabhupāda was eating several chapatis.

Paramahaṁsa Swami turned his obeisances into an art. When he became part of the entourage, he was so happy. Whenever Śrīla Prabhupāda asked to see him, upon entering the room, he would lay his six-foot body in front of the desk of his spiritual master in a full daṇḍavat. After saying the pranam mantras, he would remain on the floor chanting various Sanskrit slokas glorifying Śrīla Prabhupāda. After two years as a sannyāsī it seemed like Paramahaṁsa Swami had learned some slokas. Śrīla Prabhupāda allowed this to go on for a few days. Then one day while Paramahaṁsa was lying in front of him chanting different mantras he stopped him saying, "How are we going to get any work done lying there on the floor?" Paramahaṁsa sat up and with a big smile on his face and agreed to follow his instruction.

While travelling with Śrīla Prabhupāda in February of 1975 Paramahaṁsa and I were especially jovial. I had just rejoined the party after leaving them in Mumbai in December of 1974. I was happy to be with Śrīla Prabhupāda again and Paramahaṁsa and Nitāi were glad to have me on the party helping with the service. At that time Śrīla Prabhupāda was visiting temples in Los Angeles, Mexico City and Caracas.

Sometimes during kīrtans in the temple room Paramahaṁsa and I would look around and observe our god-brothers chanting, and then we would look at each other and laugh. We never spoke about it outside of the temple room, but these were moments we enjoyed together. I am not sure what caused us to laugh so hard but it went on for some time. I think it was partly due to the fact that we were together with Śrīla Prabhupāda again after so many weeks apart.

On February 11 Śrīla Prabhupāda arrived in Mexico City. He would take his daily massage outside in the warm sunshine. It was something he liked very much. I was massaging his back on the 13th when Paramahaṁsa Swami appeared before us on the verandah. He offered his obeisances and sat up. He looked at me vigorously massaging His Divine Grace's back and smiled broadly. For some reason, that triggered me. I started laughing at the sight of my god-brother sitting there waiting to ask Śrīla Prabhupāda a question. That opened the floodgates. We both started laughing uncontrollably. I was laughing so hard I could not do my service anymore and stopped massaging Śrīla Prabhupāda's back.

At this time Śrīla Prabhupāda inquired in a calm voice, "What is so funny?" I looked at Paramahaṁsa, hoping he had some insight into this display before our beloved guru but he sat there quietly. I had to say something. I was never very good at speaking on the spot in awkward situations, especially with Śrīla Prabhupāda, and this was one of them. Finally I said, "I do not know Prabhupada, when I see Paramahaṁsa sometimes it just makes me laugh". Śrīla Prabhupāda smiled and said, "That's okay, laughing is a Vaisnava activity." Relieved, Paramahaṁsa and I went back to our service.

A few minutes went by and Śrīla Prabhupāda began to tell us a story about his childhood. This was one of those precious times we loved so much. Whenever he told us a story we went to that place and time with him. Nothing else mattered. He began; "When I was a young boy sometimes my father, he would walk along the banks of the Ganga. He would stop at the small huts of the different sādhus there and give them ganja. Sometimes the Paramahaṁsa's they smoke a little ganja to help control their senses. So, he would provide it to them."

He stopped for a minute. Paramahaṁsa and I were speechless. We weren't laughing now. We did not know what to think or say. I was still massaging Śrīla Prabhupāda's back when he began to laugh loudly and looked directly into the eyes of his secretary and said, "But not YOU Paramahaṁsa Swami!" I continued to massage Śrīla Prabhupāda with a smile on my face and Paramahaṁsa went on with his service reading letters to His Divine Grace. Śrīla Prabhupāda sat on his straw massage mat in the sun. His golden body shined brightly, covered in mustard oil. The foremost Vaisnava, he also had a good laugh and the last laugh. It was a wonderful moment I will never forget.

Śrīla Prabhupāda, I never knew how to include this story in my memoirs. I thought it was too risky, that your followers would misunderstand. It was difficult for me to comprehend also, even though it was one of the funniest stories you told us. After all, Vaisnavas like to laugh. You have showed me that countless times while I was with you and for this I am eternally grateful. Kṛṣṇa Consciousness is joyfully performed.

A few years ago I visited my god-brother, Paramahaṁsa. He is now living near Mt. Shasta in California where his closest neighbour is a mile away. He is married and likes living in seclusion. We talked for hours about our service to Śrīla Prabhupāda. While I was there, he told me that before he was a devotee he had never been with a woman, not even on a date. However, he had one great attachment; smoking marijuana. It was very difficult for him to give that up. After he told me this I could understand Śrīla Prabhupāda's story was not just an anecdote that had the three of us laughing, it was one with insight, instructing his disciple in a sweet caring way. Śrīla Prabhupāda knew each one of us completely. He never judged us but he always encouraged us in the best possible way to chant Hare Kṛṣṇa and be happy.

After thirty years, sometimes struggling to follow the principles, I am appreciating more than ever your ability to turn fallen Westerners into Vaisnavas. You were always able to give instructions in the sweetest way to me, Paramahaṁsa Swami as well and all your disciples when necessary. Whatever was required to help us in this lifetime to become more serious. At every moment you give me instructions. You are eternally present in them. Only you could be so strict in presenting the process of Kṛṣṇa Consciousness to us and at the same time be so lenient in accepting the many bad habits your American and European disciples had as they gradually purified themselves.

I have no understanding of the degree of your compassion and mercy for us. You are the topmost messenger of Lord Caitanya and Lord Nityānanda. I look back in amazement at how you could be so happy and peaceful as you travelled around the world. You attracted everyone you saw you with your sublime form and smile. When your followers looked at your eyes filled with love of Kṛṣṇa their hearts would immediately melt. Because you were a genuine Paramahaṁsa you were able to display such qualities despite your disciples being a constant source of concern due to their bad habits and their lack of good qualities.

You patiently trained, encouraged and chastised us, thousands of children, some of them quite obstinate. Only you could have done it. You know fully the potency of the Mahā-mantra and always stress the importance of chanting our sixteen rounds and following the four regulative principles. It is a simple path by which we can become Kṛṣṇa Conscious. Like Paramahaṁsa Swami I want to prostrate myself in front of your desk and offer prayers until you allow me to serve you again.

142

"All right, let's take prasādam."

February 19, 1975 Venezuela Airlines Flight to Caracas, Venezuela

Śrīla Prabhupāda influenced everyone he was with. Travelling with him was an enlightening experience. While visiting various temples, it was amazing to see how he lifted everyone's spirits to the spiritual realm.

Being with him in planes and airports, however, offered a different opportunity. I was able to see how he changed the lives of those who knew nothing about him. It must have been his effulgence.

Once a stewardess passed by him and said, "This man looks very wonderful." Others would ask what they could do for him.

One incident on Venezuela Airlines stands alone because of its uniqueness. Śrīla Prabhupāda, Paramahaṁsa Swami, Nitāi dāsa and I were travelling from Mexico City to Caracas. I hadn't prepared any prasādam for the flight, but just before we boarded the plane an Indian Vaisnavi handed me a bag filled with puffed rice that she had made for the trip.

"All right, let's take prasādam," Śrīla Prabhupāda said shortly after takeoff.

"Do you want what is being served on the plane?" I asked.

"No, no!" he immediately said. "We have our prasādam. That's all right."

I did not ask for a plate. I simply put the tray-table down, unwrapped the aluminium foil and placed the puffed rice before my spiritual master. He immediately started to eat. Although it was a small portion, he only ate about half. Without even looking at me he said, "All right, now you can take."

This was the blessing for which we were always anxious.

Śrīla Prabhupāda always took great care of his entourage. This quality was one of many I greatly appreciated.

I took the puffed rice from His Divine Grace and split the foil down the middle, keeping half for myself and giving the rest to Paramahaṁsa Swami. We were happily eating Śrīla Prabhupāda's remnants when a young stewardess who was walking down the aisle looked at us and spontaneously reached past Paramahaṁsa and placed her hand in my maha-prasādam. Grabbing a fistful, she tossed it into her mouth.

"Oh, this is very good," she exclaimed. "What is it?"

"It's puffed rice," I said, trying to keep my composure. "It's made from rice."

Śrīla Prabhupāda looked at her with a broad smile.

"Ah, this is very good," she again stated.

"I'm glad you like it," I said, still a little shocked about what she had done.

"Are you having anything else to eat?" she inquired.

"Well, we're vegetarian," I explained. "Unless there is some fruit, we can't have anything."

"I will go up to the first-class section and get you a basket of fruit," she eagerly responded.

In a moment she returned with fruit and knives and again asked if there was anything she could get us. Turning to Śrīla Prabhupāda I asked, "Prabhupada, would you like some milk?"

"Yes, hot milk," he said.

"Okay," I told her. "He will have some hot milk and we will have some as well." She quickly went to first class and came back with the hot milk.

Śrīla Prabhupāda lectured many times about the Supersoul residing in the heart of the living entity. However, I had never experienced His presence before that day. I became convinced that only Supersoul within the heart of the stewardess could have inspired her to act in such an unprofessional manner.

Sometimes devotees would offer me money to get a taste of Śrīla Prabhupāda's remnants but I never accepted. They begged for the opportunity to render personal service. Here was this flight attendant boldly going where no one had ever gone before by the mercy of Kṛṣṇa and His pure devotee.

All glories to you, Śrīla Prabhupāda, for distributing your grace to all living entities that came in contact with you.

143

"You must worship the Deity very nicely!"

February 19, 1975 Caracas, Venezuela

When Śrīla Prabhupāda arrived at the temple in Caracas, Venezuela it was like an instant replay of his arriving in Mexico City. He took darśana of the Deities and later in his room sampled the maha-prasādam.

"These puris are terrible," Śrīla Prabhupāda again said. "The vegetable is horrible. This prasādam is not good. Deity worship must be first-class. You must worship the Deity very nicely!"

Again I was surprised. It was unusual for Śrīla Prabhupāda to reprimand his disciples by saying they must improve the Deity worship. Either way, Śrīla Prabhupāda kindly encouraged his young disciples to make advancement on the spiritual path.

It was never that Śrīla Prabhupāda was upset with us and we were doomed. He would stress the importance of performing our service with care and attention. This was the example our beloved spiritual master gave us. Everything Śrīla Prabhupāda did was with the utmost attention and devotion to the Lord.

Śrīla Prabhupāda enjoyed his stay in this part of the world and was impressed with the sincerity of the devotees. I also enjoyed being at the Caracas temple since I lived there for a few months when I first left Śrīla Prabhupāda's personal service in January of 1974. I knew most of the devotees well and, for me, it was like going home.

When we arrived in the temple room Śrīla Prabhupāda took his place on the vyāsāsana. I stood before him as the kīrtan started. As the devotees chanted I began to look around at the old familiar faces around me. I was enjoying them seeing me as Śrīla Prabhupāda's servant. As I stood there smiling broadly I felt something hit me in the head. I turned and looked at Śrīla Prabhupāda. His feet were now bare.

He took off his socks, rolled them up in a ball and threw them at my head. It was my service to remove them but being distracted I failed to notice that he wanted them off because it was warm in the temple. He graciously benedicted me for my foolishness.

Śrīla Prabhupāda, you have created a large family of Vaisnavas. You are the munificent father and grandfather of tens of thousands of devotees of Lord Kṛṣṇa. You have very kindly made it possible for your followers to go anywhere in the world, take darśana of the Supreme Personality of Godhead and enjoy the association of friends and family. This is one of the great fringe benefits of being a member of your ISKCON society. Please allow this prodigal son to remain within your family, always.

You instructed us that book distribution and Deity worship must go side by side. Your books inspire and give us knowledge to serve Kṛṣṇa. Deity worship allows us to practice devotional service. Their Lordships are the original root source of this Vaisnava family. Without them, we are lost. Your books are like attractive, cordial invitations to please come and personally serve the Deity.

See no. 140 for a similar story.

144

"You must give up everything."

February 25, 1975 ISKCON Miami

Śrīla Prabhupāda arrived in Miami after a wonderful two weeks in Mexico City and Caracas, Venezuela. He stayed in a cottage adjacent to the temple. The cottage was normally the residence of a householder couple. There were posters of devotional paintings from Śrīla Prabhupāda's books on the walls. As Śrīla Prabhupāda and I walked into the house he noticed a particular poster on the wall of Kṛṣṇa was sitting on the chariot and Arjuna standing behind Him with his left hand holding his forehead. Arjuna looked as if he was in a great deal of distress (Plate 5, *Bhagavad-gītā* As It Is).

Śrīla Prabhupāda began laughing.

"Yes, this picture," he said. "I like this picture very much. This picture is very instructive."

Unaware of any correlation to my own situation in life, I naively inquired, "What is that Śrīla Prabhupāda?"

Knowing me completely, he replied, "Well, Kṛṣṇa is saying to Arjuna, 'You must give up everything.' He is telling Arjuna, 'Give up all your family. You must kill them. You must kill your family members.' So this is the point. One has to be ready to give up everything for Kṛṣṇa and do what Kṛṣṇa desires. You must be prepared to give up a wife, children, everything. One has to be ready to kill their relatives if Kṛṣṇa desires what to speak of giving them up. If Kṛṣṇa wants, you kill your relatives. This is a devotee. A devotee is prepared to kill their relatives for Kṛṣṇa. So, at this point, Arjuna is ready. He is having to accept. Then everything is all right. As devotees, we must be able to give up all of these family relationships."

At this point I became overwhelmed with my own internal turmoil since I still considered myself a newlywed with a wonderful baby boy. I was just embarking on family life, certainly not ready to give them up, much less kill them. This point of surrender was so extreme. I just gave in to the fact that I could not yet understand. Burdened by my own ignorance, I looked down at the ground and quietly responded, "Yes, Śrīla Prabhupāda."

After explaining the picture, Śrīla Prabhupāda continued into the cottage. I began to unpack his suitcase while considering his valuable instruction. I longed for the comfort of family attachment. I was tormented with the fact that I left my infant son and young wife.

The way His Divine Grace explained Arjuna's dilemma was completely objective. Śrīla Prabhupāda was so expert. He was not telling me to leave my family, he was gently persuading me to come to my own conclusion. There was no indication in his voice that this was my predicament, yet it was obvious to me that this was my exact predicament. I was attached and determined to stay with my family. Śrīla Prabhupāda philosophically prepared me to make the important decision that was to come in the near future.

I had enlisted in Śrīla Prabhupāda's army. Instead of Uncle Sam on the billboard, Prabhupada pointed, saying, "Kṛṣṇa wants you!" We were at war with māyā. Śrīla Prabhupāda, our commander and chief, called upon us to implement emergency measures. As volunteer warriors, this required great personal sacrifice. We could choose frontline preaching work or be involved in behind the scenes support. In my case it involved personally serving Śrīla Prabhupāda and for many others it involved long hours of sankīrtan.

Somewhat weary from battling māyā, I became aware that the war was never over. Somehow or other, I realized that making one stab at surrendering to Kṛṣṇa was not enough. The magical panacea of mitigating all stress through instant, total Kṛṣṇa Consciousness no longer seemed possible for me. I could make the wonderful choice of staying properly situated at the lotus feet of Śrīla Prabhupāda, but it did not mean my mind would be willing to be taken hostage by my intelligence. My intelligence battled daily with my rebellious mind. In the past, this struggle had caused my body to succumb to illness.

I was secure in the fact that my family was being provided for at the Hawaii Temple. It was not as if I had abandoned them. I was just called away on a tour of eminent duty. I had only been with Śrīla Prabhupāda for two weeks after leaving Hawaii. I took comfort knowing that when His Divine Grace left the United States, I would be back in the loving arms of my family. After all, the agreement made with Paramahaṁsa Swami, Prabhupada's secretary, was that Nanda Kumar would be Śrīla Prabhupāda's servant while touring India. I was very attached to this arrangement.

However, Śrīla Prabhupāda seemed to be preparing me for more loving service by instructing me on a much different level. He was giving me the opportunity to surrender to Kṛṣṇa and stay with him as his personal servant. It appeared that he was telling me I should give up my attachment to my family and continue to be his personal servant. He said nothing more about it while he stayed in Miami. Out of apprehension, I never mentioned it again.

Always one hundred percent percent Kṛṣṇa Conscious, Śrīla Prabhupāda continued to teach us how to surrender to Kṛṣṇa

During the course of his preaching work, Srila Prabhupada was faced with many obstacles and difficulties, yet he always remained calm. He dealt with the problems as they arose. With fearlessness and expertise, he depended fully on Krishna for the result and the challenges he faced never interfered with his personal meditations.

Srila Prabhupada never ceased to make himself avaiable, whether to his disciples on a morning walk, such as here with Paramahamsa Swami at Juhu Beach, or receiving a guest into his quarters in Melbourne, Australia. His disciples were always keen to accompany him, especially for prasadam at a Life Member's, as here in London.

Srila Prabhupada takes his morning walk—here on the streets of Brooklyn during the summer of 1973. His disciples gather as he leaves the temple. (Opposite) In the early hours at Mayapur, his servant is ever ready with the reel to reel Uher tape recorder, eager to capture his words. To please Srila Prabhupada was the greatest happiness for his devotees.

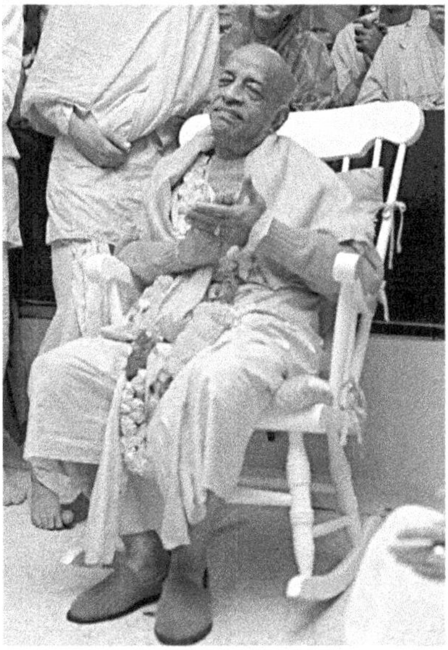

No matter how small the offering, he was easy to please. Whether a flower, a devotional drama, or a new edition of one of his books—here the Dutch translation of his Bhagavad-gita As It Is—De Bhagavad-gita Zoals Ze Is—he took great pleasure seeing his children grow in their Krishna Consciousness.

TAA

and declare war on māyā. I, on the other hand, was not Kṛṣṇa conscious. I had glimpses, but no real vision, so it was hard for me to always stay in the fire of Kṛṣṇa Consciousness. It was hard to stay on the front line. I was tired and in need of some relief, some sense gratification. Although, I very much appreciated being with Śrīla Prabhupāda, my senses always churned. I was always looking for some way to pacify them. It did not matter where we were, I was always eager to go to the next temple. Unable to be at peace, I always promised myself that satisfaction was just around the corner, so I was always ready to be on the move.

Somehow or other, despite my transient nature, Śrīla Prabhupāda was satisfied with me as his servant. This is an important fact. Śrīla Prabhupāda was satisfied with whatever Kṛṣṇa provided. Fortunately, he did not give up on me. In spite of all of my many flaws, he never told me to leave his personal service and do something else. He allowed me to stay at his lotus feet and render intimate service, no matter how disturbed my mind was. I took solace massaging the soft lotus feet of His Divine Grace and became peaceful.

My loving master, you are very compassionate. You always encouraged me in the sweetest possible way to stay under your care and perform devotional service. I was so unfortunate that I was unable to surrender to your desire. There is not one day that goes by that I do not lament my foolish behaviour. I pray that someday I will get the chance to once again rub your lotus feet. If it happens, I hope to remember how easily I gave up such a covetable service, so that I will never again let go of those soft, golden lotus feet.

145

"Why, here you have dirt?"

February 26, 1975 ISKCON Miami, Florida

One day Śrīla Prabhupāda took his morning walk on the temple grounds in Coconut Grove. While walking in the yard, he turned to the temple president and asked, "Why everyone else's yards are clean? Here there are only leaves on the ground?"

"Well, under the leaves there is nothing but dirt," the devotee responded. "The leaves keep the dirt from rising."

"There are lawns everywhere," Śrīla Prabhupāda replied. "Why, here you have dirt?"

Śrīla Prabhupāda always wanted everything to be done first class. He knew that sometimes we had 'hippie mentalities'. He wanted our temples to be very clean, the deity worship done properly and for us to be dressed nicely and kept clean. He particularly disliked to see the men with long hair and beards.

Śrīla Prabhupāda, you had to instruct us how to do everything, how to dress, cook, and keep ourselves clean. There was very little we knew how to do. For years you taught your children without losing your patience. It was more wonderful that you enjoyed associating with us, your Vaisnavas in training. Thank you for never renouncing your service.

146

"Caitanya Mahāprabhu even does not demand ..."

February 28, 1975 ISKCON Atlanta, Georgia

Śrīla Prabhupāda's visit to the Atlanta temple lasted only a few days, but it was packed with mystical experiences.

Śrīla Prabhupāda flooded the devotee community with love of Godhead. When His Divine Grace arrived, he delivered the following short, sweet lecture to the devotee congregation in front of Their Lordships.

Śrīla Prabhupāda: So I am very glad to see you, and I am coming first of all to Mexico City?

Devotee: Yes.

Prabhupada: So Mexico City, then Caracas, then . . .

Devotee: Miami.

Prabhupada: Miami. So I see your temple is the best.

Devotees: Jaya! Hari bol!

Prabhupada: So, Caitanya Mahāprabhu is very kind. *Parama karuna pahu dui jana.* Two Lords, Nitāi-Gauracandra. Nityānanda Prabhu and Śrī Caitanya Mahāprabhu. They are very kind, you see? They have appeared just to reclaim the fallen souls of this age. So They are more kind than Kṛṣṇa. Kṛṣṇa, He is also very kind. He comes to deliver. But, Kṛṣṇa demands that first of all surrender. Caitanya Mahāprabhu even does not demand surrender. He is so kind. (Voice choking) So, take shelter of Śrī Caitanya Mahāprabhu and be happy. Thank you very much. (Weeping)

Seeing Their Lordships, Śrīla Prabhupāda melted in joy. Inundated by the flood of love of Godhead, tears flowed from Śrīla Prabhupāda's eyes. He was overjoyed to see the Deities being taken care of so well. What good fortune! How incredibly moving it was to witness Śrīla Prabhupāda's encounters with Their Lordships! It is not possible to adequately describe His Divine Grace as he gave us a hint of his divine personality. Śrīla Prabhupāda saw the Lord before him. I, on the other hand, saw beautiful Deities made of metal. I did not understand the real nature of Arcā-vigraha. I could only imagine what Śrīla Prabhupāda was experiencing.

Śrīla Prabhupāda rarely revealed his symptoms. On a previous occasion in Mayapur, he apologized after he went into a trance.

This was the only time I was fortunate enough to witness Śrīla Prabhupāda in this mood. Stunned and astonished, everyone remained motionless; mesmerized by Śrīla Prabhupāda's transcendental mellows. We stood in rapt attention as our spiritual master left external consciousness while each moment seemed like twelve years or more. Mysterious time stretched out around us like the great unknown. Astounded, we stood and awaited Śrīla Prabhupāda's return. As His Divine Grace rejoined us, he nodded for kīrtan to begin.

What amazed me was Śrīla Prabhupāda's ability to refrain from such symptoms on a regular basis. He expertly controlled himself in order to instruct us and to push on Lord Caitanya's movement. We were not capable of fully understanding Śrīla Prabhupāda's ecstasy, so he compassionately trained us, beginning with the neophyte level. Devotional service is so full of spiritual sweetness that foolish rascals easily consider such emotion to be like ordinary, mundane feelings, because that is all they know. Śrīla Prabhupāda carefully lived an exemplary life by teaching us what we were ready to learn.

Also, while in Atlanta, he played mṛdaṅga on the vyāsāsana during a kīrtan. This was the only time I was able to witness such a wonderful event. Everyone was treated to very rare and glimpses of their divine spiritual master.

My dear Śrīla Prabhupāda, I realize that if I meditate on any day of your life, I can become Kṛṣṇa Conscious. Every minute in your presence was filled with waves of inspiration that continually poured from your divine form. I am still unable to appreciate the love of God emanating from you, because my consciousness is filled with the desire to enjoy. Śrīla Prabhupāda, please give me the eyes needed to see you.

147

"If I say you can do it, then it is all right."

March 1, 1975 ISKCON Atlanta, Georgia

Paramahaṁsa, Nitāi and I received unique, and rare treasures during our stay in Atlanta. When Śrīla Prabhupāda arrived the weather was rather cold. The devotees presented Śrīla Prabhupāda with warm socks and a pair of canvas walking shoes. The next morning, before the walk, I assisted Śrīla Prabhupāda by sliding his toes into his new pair of shoes with his blessed shoe horn. After his walk and morning programme, Śrīla Prabhupāda rang his bell. I found my way to his new quarters . "These shoes do not fit me," he said. "If they fit, you can use them."

"I can't wear your shoes, Śrīla Prabhupāda," I immediately answered. "That would be offensive."

"If I say you can do it, then it is all right," he gently replied.

I was startled. Śrīla Prabhupāda was always full of surprises, but I never imagined walking in my Guru Mahārāja's shoes! Like a young boy, I grew increasingly excited with the idea of walking in my spiritual father's shoes. I had heard one should not use the spiritual master's shoes, so this made the idea even more intriguing. The notion that I could do it was controversial! I liked it! I had firm faith that when Śrīla Prabhupāda said something was all right, then it was definitely all right. I felt safe and was excited knowing his shoes were filled with incredible potency. Smiling, I agreed to take them. Śrīla Prabhupāda's generosity continued to flow in my direction.

"Do you need any socks?" he asked.

I have to admit, although it was a gluttonous thing to accept gifts from your spiritual master, I thoroughly enjoyed it. With heightened desire, I cheerfully, yet shamefully, replied, "Yes, I guess I do."

"All right," he said. "Take some socks for yourself and give some to Paramahaṁsa and Nitāi also."

I happily complied with his instructions. I offered my obeisances, filled my arms with his shoes and some socks and dashed out of the room. The first thing I did was hurry to a secluded spot like a mischievous child and tried to place my feet into his prized footwear. Much like the evil stepsister, my feet were regrettably too big to fit into His Divine Grace's shoes. Persistently, I kept trying to squeeze my locust feet into Śrīla Prabhupāda's magical shoes. Finally, I understood the profound lesson. I practically and symbolically could never walk in Śrīla Prabhupāda's shoes.

Being playful, I unfortunately did not linger upon the depth of this message. My rascal nature made me rush to my godbrothers where I capriciously handed them Śrīla Prabhupāda's socks. I explained that His Divine Grace wanted them to have them. They resisted, chastising me for my improper behaviour. They reacted exactly as I had anticipated. I confidently passed on Śrīla Prabhupāda's benediction in spite of their hearty objections. The controversy was confirmed by their criticism and sweetened the adventure. Contented, I guaranteed that Śrīla Prabhupāda had given his personal endorsement. They could rest assured that he had given his seal of approval and it was all right to wear them. Hearing this, they excitedly grabbed the socks from my hands and happily put them on to warm their cold toes.

Śrīla Prabhupāda personally utilized everything in Kṛṣṇa's service or engaged others in this principle of utility. So, trying to follow in his footsteps, not in his shoes, I quickly got over the fact that the shoes did not fit me. The next time I saw the temple president, I explained that the shoes did not fit Śrīla Prabhupāda properly, so he could have them.

He took them and placed them at the foot of Śrīla Prabhupāda's vyāsāsana. Embarrassed, I could not bring myself to tell him what had transpired. I took comfort, however, knowing that it was not possible to contaminate anything that came in contact with our completely pure spiritual master.

Śrīla Prabhupāda, you have showered so many blessings upon me. I have often heard it said, "Familiarity breeds contempt." I know I was always offensive by not fully comprehending your glorious presence. Contrary to mundane relationships, the more you benedicted me with your association, the more I appreciated your greatness. You continually express your love to everyone. You reciprocate with genuine affection. As you warmly express your love for your disciples, I have become more and more enchanted and attached to you. You embody all that you preach. You freely give your spiritual love to everyone. Since your love is unmotivated and unconditional, it never diminishes or becomes cheap. Your love crosses time and space and touches the heart of anyone fortunate enough to receive your precious literature. You stay ever-close to the hearts of your faithful disciples, who adhere to your Bhāgavata vāṇī. Please forgive me for thinking I could walk in your shoes. No one compares to you. I should have known better. Although I can never fit into your shoes, I pray that someday I may follow in those divine footsteps that you have placed clearly before me.

148

"You offer your obeisances!"

March 2, 1975 ISKCON Atlanta, Georgia

Morning Massage

Every morning at approximately 11:00 am, Śrīla Prabhupāda began his morning massage which lasted about one and a half hours. There were no hard and fast rules for the length of time he took his massage. Sometimes during his massage, Śrīla Prabhupāda's secretary read him his mail and took dictation for replies. His Sanskrit editor also came in with questions regarding Śrīla Prabhupāda's morning translation work.

While I massaged him one day, his Sanskrit editor came and went several times from Śrīla Prabhupāda's room. The first time he entered the room he carefully offered his obeisances. The next few times he entered he knelt quickly, momentarily touched his head to the floor and hastily sat up and asked questions. Again he left the room. The next time he entered the room, he touched his head to the floor for a moment.

"What is this hatchet?" Śrīla Prabhupāda said, chastising him as he sat up. "You offer your obeisances! This hatchet is not good." As he said the word 'hatchet' he took his right arm and swung it up and down like one would when using an axe.

This incident happened years ago. It was another instance of how well Śrīla Prabhupāda picked his words. A hatchet is often used to cut down trees and creepers. Our devotional creeper is very fragile. While rendering personal service to the spiritual master, we can easily damage our devotional creeper by carelessly swinging our hatchet-like egos. To be Kṛṣṇa Conscious means we must be conscious of our activities at all times. We can not take short cuts in the process of devotional service.

Śrīla Prabhupāda your compassion to your disciples was endless. Your chastisement came from such great compassion for us. When you saw one of your disciples acting in a way that was damaging to their devotional creeper, you would try your best to correct them. You often told us that devotional service was voluntary and no one could be forced to surrender to Kṛṣṇa. Still, you did your best to encourage us in our fragile state. If we listen carefully we can hear your instructions. If we read your books sincerely and regularly we will know them without a doubt.

All Glories to Śrīla Prabhupāda, the most expert gardener who lovingly tends to our devotional creeper! Jai Śrīla Prabhupāda!

149

"What shall we do?"

March 3, 1975 ISKCON Dallas, Texas

Śrīla Prabhupāda travelled quickly through the western world. Normally, he spent only a few days, or at most a week, visiting each temple. The two places he blessed with his divine association for extended periods were New Dvārakā in Los Angeles and New Navadvīpa in Hawaii.

After visiting the Atlanta yatra for two days, Śrīla Prabhupāda and his entourage proceeded to the Dallas centre for another two days. My mind was fixated on the agreement I had made with Paramahaṁsa Mahārāja about returning to my wife and son in Hawaii before Śrīla Prabhupāda departed for India. Part of me longed for the comfort of society, friendship and love that devotional householder life offered. Another part of me was racked with guilt for wanting to leave my beloved

Guru Mahārāja. With a restless heart, it was hard for me to sit alone in the servants' quarters hour after hour, day after day, waiting to be called. My senses churned, pushing me to press Paramahaṁsa Mahārāja into action.

I decided to speak with Paramahaṁsa in Dallas since it was the closest temple to the devotee who was to replace me in Los Angeles. I told him it was time to set up the exchange. Śrīla Prabhupāda's next stop, before leaving for India, was New York. I feared going to India. It generally resulted in my extreme illness. I wanted to make certain that the arrangements were made effectively. It was a simple matter of arranging for Śrīla Prabhupāda's next servant's flight to New York and my flight could go directly from Dallas to Hawaii.

Late that morning, while I energetically massaged Śrīla Prabhupāda, Paramahaṁsa Mahārāja, His Divine Grace's secretary, walked into the room and offered his obeisances.

"Śrīla Prabhupāda," he said. "Should we send for your other servant in Los Angeles? Shouldn't he come now to replace Śrutakīrti? Shall we set it up?"

For me this was the moment of truth. I was in great anxiety as I waited for Śrīla Prabhupāda's reply. I did not know what to expect, but understood anything was possible. It was curious as to how often decisions were made when I was massaging Śrīla Prabhupāda's back, unable to see the expressions on his beautiful golden face. I sat crossed-legged behind Śrīla Prabhupāda rubbing vigorously and holding my breath. My wait was over quickly.

"I am not very anxious for this boy to come with me," he said. "He is too whimsical. Some woman will walk by and he will go away. And then, finished. Then, it will be all over. He is very good, he is very qualified. But, he is too whimsical. A girl will cross his path and then finished. He will be gone."

"Well, Śrīla Prabhupāda," Paramahaṁsa said. "What shall we do? Śrutakīrti should come to India?"

There was about three seconds before Śrīla Prabhupāda replied. It was as if he was waiting for me to say something. He was giving me a choice. My ambivalence kept me silent. I broke into a cold sweat realizing that in spite of my apprehension, most likely, I would return to India with my beloved Śrīla Prabhupāda.

"Yes, he can come," Śrīla Prabhupāda said.

Again, Śrīla Prabhupāda, very thoughtfully and gently, gave me another opportunity to make a choice. My heart melted. My Guru Mahārāja wanted me to come with him! I felt my beloved Guru Mahārāja needed me. Śrīla Prabhupāda made me feel heroic, so, courageously, I agreed to come to India. That was all that was said during the remainder of the massage. Paramahaṁsa offered his obeisances and left the room. I continued to massage my loving spiritual master until he told me to stop.

Returning to the servants' quarters, I had a good laugh with my god-brothers. Deep down, I figured this would happen. After Śrīla Prabhupāda made his decision, I felt great relief. Something very special had taken place; Śrīla Prabhupāda expressed that he liked having me as a servant! It may seem silly, but it meant a great deal to me. Śrīla Prabhupāda never said much about what I did day after day. He was always, serving the Supreme Lord, and accepted all situations as the mercy of the Lord. On that day he said he wanted me to come with him. Śrīla Prabhupāda spent a lot of time training me and was pleased with the results. It was a good feeling. Śrīla Prabhupāda always let me know he appreciated what I did, but on that day, he confirmed it.

Sometimes devotees inquire about the nature of a first-class personal servant. In retrospect, I think a good servant invisibly assists by anticipating the needs of the master. He satisfies the master's needs without being asked. A good personal servant does not ask for much in return, does not need much encouragement or many problems solved. A good personal servant does not manufacture questions and only speaks when spoken to. A good personal servant does not try to manipulate the master. A good personal servant does his service and stays out of the way. A good personal servant only renders an opinion if asked. Any questions should be tendered with sincerity and submission. A good personal servant is influenced by the guru and seeks not to interfere in the guru's mission.

> *Gurudeva, it made me feel wonderful knowing you wanted me with you. Now, I feel only sadness because my desire was not strong enough to stay with you. Śrīla Prabhupāda, every day I lament and these feelings gnaw at me. I am the most unfortunate person on the planet. You never sent me away, yet I left you. Being short-sighted and foolish, I thought you would be with us forever in your vapu. Please forgive me for my ignorance. I pray that you allow me your darśana once again. I am in a hellish condition, alone and lost without seeing your smile and feeling the touch of your silky, soft lotus feet.*

150

"Daton is there?"

March 7, 1975 New York, New York

There were countless mornings when Śrīla Prabhupāda passed by me on the way to his bathroom.

"Daton is there?" he would ask.

When he said that I knew it meant I had forgotten to put his twig in the bathroom so he could brush his teeth. When I was with him, Śrīla Prabhupāda used a twig to brush his teeth, not a toothbrush. The best was from the neem tree. This was easy to get in India. You could go to a store and buy them by the bunch.

In New York City, however, it was not easy to get any kind of twig. Somehow, I always managed to get something. The important feature to look for was a wood that became bristly when chewed on the end.

As his personal servant I was supposed to ensure that wherever Śrīla Prabhupāda travelled, he would have the facility to follow his schedule. It was amazing. He did so much travelling, but maintained his regulation as if jet lag was only imaginary.

∽ 151 ∽

"My mother, she made very first-class puffed rice."

March 20, 1975 ISKCON Juhu Beach, Mumbai, India

One evening Śrīla Prabhupāda called me into his room.

"This evening you can make me some puffed rice and peanuts," he said. "It will fill me, but it is not heavy. What I ate last night made it difficult for me to get up and do my translating work. With puffed rice there is no indigestion."

I offered obeisances and left the room smiling and shaking my head. I did not say anything to him but I wanted to ask how it was so. He was always getting up around 1:00 am to do his translating work.

I left his room and began to prepare the puffed rice and peanuts. He told me to serve it with sliced cucumber and ginger root on the side. First, a chaunce was made and then the puffed rice and peanuts were put into the wok and cooked until all the grains were toasted. I brought it to his room along with hot milk that was sweetened with sugar. Shortly after he finished his meal he called me in and told me it was time for his massage.

For his evening massage he either sat up or lay on his back. While in his Juhu flat I sat on his bed beside him because the mosquito net surrounded his bed. The room was very peaceful.

The massage started out innocently enough. The weather was always warm in Juhu. Śrīla Prabhupāda was lying down in the bed. It was so warm there was not a need a sheet over him. I began massaging his legs. It was my favourite time of the day. No one ever walked into his room at this time, not his secretary or his Sanskrit editor. It was the time of day that was reserved for his personal servant. What a privilege to be there with him.

During this time it was difficult to imagine that he was spiritual master for the whole world. It was not difficult to see that he was completely aloof from such considerations. He exhibited it at every moment. He was detached from the results of everything going on in the society but his determination to serve Kṛṣṇa was unparalleled.

I had been massaging his legs for about ten minutes when without even opening his eyes, he began speaking to me. "My mother, she made very first-class puffed rice," he said as I massaged his legs. "She had a special wok. A very thick wok, so you could make it hot. You put sand in the wok and fire it very hot. You would throw the rice in and mix it up. It would puff in the hot sand. Then you sifted it so all the sand would fall through. When sifting, you had to be sure and clean it very well until all the sand was gone."

He stopped for a moment and then continued, "She would give it to us often. This puffed rice is very nice. She was a first-class cook. Everything she made, she made nicely. It was natural. My sister also, she was a very good cook. She learned from my mother. I also learned to cook, just by watching my mother.

In the Vedic society it was the woman's duty. All day the women were engaged in cooking. The husband and children, they took nice prasādam and everyone was happy. The woman's day was spent cooking and drying out foodstuffs. Storing and preparing all different kinds of foodstuffs and cooking down milk and making ghee. In this way they were all very expert. In the Vedic culture, whenever there was some gathering, all the women would get together. Whatever feast there was, everyone would bring something. In this way they could have big festivals."

Still absorbed in his childhood pastimes he continued, "When we were young there was no want of food. We always had plenty of food. In mango season we would have a bushel basket of mangos in the house. When we were children, we would run through the house, playing. We would grab mangoes as we were running through. All through the day we could eat mangos. It was not you had to think, 'Oh, can I have a mango?' Plenty of food was there. So life was simple. My father, he did not talk much, but he always provided enough food. There was no difficulty." I continued to massage his legs and feet as he lay there peacefully. I did not say a word. What could I say? I just felt bliss.

Śrīla Prabhupāda, being with you made clear to me the meaning of the term "causeless mercy" became clear to me. There was no amount of pious activities one could perform to be able to have your association, what to speak of being with you at such moments. To sit here and try to describe it impossible, still I am trying. They are eternal moments. Please allow me to serve you eternally.

∽ 152 ∽

"They are trying to blackmail me"

March 21, 1975 ISKCON Kolkata, India

What I found amazing was how proficient Śrīla Prabhupāda was, considering he had to deal with so many young, inexperienced disciples. Śrīla Prabhupāda was expert at everything. He spent almost two hours talking about the workings of a car engine to a world champion race car driver in his room at Bhaktivedanta Manor. And then there were his disciples; we were expert at wasting money, changing his directives, and mis-quoting his desires.

It was just a few weeks before the scheduled opening of Kṛṣṇa Balarāma Mandir. There had already been so many setbacks. Śrīla Prabhupāda disliked delays and he could not tolerate wasting money. Sometimes it seemed that he expected things to happen without spending any money. At least he expected that his disciples should acquire the required funds without approaching him for it. In 1975 most of the money for developing the temples in India came from the West.

On this day he was sitting in his room in Calcutta. In front of him were half a dozen of his senior disciples. A phone call came from Vṛndāvana. One devotee transmitted the message. He told Śrīla Prabhupāda that they were requesting still more funds to complete the construction and have the grand opening. Śrīla Prabhupāda did not want to hear another word. He pounded his fist on the desk and shouted, "My disciples, they are trying to blackmail me by not putting this festival on in time. They are simply taking so much money and now they want more money and this festival is not going to happen."

I sat in the corner of the room, numb. I always struggled in these situations feeling helpless, unable to do anything for my spiritual master. I could feel my heart beat almost as loud as his fist pounding the desk. He continued, still angered by our incompetence. "I do not care if it happens. I do not want anything more to do with it." He then ordered everyone out of the room.

Who could understand the mind of the pure devotee? I certainly could not. I just wanted to see Prabhupada relieved of the anxiety we caused him. He worked so hard for years to give us what we now have. I think only a few of his followers can appreciate how hard he worked to create this society and establish temples all over the world. Now, travelling around to temples, it is easy to take for granted the countless conveniences we have, the easy facility to perform our service.

A few minutes later Ramesvara and I went back into his room and offered obeisances. Śrīla Prabhupāda sat behind his desk, appearing very grave. Ramesvara said, "I can try to make some arrangement and get the money from America." His Divine Grace replied, "If you want to do it, do it, but I do not want to hear anything about it. I do not want anything to do with it anymore." Ramesvara went into the city and made a series of phone calls and arranged that the required money would be sent to Vṛndāvana.

Of course the opening went on according to schedule. When he arrived in Vṛndāvana Śrīla Prabhupāda took charge. It was essential that every thing was done in a first class manner. He wanted his western Vaisnavas to be taken seriously. He put his senior GBC men in charge of all departments. Jayatīrtha was the head pujari, Bhavānanda was in charge of seeing everything was properly clean. Another was in charge of accommodations. Śrīla Prabhupāda never missed a thing. He always knew what was going on, without leaving his room. Each day I must have walked miles, going back and forth to his quarters. He would call me in his room and say, "Go find Surabhi.... Go get Jayatīrtha... Bring me Bhavānanda."

He knew all our defects and our limited abilities. He

mercifully allowed us to engage in his devotional service, in the holiest of Dhāmas. He was, is and always will be our Ever will wisher.

Śrīla Prabhupāda, your mercy was not always easy to understand. You entrusted so much service to your leaders. With that increased service came increased responsibility. Sometimes, standing before the Deities, in a very grave voice you would tell us that we had to understand we were serving Kṛṣṇa. You said it with the full realization that you were serving Him. You also understood that we did not have that same realization.

You could help us in so many ways. But like you told me in New Dvārakā, "In the end we all have to fly our own aeroplane."

Māyā is very strong and the more service we perform the more we are tested. By following your instructions carefully, one is protected by you. You also said many times, 'By chanting sixteen rounds daily and following the regulative principles Mayācan not touch you'.

153

"Are they getting cows' milk to drink?"

March 24, 1975 ISKCON Mayapur, India

During my first trip to India with Śrīla Prabhupāda in 1972, I contracted jaundice, malaria, colitis and, of course, dysentery within the first two months. The effects continued to linger and my health was somewhat fragile. Śrīla Prabhupāda's tour of India lasted about two months and due to the mercy of my beloved Gurudeva, I stayed healthy the entire time.

I am embarrassed to speak about my activities, but I must because Śrīla Prabhupāda personally saw to it that I received all I required to stay healthy. I ate fresh fruits, yogurt and cheese made from cows' milk. In addition, I ate steamed vegetables and rice. For breakfast, I also ate oatmeal. Of course, I ate Śrīla Prabhupāda's remnants whenever the opportunity arose. At different times he asked me if I was getting fresh cows' milk and sufficient fruit to eat. He would tell the mataji arranging his cooking to see that I was getting what I wanted. Śrīla Prabhupāda nurtured me, not like a father, but more like a loving, concerned mother. His Divine Grace endeared himself to all he met. I was enchanted with his kindness. He cared so much about us all. He still does. I am ashamed to say that I never deserved such favour.

Śrīla Prabhupāda's wonderful quality of mercy was not for me alone. He loved all of his disciples. When he arrived at the Kṛṣṇa Balarāma Mandir for the temple opening he called the leaders into his room and asked, "How is everyone being taken care of? Are they getting cows' milk to drink? They must get cows' milk. They shouldn't be drinking buffalo milk."

I cannot emphasize enough how many times Śrīla Prabhupāda spoke about the importance of serving nice prasādam to the devotees. One of the first lessons Śrīla Prabhupāda taught me was that every visitor must take prasādam before leaving, even if it was one piece of fruit.

During the Utsava, the opening festival of Kṛṣṇa Balarāma Mandir, devotees stayed in various guest houses near the temple because there was not sufficient facility at the temple. Śrīla Prabhupāda told those in charge, "Be sure the devotees have nice facility. They should not be uncomfortable." It was delightful to watch a Kṛṣṇa Conscious person in action. Śrīla Prabhupāda was fully cognizant of everything going on around him and everything not going on around him. Śrīla Prabhupāda's loving attention influenced all the devotees to do their best.

Śrīla Prabhupāda made sure that everyone in his entourage received all necessities and had nice prasādam. He told the leaders to be sure that everyone under their care received the same. I never heard Śrīla Prabhupāda tell anyone they were eating too much. However, it was common for His Divine Grace to tell his disciples they were getting up too late, if they were not rising in time to receive the spiritual benefits of Brahma Muhūrta.

> *Śrīla Prabhupāda, you always set the perfect example by showing us how to act in all circumstances. When you were ill, you continued your service without complaining, but when I complained of illness you compassionately catered to my desires. I owe you my life and more. You accepted whatever Kṛṣṇa provided, but for your disciples you strived to provide them with the comforts to which they were accustomed. You were pleased to see your disciples happily engaged in devotional service and free from anxiety. Please bless me with the desire to treat my god-brothers and god-sisters with the same love and care you bestow upon them.*

154

"Just chant Hare Kṛṣṇa."

April 6, 1975 ISKCON Mayapur, India

Many joyful adventures took place daily while travelling with Śrīla Prabhupāda. So much sweetness flowed from the regulated activities of personally serving our glorious Gurudeva. Who could imagine anything more wonderful than cooking, massaging and tending to the needs of His Divine Grace, except for being present when His Divine Grace exhibited ecstatic symptoms? It was the rarest of treasures. These exceptional events invariably took place while Śrīla Prabhupāda sat on his vyāsāsana in the temple room during his lecture. The most widely known, example took place during the Māyāpur festival.

Hundreds of devotees were assembled in the temple room while Śrīla Prabhupāda spoke. Suddenly, he stopped and became silent with his eyes closed. Everyone in the room became still, not wanting to disturb him. A pin drop could be heard. We dared not breathe too loudly. This went on for some time. Hundreds of devotees were transfixed on His Divine Grace's internal state, each being transported by his rapture. Our minds were overwhelmed with anticipation. Śrīla Prabhupāda carried us all to another realm.

Suddenly, one sannyāsī seated near the vyāsāsana began loudly chanting, "Nama Om Visnu-padaya..." I felt jolted from a heavenly realm. Gradually, the reluctant devotees began to join in the kīrtan. Soon, Śrīla Prabhupāda regained his external consciousness and joined his disciples in the kīrtan.

After the kīrtan, there was disagreement amongst the devotees. Some criticized the sannyāsī saying, "How could you do that? Śrīla Prabhupāda was in ecstasy. You could see no one else was chanting. You should have stopped."

"Oh, I thought I would chant," he replied. "It seemed like the right thing to do." Brahmānanda Mahārāja was Śrīla Prabhupāda's secretary at the time. He was trying to mediate in this matter, but no one could arrive at a conclusion. So, he agreed to take the issue to Śrīla Prabhupāda. We went into Śrīla Prabhupāda's room in the afternoon.

"Śrīla Prabhupāda," Brahmānanda Mahārāja said. "Do you remember at the lecture when you stopped speaking and went into ecstasy?"

Before he could continue, Śrīla Prabhupāda responded in the sweetest voice, sounding a little embarrassed.

"I do not do that very often," Śrīla Prabhupāda said.

"No, Prabhupada," Brahmānanda said, understanding Śrīla Prabhupāda's humility. "But, when it does happen, what should we do? Should we just sit there, Śrīla Prabhupāda? Or should we chant japa?"

"Yes, just chant," he said. "Chant Hare Kṛṣṇa. Why are you making it such a big thing? What is to be done? Just chant Hare Kṛṣṇa. That is all right."

As always, there is no way to properly describe how Śrīla Prabhupāda spoke. When he said, "I do not do that very often," it was the most innocent voice I had ever heard. The gentle grace and humility he displayed was amazing. He was apologizing for exhibiting the symptoms of a pure devotee. It appeared that Śrīla Prabhupāda felt awkward exposing us to his personal moments with Kṛṣṇa.

One of the most wonderful things about His Divine Grace was the way he always made us feel that if we just followed the process of Kṛṣṇa Consciousness, then we could advance to the perfectional stage without difficulty. It seemed that he did not want to discourage us by showing how special he was, thus allowing us to consider Kṛṣṇa Consciousness too difficult for neophytes. He gave us hope. He made us feel that Kṛṣṇa Consciousness was for all of us. He always spoke of himself in the plural, "We are Kṛṣṇa's servant." Śrīla Prabhupāda included us. Just as he transported us on that special day in Mayapur, he continues to take us "Back to Home, Back to Godhead."

Śrīla Prabhupāda, thank you for a peek into your private moments. I would have loved the opportunity to sit at your feet in that temple room for hours. I can only imagine where you were. I take great pride in knowing that you are the topmost personality within these three worlds. Still, you spoke humbly about revealing a glimpse of your internal ecstasy. I beg for the chance to hear your sweet voice again and again.

155

"You may come back."

April 11, 1975 ISKCON Hyderabad, India

I can remember only a few times when it was difficult being in the same room with Śrīla Prabhupāda. Obviously, one could easily imagine yearning to be in His Divine Grace's presence twenty-four hours a day. However, the presence of others sometimes changed the atmosphere in Śrīla Prabhupāda's room.

One day, Devānanda Mahārāja came to visit Śrīla Prabhupāda. He had been initiated by Śrīla Prabhupāda and was now a sannyāsī. He had also been his personal servant for a short while in 1970. He asked to see Śrīla Prabhupāda and was allowed darśana even though he was no longer a member of ISKCON. Śrīla Prabhupāda was seated behind his desk and upon entering Śrīla Prabhupāda's room, Devānanda did not offer his obeisances. Brahmānanda Mahārāja and I were also in the room. Devānanda wore bright orange satin robes and his long hair and beard were matted. He had a very strange smile on his face. He began to speak to Śrīla Prabhupāda in such a peculiar way that I could not understand anything he was saying. He moved his hands about as if he were doing some type of mudra. It was too bizarre to watch. He appeared to have had too much intoxication.

Śrīla Prabhupāda tolerated his nonsense for a few minutes. There was no conversational exchange as Devānanda was incoherent. Finally, his all merciful spiritual master, Śrīla

Prabhupāda, said, "If you want to come back, you do like him." He pointed to Brahmānanda Mahārāja and continued. "You shave your head and face, put on a dhoti and then it's all right. You may come back."

Devānanda continued flailing his arms.

"No. This is not why I am here," Devānanda said.

He continued to move his body about while speaking nonsense. Śrīla Prabhupāda had enough.

"Get out!" Śrīla Prabhupāda shouted.

Devānanda started to shake with anger. Brahmānanda Mahārāja grabbed him and forcefully escorted him out of the room. Śrīla Prabhupāda was furious. Even though his anger was not directed toward me, I felt like I had been struck by lightning. Just being in the vicinity of Śrīla Prabhupāda's anger was frightening. If I could have disappeared, it was the time to do so. It is difficult to describe the spiritual potency generated by Śrīla Prabhupāda's rage. His total commitment to his disciples was obvious by this encounter.

This was one of the most difficult experiences I faced while being with Śrīla Prabhupāda. It was amazing how he tolerated Devānanda's bizarre behaviour. He offered to accept him back as his disciple even though Devānanda had strayed far from the Kṛṣṇa Conscious path and had obviously crossed the threshold of sanity into madness. When His Divine Grace saw he had no interest in accepting instruction, he mercifully sent him away before he could commit any more offences.

Śrīla Prabhupāda, I beg you to protect me from myself. I do not want to ever do anything that would cause you to become so angry. The greatest danger is to lose the shelter of your lotus feet. My senior god-brother was steeped in illusion, wallowing in the mode of ignorance and drowning in the quagmire of false ego. By your potency you had elevated him to a high post and by your grace he had achieved a grand standard of service as a sannyāsī. Even while you were with us, some of your disciples became under illusion, thinking they needed to go elsewhere to find perfection. The result of his deviation was apparently disastrous.

Perfection for me is to sit in my servants' quarters and wait for you to ring the bell. I pray to answer your call by running to your room, offering my obeisances and seeing your lotus feet as they peek out from under your desk.

*(Devānanda later died of self-induced starvation in a cave in South India).

156

"So, your mother is very beautiful?"

April 16, 1975 Kṛṣṇa Balarāma Mandir, Vṛndāvana, India

It was, if it is possible to say, a typical day in Vṛndāvana Dhāma. I was alone with Śrīla Prabhupāda in his new quarters giving him his midday massage. He was sitting cross-legged on his mat and I was sitting to his right massaging his legs with mustard oil. However, something was different and I felt uncomfortable. I even started feeling embarrassed because it seemed that he was staring at my feet as I was rubbing his legs. This went on for what seemed like a very long time. I did not dare ask him what he was looking at. What could I say?

Suddenly I was feeling very self-conscious in the presence of my spiritual master. This was unusual. Śrīla Prabhupāda was expert at helping one feel at ease around him, what to speak of me, who had been with him for so long. How could one perform personal service if they were feeling any other way?

I have often mentioned how he rarely spoke to me when I was massaging him, except for when I was behind him. It seemed to be a tradition we had developed. He would ask me interesting questions or tell me wonderful stories as I massaged his back. I am sure part of the reason was that I spent about an hour massaging his back each day and another half hour massaging the rest of his body.

I continued to rub his legs but now I tried to hide my feet under my gamcha because he was still staring at them. Finally it happened, still gazing at them he nonchalantly said, "So, your mother is very beautiful?"

Wow! What a question to ask your twenty three year old disciple, struggling to see every woman as his mother. 'Beautiful' was not a word we would think of using talking to Śrīla Prabhupāda about women. He was full of surprises. I gathered myself and tried to appreciate my wonderful spiritual father. He allowed me to enter into such intimate moments with him, on so many levels. I was unsure what his purpose was but I learned that the best thing was to be completely open to whatever he wanted. After all, he knew me completely. I did not even understand that I was not my body; consequently, I was not those feet either.

"Well, she is around fifty years old now." I responded. "But, yes, she is a very beautiful woman." I had done it. I put my foot out, the one he was looking at, and called a woman beautiful. My mother! He smiled and, looking at me, said, "Yes, I can tell, I was noticing your feet. Your feet are very nice. They say that means your mother is beautiful. I was checking. I wanted to see if it actually worked."

He then closed his eyes, satisfied with the conclusion and I continued to rub his soft, golden body. I did not feel self-conscious any more. I felt still closer to Śrīla Prabhupāda. Is there anyone more endearing? I have never met anyone that was. I can not imagine how beautiful Śrīla Prabhupāda's mother must have been.

> *Śrīla Prabhupāda your lotus feet are sought after by great souls all over the three worlds. Followers want to take shelter of those feet, birth after birth. I beg that you give me darśana of your feet eternally. Please let me massage them again and again.*
>
> *Śrīla Prabhupāda was always very personal with his disciples. He cared for us, looked out for us and was interested in us.*

157

"Just see, 45 minutes... finished"

April 17, 1975 Kṛṣṇa Balarāma Mandir, Vṛndāvana, India

Particularly in Vṛndāvana, Śrīla Prabhupāda often boasted to guests about how his servant could cook lunch so quickly.

"Śrutakīrti," he said. "He can cook my entire lunch - rice, dahl, chapatis, and three or four subjis in just forty-five minutes." Looking at me, he then said, "Is it not?"

"Yes, Śrīla Prabhupāda," I said nodding. "And I give you massage while the cooking is going on."

Now, widening his eyes he said, "Just see, forty-five minutes and all bodily maintenance business . . . finished. This is Kṛṣṇa Consciousness. We minimize bodily maintenance as much as possible, so we have more time for devotional service."

Śrīla Prabhupāda's humility was so endearing. He was always engaged in serving Kṛṣṇa and required so little to be done for him. During the morning massage he would often have his secretary read mail to him and it was also when his

Sanskrit editor would come in and ask questions. He utilized every minute in Kṛṣṇa's service. He slept an average of three to four hours a day. While I was with him sometimes he would look at me when he was about to take rest and say, "Now I am going to waste my time." I would offer my obeisances and leave the room, shaking my head, knowing he was the dear most servant of his spiritual master.

158

"This is first class servant."

April 18, 1975 Kṛṣṇa Balarāma Mandir, Vṛndāvana, India

Another example demonstrating Śrīla Prabhupāda's efficiency with minimal effort took place in the privacy of his quarters. Śrīla Prabhupāda instructed me without saying a single word. While sitting in his room, he looked up at the ceiling fans. If they were on, it meant I should turn them off. If they were off, it meant I was to turn them on. Other times, he looked at the French doors. If the curtains were open, I closed them. If they were closed, I opened them.

"This is the first-class servant," Śrīla Prabhupāda said. "He does his service without being asked. The second-class servant, you ask him and he does it. The third-class servant, you ask him and he does it begrudgingly or doesn't do it at all."

I pray to hear the shuffling of his feet, see his glances, hear his words and get the opportunity to serve him life after life. Śrīla Prabhupāda is Ācārya.

Jai Śrīla Prabhupāda!

159

"Ok, then you can take mine."

April 19, 1975 Kṛṣṇa Balarāma Mandir, Vṛndāvana, India

Śrīla Prabhupāda was always very kind to his disciples. Sometimes when he received new clothes, he fulfilled our desires by distributing articles of prasādam clothing he had worn. Śrīla Prabhupāda did not accumulate many belongings because he was always giving things to his disciples. One item that was particularly covetable was Śrīla Prabhupāda's well-worn gray, woolen chaddar. I meditated on this chaddar and imagined Śrīla Prabhupāda had worn it during his transatlantic voyage on the Jaladuta. I imagined he had worn it for years and years. This chaddar's magical value increased each time Śrīla Prabhupāda wore it. For years, I saw His Divine Grace wear it to warmly wrap his perfect form on morning walks. This chaddar had water spots sprinkled in a few places. It was the chaddar Śrīla Prabhupāda showed me how to fold during my first morning walk as his personal servant in Dallas.

Two years later in Mayapur, a group of sannyāsīs put their money together and bought a beautiful pashmina chaddar for Śrīla Prabhupāda. It cost several thousand rupees. It was brown and decorated with a very fancy border. It had been made in an area known for its fine cashmere. I think it was called pashmina wool, well known for its soft, thin, yet warm quality. It was said that a full-sized chaddar made of this pashmina could be pulled through a small ring to demonstrate its lightweight texture. The wool came from the chin of goats that lived on the steepest peaks of the Himalayan Mountains.

With great pride, the group of sannyāsīs presented the new chaddar to Śrīla Prabhupāda in his sitting room. One sannyāsī had already decided that when Śrīla Prabhupāda accepted it and gave away his old chaddar, he would be the fortunate one to keep it.

Śrīla Prabhupāda smiled as he received the gift.

"When I was young, I was given one of these every year," Śrīla Prabhupāda said. "One gentleman, one of my father's friends, would go back and forth to Kashmir. He would deal in these chaddars. Every year I was getting one."

Śrīla Prabhupāda accepted the chaddar, but never offered his old one to any of the sannyāsīs present. His disciples left the room with a little more understanding of their spiritual master's position. Śrīla Prabhupāda did not wear the new chaddar very often. He continued wearing the well-worn gray chaddar on his morning walks.

One week later Śrīla Prabhupāda was at the Kṛṣṇa Balarāma Mandir. My desire for Śrīla Prabhupāda's gray chaddar increased because everyone else wanted it as well. I was a householder with a few hundred rupees in my pocket, so I decided to buy Śrīla Prabhupāda a gray chaddar just like the one he had. I felt confident that if I gave him an exact replica of his old chaddar, he would immediately give me his blessed old one. Since I never left my servants' quarters, I arranged for a devotee to go to Delhi to purchase one. He soon returned with a new, gray, Lohi-brand chaddar. It cost me one hundred and fifty rupees which was about seven dollars at that time.

The next afternoon, aware of my selfish motives, I sheepishly walked into Śrīla Prabhupāda's room with this conditional gift neatly tucked into my hand. I offered my obeisances. My Guru Mahārāja was sitting quietly behind his desk, looking as effulgent as ever.

"Śrīla Prabhupāda," I said. "I just bought this chaddar for myself, but I decided that you should have it because it is new. Your chaddar is so old."

Śrīla Prabhupāda, as always, knew my childish mind. He looked right through me and said, "You need a chaddar?"

"Well, yes. I need one," I replied.

"So, you keep it," he said. "That's all right."

Śrīla Prabhupāda was making it difficult for me. He did not allow me an ounce of deception.

"But Śrīla Prabhupāda," I said, squirming. "I'd really be happy if you would take this new chaddar. I would rather you have it. You are my spiritual master."

Śrīla Prabhupāda enjoyed my predicament.

"No, that's all right," he said. "Mine is sufficient. I do not require a new one."

I understood he was not allowing me a thread of duplicity. Śrīla Prabhupāda, knowing my heart, toyed with me. I surrendered and finally came clean.

"Actually, Śrīla Prabhupāda, I would much rather have your chaddar than this new one. Yours is prasādam. I want yours," I admitted.

Śrīla Prabhupāda smiled with great pleasure.

"Okay, then you can take mine," he said. "I will take the new one."

I placed the new chaddar on his desk and offered my obeisances. The truth really does set one free. Feeling quite blissful and very relieved, I took Śrīla Prabhupāda's old chaddar and triumphantly floated back to my room.

Śrīla Prabhupāda, I still have your chaddar. Once you instructed, "When the spiritual master leaves the planet all of his paraphernalia is worshipable. Until that time, everything can be used by the disciple, except for his shoes."

Your chaddar is being used on your murti. Your life size form is seated in my family's temple room. In the winter you wear it as you did for so many years travelling around the globe. When I see it on you, I remember all of the generosity you bestowed upon me. You gave me your blessings in exchange for the insignificant service I performed. Whenever I wear your chaddar, I knew māyā could not touch me. Your mercy shields me. Now I know I must wear your instructions as my protective cover by chanting sixteen rounds and following the four regulative principles. I want to be with you always and pray I may eternally serve your instructions.

160

"My job is to instruct."

April 22, 1975 Kṛṣṇa Balarāma Mandir, Vṛndāvana, India

During this two-week visit at Kṛṣṇa Balarāma Mandir, everyone was busy preparing for the opening of the temple. Śrīla Prabhupāda took daily walks through the temple compound and advised Surabhi Mahārāja, the architect and engineer, on necessary corrections. Śrīla Prabhupāda's quarters were also being finished, although they were quite liveable. As the glorious day approached, Surabhi Mahārāja was getting very little sleep. He was constantly running around supervising hundreds of carpenters and masons working on the premises.

One day Śrīla Prabhupāda called for me. I entered his room and offered my obeisances. He was upset.

"They have used a plastic toilet seat in the bathroom and already it has broken," he said. "Call Surabhi."

I walked around the property and told Surabhi about the situation. Together we hurried back to Śrīla Prabhupāda's quarters.

"The toilet seat is already broken," Śrīla Prabhupāda told Surabhi. "I need a new one. Otherwise, how can I sit down? I am an old man. I have to sit down."

"Yes, Śrīla Prabhupāda," Surabhi said. "I will arrange it."

Two days passed, but there was no change in Śrīla Prabhupāda's bathroom. Śrīla Prabhupāda called for me and said, "Where is my toilet seat, call Surabhi."

Again, I found Surabhi and went with him to see Śrīla Prabhupāda.

"Where is my toilet seat?" Śrīla Prabhupāda inquired sharply.

"Śrīla Prabhupāda," Surabhi said. "They are looking for one in town today. They could not find one in Vṛndāvana, so today they are going to Mathura."

"No! I do not want one of these plastic seats," Śrīla Prabhupāda said. "They are cheap and will break again. Have one of the carpenters carve one from wood. I want it today."

Surabhi called one of the workers.

"Guru Mahārāja wants a toilet seat carved from wood," he explained. "You make him a very nice seat."

The Brijbasi carpenter was excited for the opportunity to perform personal service for Kṛṣṇa's pure devotee. Naturally, things did not go as planned. Surabhi was extremely busy and did not take the time to supervise the carving of this important seat. The mistris were expert, but incredibly slow, as everything was done by hand with the simplest of tools. That afternoon Śrīla Prabhupāda called for me.

"Where is my toilet seat?" he asked.

"I will find out Śrīla Prabhupāda," I said.

I left his room in a hurry not wanting to be on the receiving end of Śrīla Prabhupāda's annoyance. Within minutes we were prostrating ourselves in His Divine Grace's room.

"I'm sorry, Śrīla Prabhupāda," Surabhi said. "I can't keep up with all of the people. I told him to have it ready. I thought you would have it installed by now."

"I want this seat now," Śrīla Prabhupāda said. "It has to be here. It must be finished."

We both offered our obeisances and hastily left the room. Overwhelmed with stress, my wounded false ego silently made excuses for not having fulfilled the expectation of His Divine Grace. Surabhi and I rushed to the mistri.

"You must get this seat finished or you are fired," Surabhi shouted. "You must finish it immediately."

I was amazed when I saw the simple tool being used to carve this seat from a piece of wood.

"Does Guru Mahārāja want designs carved into the seat?" the man calmly asked.

"Just get the seat finished," Surabhi said rolling his eyes. "Now!"

Finally, the mistri brought the seat into Śrīla Prabhupāda's quarters and offered his obeisances. He went into the bathroom and installed the hand-carved teakwood seat. The mistri was thrilled to have the chance to enter Śrīla Prabhupāda's sanctified rooms. He understood he was fortunate to be doing important personal service for the guru. Whatever important service we appeared to be doing, Śrīla Prabhupāda always reminded us that our real business was to serve our Guru Mahārāja. We may be empowered to do some important project, but our real position is the servant. By remaining humble, we are guaranteed the continuation of eternal devotional service to our beloved spiritual master.

After everyone left, Śrīla Prabhupāda said, "Rub some mustard seed oil into the seat until it stops absorbing."

I happily complied with his instructions, relieved that the incident was coming to a close. After oiling the seat, I informed Śrīla Prabhupāda that his bathroom was ready for use. Later, Śrīla Prabhupāda entered the bathroom.

"It is all right," he said nodding, as he came out of his bathroom.

Śrīla Prabhupāda applied a strict standard of Kṛṣṇa Consciousness in Vraja Dhāma. He expected his resident disciples to live exemplary lives. This was apparent in every aspect of life at Kṛṣṇa Balarāma Mandir. Being inferior, we struggled to comprehend the importance of his superior vision. Therefore, His Divine Grace never recommended ordinary or mundane residence in Vṛndāvana. If devotees could not live up to the highest standards of Kṛṣṇa Consciousness, then they had no business living in Vraja Dhāma. Since life was like a razor's edge in this holiest of Dhāmas, Śrīla Prabhupāda vigilantly supervised our devotional practice.

I was always in awe of Surabhi. Daily, Śrīla Prabhupāda called him into his room and chastised him about different aspects of the construction. The pressure on Surabhi was immense as the opening of the temple approached. Śrīla Prabhupāda wanted everything perfectly executed and it was Surabhi's service to see that His Divine Grace's desires were fulfilled. One day while walking, Śrīla Prabhupāda looked at the Deity rooms saying, "Why aren't the doors up yet?"

"I'm trying, Śrīla Prabhupāda," Surabhi said. "But, there is so much to be done. It is difficult."

"Never mind," Śrīla Prabhupāda responded. "You have to get it done. These men, they are all cheating you. Do not let them cheat you. You have to be on top of things and make sure everything gets done."

This continued for a week as Śrīla Prabhupāda would ask Surabhi, "Why aren't the Deity doors on yet? Why aren't the front gates on?"

Surabhi would reply that he was working on it. Finally, by Kṛṣṇa's mercy, everything started to come together during the last few days before the opening of the temple. On one morning walk with Śrīla Prabhupāda through the temple compound the devotees were admiring how magnificent the temple looked.

"Surabhi has done a very good job, Śrīla Prabhupāda," one disciple said. "He has worked very hard. His work is excellent."

"Yes, everyone is saying, 'Surabhi has done a very nice job', but me," Śrīla Prabhupāda said laughing. "I am simply criticizing, saying, 'Why are you doing such a slow job? Why are you working so badly?' Everyone is complimenting him, but me. My job is to instruct him. Therefore, all the time I am criticizing him. That is my duty. I am his spiritual master. Therefore, I must guide."

I am not sure, but I think I noticed Surabhi Mahārāja take his first breath in two weeks.

Śrīla Prabhupāda, I stand in awe when I see the service my god-brothers and god-sisters have done for you over the past thirty years. My service has been insignificant. I was not even able to accept your chastisement without brooding. You were always gentle with me, realizing how fragile my faith was. I pray to develop unflinching faith in your order so I may properly serve your lotus feet regardless of how you reciprocate with me. Allow me to be present for your pastimes and never again stray from your lotus feet.

161

"The difficulty is none of my disciples believe ..."

May 3, 1975 ISKCON Delhi, India

Being with Śrīla Prabhupāda was always stimulating. I especially enjoyed when he gave us a glimpse of his life before coming to America. It was a wonderful expression of his love for us. Śrīla Prabhupāda also took great pleasure in describing different aspects of his life with his disciples. One afternoon he began describing his life as a sannyāsī to Paramahaṁsa and me.

"While I was living in Vṛndāvana," he said. "Sometimes I would go to Delhi for a few days to make arrangements with my publisher. I would stay in one room during these periods. During the winter, it was so cold. I would have to crack a thin layer of ice with my lota in my bucket of bath water. Then I would bathe with that water."

At Bhaktivedanta Manor, a few ladies came to visit Śrīla Prabhupāda on a number of occasions. They knew His Divine Grace was a very saintly person. They were hoping that he could help them solve their predicament. They described to Śrīla Prabhupāda how poltergeists had inhabited their flat. They had tried many things to rid their home of the pesky spirits but nothing worked. They informed Śrīla Prabhupāda that different items were being broken while being tossed around the rooms. One of the women asked Śrīla Prabhupāda if there was any particular prayer or mantra they could chant to force the entities to leave the premises forever. It was no surprise to his disciples when Śrīla Prabhupāda advised them to chant the Mahā-mantra. He sweetly told us of his own experience with the "supernatural." He described that when he was a grihasta, he bought a large haunted house in Kolkata for a very good price.

"No one would buy the place," he said smiling. "It was a very nice, big house, but because it was haunted, everyone was afraid. So, I bought it and lived there. Sometimes, I remember sitting down and you could see things moving about in the house. I would sit in my chair and chant 'Hare Kṛṣṇa.' One time, one of my servants came up to me and said, 'Swamiji, how can you stay here with these ghosts?' I told him there was nothing to worry about. Just chant Hare Kṛṣṇa. So, I was living there and so many things would go on, but nothing frightened me."

One day in the spring of 1973, Śrīla Prabhupāda was in his room in New Dvārakā. He was walking around chanting japa. I was fortunate to be sitting on the floor watching him. Suddenly, he looked at me and in a very serious tone said, "The difficulty is that none of my disciples believe Kṛṣṇa is there. Actually, no one has any faith that Kṛṣṇa exists."

I sat motionless as Śrīla Prabhupāda continued to chant japa. My faith was microscopic, at best. I was in illusion, but not enough to disagree with his profound words. Besides, I could not think of anything to say. Śrīla Prabhupāda had already said it all.

Śrīla Prabhupāda, my faith is very weak and my ghost-like senses powerfully haunt me. Please purge my soul of these demons. Let me hear the holy name from your courageous lotus lips. Please guide me in your service. I do not know Kṛṣṇa, but I have experienced the shelter of your stalwart lotus feet. I have complete faith that you lovingly experience Kṛṣṇa at every moment. If I hang onto your fearless lotus feet, by your mercy, I will come to serve the Lord. Your Kṛṣṇa Consciousness was evident in every word you spoke, every glance you gave and every move you took. Please bless this misguided soul and mercifully glance upon me once again. Without hearing you chant the Holy Names, I am lost and full of fear.

162

Lotus feet on Transcendental World Airways

May 6, 1975 Flying TWA to Perth, Australia

Wherever the pure devotee resides is Vaikuṇṭha and he distributes his causeless mercy to the conditioned souls whether they like it or not. While travelling by plane, Śrīla Prabhupāda always kept me smiling because he never changed his habits. In the presence of materialistic persons these activities were sometimes unconventional.

Śrīla Prabhupāda liked to look out the window during takeoffs and landings. He especially enjoyed looking out the window upon landing. If we took a long evening flight, Śrīla Prabhupāda's secretary and I would leave our seats next to Śrīla Prabhupāda so he could lie down and rest. On this particular occasion, Śrīla Prabhupāda's effulgent body was stretched across the seats. His head lay peacefully on a pillow by the window. He appeared completely relaxed, something I still do not know how to do on a plane. His feet went under the armrest reaching about 6 inches into the aisle. They looked so beautiful, with or without saffron socks covering them. On this particular evening his lotus feet were snugly covered. As he rested for about an hour, the passengers walked up and down the aisle brushing against his beautiful lotus feet. Sometimes they accidentally hit them and he would move slightly, but he never pulled in his feet. He left them there benedicting everyone fortunate enough to pass by.

Śrīla Prabhupāda's entourage watched from the next row and wondered what these people had done to be given such an opportunity. Perhaps, Śrīla Prabhupāda forcibly benedicted them, whether they liked it or not.

Thank you, Śrīla Prabhupāda, for allowing me to witness one of the countless ways the pure devotee benedicts those who come in contact with him. Please force your benedictions upon me again and again as you have compassionately done so many times in the past.

163

"You must accept!"

May 8, 1975 Perth, Australia

While in Perth Śrīla Prabhupāda engaged his disciples in many lively conversations during the morning walks. Around this time he had been translating the Fifth Canto of *Śrīmad-Bhāgavatam* regarding the structure of the Universe and the movements of the planets. Śrīla Prabhupāda would have mock debates. His disciples would pose as materialistic scientists. This would always be very exciting. I would sometimes get involved but Paramahaṁsa Swami took much more pleasure in it.

Sometimes he would call us into his room and discuss the Vedic cosmology. One day he told us the different planetary orbits were all independent and that the so-called law of gravity was not mentioned in the Vedic literature. Once Paramahaṁsa Swami asked Śrīla Prabhupāda, "How is it that the sun is always shining somewhere on the earth planet if it is going behind Sumeru Mountain? Wouldn't it be dark on the entire planet?" Śrīla Prabhupāda was silent for a moment and then replied, "We are not so interested in these details. The *Śrīmad-Bhāgavatam* is just a very short summary to give some idea of the creation of the Lord but it is not scientific. We are not interested in science. We are interested in developing love of God."

It was evident to us that Śrīla Prabhupāda did not want us to become sidetracked from that goal he worked non-stop to teach us. He continued, "If this were to be scientific it would take volumes to explore how the creation is done. But this was not Śukadeva Gosvāmī's purpose in speaking, to explain very scientifically the creation. He just wants us to understand, 'Kṛṣṇa has created everything. Develop love of Kṛṣṇa.' That is all. If you can't understand it, you accept it because it is there in the scriptures. We do not bother our minds trying to understand how it could be like this. It seems very difficult. We are not concerned. We just want to develop love of God. Actually, I am not giving any more information, simply what is there. I am not an astronomer, so I may not understand all the details. Those details are given in another part of the Vedas. ŚukadevaGosvāmī is giving some basic summary ideas of the universal operation."

During his visit to Perth, Śrīla Prabhupāda would often take his massage by the swimming pool. When it was very warm he would take his bath in the pool. It was heart warming watching him walk down the pool steps and begin splashing water over his body. However, one day in particular was difficult for me. In the company of my god-brothers I was comfortable discussing topics of universal proportion with Śrīla Prabhupāda but I never did it while I was alone with him. I was fearful due to my lack of understanding on the subject matter. One morning just before noon, during his massage, I had no alternative. I remember the day clearly.

I was sitting behind Śrīla Prabhupāda, massaging his back with mustard oil. If his massage lasted for two hours it is likely that one hour of it was massaging his back. So, it was not uncommon that when he spoke to me I was massaging his back. However, it ALWAYS seemed like I was massaging his back when he asked me a question. It started out innocently enough. I was rubbing his back vigorously and he inquired, "So, we have to accept the śāstra. Śāstra is our mother. If you want to know who your father is, you have to know from your mother. Is that right?" I immediately agreed.

Then he asked, "What do the scientists say about that?" I was alone and Śrīla Prabhupāda was engaging me in a mock debate. I thought for a moment, not nearly long enough, and responded. "Well Prabhupada, the mother is there, but you have to accept that she is telling you the truth when she says that this person is your father." Much to my surprise Śrīla Prabhupāda became very upset with me. He shouted, "If you do not accept that is the truth, then what are you doing here? If you do not accept the śāstra then why are you here?" I had no idea what I did wrong. I thought I was playing the devil's advocate. I quickly confirmed saying, "I accept Prabhupada!" He emphatically said, "Yes, you must accept! If you do not accept you have no business here. This Kṛṣṇa Consciousness is there. We must have faith. If there is no faith, then what are you doing here?"

I continued to massage his back. My mind was reeling. I did not know what to think. Did I have doubts? I did not think so. I thought I was role-playing and considered my response to be reasonable. I could only respond, "Yes, Prabhupada." I tried to concentrate on my service knowing how much he liked me to use all my strength while massaging his back. I put my energy into rubbing as firmly as I could. A few minutes went by, although it seemed much longer.

Śrīla Prabhupāda again asked, "So, what do they say? Mother is there; only the mother can tell you who is your father. What would they say about that?"

I continued massaging but wished it was someone else doing it. I did not know what to say. I was already in shock but Śrīla Prabhupāda seemed to be as calm as ever and put me at ease. I had lost all composure and had another lapse of reason. Being 'fool number one' I had learned nothing. He wanted a response and I gave the same reckless one trying to be sure it sounded like it was coming from the materialist.

Again I responded, "They would say, that even the mother may know, we have to be sure the mother is telling the truth."

It was definitely the incorrect response. He was more emphatic then previously. "It must be the truth," he said with conviction. "Why you do not accept the truth?"

The only thing that kept me conscious was that I did not have to look directly into his eyes. I was still behind him, rubbing his back with oil. I responded in a confused, quiet tone, "I accept, Prabhupada." He said, "Yes, you must accept. "He waited a few moments and added, "I am not going to say anything more. I do not want to speak about this subject."

The rest of the massage went on quietly. I did not dare try to explain that I was trying to play the role of a mundane scientist who wants proof of everything. At least I thought I was. I retreated to my role as servant who spoke only when spoken to. As I massaged I began to ask myself, "Did I have such doubts?" Whatever I thought I was doing, Śrīla Prabhupāda was giving me an instruction. One that I could never forget.

> *Śrīla Prabhupāda, thirty years have gone by since that day by the pool when you exposed my lack of faith. I see much clearer now. I have no faith in this material civilization or their science. By your mercy all that you have told us about this modern society is more apparent. Everyone is gliding quickly to hell as Kali Yuga advances rapidly due to the greed of the demoniac. Because of the sinful activities of the western civilization suffering is increasing. You would sometimes mock the scientist saying, "They know everything except who they are." You came to this hellish place to teach us that Kṛṣṇa is God and we are His eternal servants. We can only know this fact through the śāstra, the Śrīmad-Bhāgavatam, and by serving you, Kṛṣṇa's pure devotee. You are that person Bhāgavata who dispels all doubts and myths by your Vani and Vapu. By following the principles of devotional service and serving you one gets the unflinching faith in Kṛṣṇa and His pure devotees that you always exhibited to me.*

164

"You will not leave, will you?"

May 9, 1975 Perth, Australia

During his visit to the temples in Australia Śrīla Prabhupāda often spoke about the positions of the planets within the solar system. He described the differences in calculation between the astronomers and those mentioned in *Śrīmad-Bhāgavatam*. One difference he focused on was the modern scientist version that the moon is nearer to the earth than the sun. He said, "Actually the moon was far, far away and could not be approached by a so-called moon expedition". In the car while going for his morning walk Śrīla Prabhupāda spoke more about Vedic cosmology. He gave very elaborate details of the dimensions of the universe.

"They have not gone to the moon," he said. "The whole diameter is pancasata koti yojana. One yojana equals eight miles, and one koti is ten million. So, pancasata, fifty by ten million by eight. That's 4,000,000,000 miles."

Śrīla Prabhupāda exited the car and within minutes continued the discussion as he walked in the park. Śrīla Prabhupāda said with full conviction, "The moon is far, far away. Their conclusion is wrong. They are going to the wrong planet. They are bluffing only. I am repeatedly saying that they have never gone. Simply bluff!"

It was so enlivening for me to see Śrīla Prabhupāda's firm faith and conviction in the words from *Śrīmad-Bhāgavatam*. He did not need to hear from any other source. Years earlier he was convinced and told us it was impossible to go to the moon planet without proper qualification. Now, while translating for us, he was giving us the same opportunity to understand from the Supreme Lord and from His pure devotees what the Absolute Truth was and what speculation was.

One evening, after days of discussion about the moon planet and other topics on the cosmology of the Universe, I was massaging Śrīla Prabhupāda's legs and feet while he laid in bed. Most of the time when I massaged him in the evening, he would lay quietly while I rubbed his feet and kneaded his legs gently. In the small room I felt very peaceful as I performed my service. Suddenly Śrīla Prabhupāda looked at me and asked, "So, you have heard me speak so many things. Do you believe what I say, that these scientists, they have not gone to the moon? Do you accept it...do you understand? You will not leave, will you?"

I was surprised but comforted by his question. He was concerned for my spiritual well being and did not want doubts to drive me away from his lotus feet. I said with a smile, "Yes, Prabhupada. It's all right." With compassion he said, "Yes! I want that you understand. I once had a servant, Purushottama. When I said that 'we did not go to the moon' he became very outraged and left. So, you are all right? You can accept it?"

I felt completely sheltered by His Divine Grace. His genuine concern for me increased my love for him and also increased my faith in every word he said. I looked at him as I rubbed his exquisite, golden, lotus feet and assured him saying, "Yes, Prabhupada. It's all right. I believe you and I believe we did not go to the moon." He continued to look at me with a smile and relief in his voice said, "That's good, because I do not want you to leave like our Purushottama"

Śrīla Prabhupāda, until today I could never understand why you were so concerned when you asked me about accepting the śāstra as my authority only a day earlier. I finally comprehend your compassion a little more. You were protecting me as you always have, doing everything possible to keep me from leaving you. You have continually done it to this day. The most amazing thing happened as I had this realization. As I sat in the flat in Rishikesh writing this and realizing your potency and purity, the entire building started to shudder as if in agreement with my thoughts. I stopped writing as the shaking continued for over a minute. Items in the room gently moved to and fro as I contemplated my new insights.

Today is October 8, 2005 and it turned out the tremors were from an earthquake in Pakistan. All over the world calamities are increasing, just as you said they would thirty years earlier. I believe all that you said and need your protection. It has taken an earthquake to bring me to my senses and better understand your instructions. Thank you Śrīla Prabhupāda!

165

"Is a devotee simple or crooked?"

May 10, 1975 Perth, Australia

A Morning Walk

Going on a morning walk with Śrīla Prabhupāda was never dull. Sometimes His Divine Grace would not say a word, chanting japa throughout the walk. This disappointed some disciples who did not often get such an opportunity. They sometimes asked a question, hoping that Śrīla Prabhupāda would engage in a debate or conversation, but this was risky business. Śrīla Prabhupāda was never subject to our whims. Sometimes he gave a short response to such questions and continued to walk in silence.

One day, however, Śrīla Prabhupāda was in a talkative, humorous mood.

"Is a devotee simple or crooked?" he asked smiling.

"He is simple, Śrīla Prabhupāda," one disciple answered.

"Are you sure? Is he simple or crooked?" He again asked with a rascal-like gleam in his eye.

"Yes, a devotee is simple!" the disciple enthusiastically responded, not realizing he had fallen for a trick question.

Śrīla Prabhupāda then sprang the unexpected punch line.

"Actually, the devotee is crooked!" Everyone stood there with their mouths gaping.

"Take me for example," Śrīla Prabhupāda explained. "I came to your country and everyone was eating meat, taking intoxication, and doing so much nonsense. I tricked everyone. I've tricked all of you into becoming Kṛṣṇa Conscious. So, in that sense the devotee must be crooked, because he must be able to trick. Just like I have tricked everyone. No one wanted Kṛṣṇa Consciousness, but I have tricked you."

he demonstrated the art of tricking us.

Śrīla Prabhupāda, human society without Kṛṣṇa Consciousness is a society of cheaters and the cheated. Almost everyone is doing both. You explained that your trick was telling us we could just 'Chant Hare Kṛṣṇa'. The tricky part that you did not tell us was we had to surrender our lives to you. There is nothing sweeter for us then to give our lives to you in service. One who lives their life completely dependent on the mercy of the Lord is considered most fortunate. I am completely dependent on your mercy. Thank you for tricking me.

৩ 166 ৩

"The devotee is proud to be the servant of Kṛṣṇa."

May 12, 1975 Perth, Australia

A receptive devotee could learn so many things just by sitting quietly and watching Śrīla Prabhupāda. Once, Śrīla Prabhupāda sat up very straight in his garden in New Dvārakā and said, "The devotee is proud to be the servant of Kṛṣṇa." This was a very important lesson for me because balancing humility with the pride of being Kṛṣṇa's servant was a bit confusing.

I was somewhat timid in the execution of my service when it involved requesting help or some service from people outside the devotee community. I mistook devotional humility for mundane bodily apprehension. Instead of being proud of being Kṛṣṇa's servant and Śrīla Prabhupāda's servant, I was apologetic. I denied pride, not realizing that I was misdirected. Deluded, I thought I needed to exude humility.

Śrīla Prabhupāda adorably personified pride in being Kṛṣṇa's servant. Sometimes, when he returned to his sitting room after a morning programme, he turned to me and said smiling, "Did your record the lecture today?"

"Yes, Śrīla Prabhupāda," I said.

"Play it back," he instructed. "I want to hear it."

On other occasions he would be sitting behind his desk in his room and when his disciples entered the room he would smile and ask, "So, the lecture was all right today?" Of course, his disciples always responded enthusiastically, cherishing every word that flowed from the lotus lips of their spiritual master. The devotees recognized special messages within some of his lectures, and even the dullest of living entities could understand the one point Śrīla Prabhupāda continuously and clearly drove home.

It appeared that Śrīla Prabhupāda took special pride in

certain lectures. He seemed to immensely enjoy smashing the Mayavadi philosophy. He proudly presented Kṛṣṇa to everyone, defeating their bogus arguments. He was very proud that Kṛṣṇa was his Lord and Master.

Śrīla Prabhupāda also expressed pride in his disciples. One beautiful afternoon in July of 1973, Śrīla Prabhupāda sat on the lawn at Bhaktivedanta Manor with some of his disciples and Indian guests. I was reading *Lord Caitanya in Five Features*, an early and partial printing of *Śrī Caitanya-caritāmṛta*. I was doing my best to pronounce the Bengali by using the transliteration. Much to my surprise, after reading for about ten minutes, Śrīla Prabhupāda said, "Just see how nicely he pronounces the Bengali. Although he has never read Bengali in his whole life, with this method, he can pronounce it very nicely."

Many times Śrīla Prabhupāda praised his western disciples before the Indian community. He accomplished many things by doing this. He encouraged his disciples to further their progress in Kṛṣṇa Consciousness. He encouraged the Indian community to take more seriously that which was their birthright. He showed everyone that by the mercy of guru and Gaurāṅga and the potency of the Holy Name even mleccha and yavanas could advance in spiritual life. Śrīla Prabhupāda always credited his Guru Mahārāja and the potency of chanting the Lord's holy name for all that he accomplished. Once in his quarters in New Dvārakā, Śrīla Prabhupāda said to me, "You western boys and girls have taken so much intoxication. If not for the chanting of the Mahā-mantra, you would not be able to accomplish anything."

In May of 1975 in Perth, Australia, Śrīla Prabhupāda was having a conversation with a professor. Śrīla Prabhupāda spoke very strongly about different classes of human beings. Paramahaṁsa Mahārāja and I were sitting in the room relishing our spiritual master expressing to the fairly receptive gentleman how almost everyone was a fourth-class man.

"You also are a fourth-class man," he told the professor.

"Well, what can I do?" the professor responded.

"You must become a pure devotee like them!" Śrīla Prabhupāda energetically said.

As he finished the sentence, he pointed to Paramahaṁsa and me as examples of pure devotees. My god-brother and I looked at each other and broke out in huge smiles. We knew we were not pure, but we loved being used as illustrations for our dear most spiritual master. We knew that Śrīla Prabhupāda would never say, "Become a pure devotee like me." That was one of the beautiful qualities of my spiritual master, the pure devotee of the Lord.

Śrīla Prabhupāda, anything I may have accomplished in this life is due only to you. I am always consumed by false pride, but my greatest pride is to identify myself as your servant. You are my master and I am very proud of being your servant. I pray to always remain as such. Please give me the intelligence to never forget my eternal position. Although I have no qualifications, I have faith in your words as you pointed to Paramahaṁsa and me. I know that you benedicted us both to attain pure devotional service in this life or some future lifetime. From your mouth to Kṛṣṇa's ears! All glories to you, Śrīla Prabhupāda!

167

"You are worse than karmīs"

May 13, 1975 Perth, Australia

Śrīla Prabhupāda arrived in Perth from Mumbai on May 6, 1975. Paramahaṁsa Swami and I accompanied him. I brought some mangoes with me from Mumbai, some of Śrīla Prabhupāda's favourites. When we arrived the Australian quarantine officers confiscated them. I asked them why they allowed dried meat but not mangoes. The men told me that according to their laws imported mangoes were potentially more dangerous than dried meat.

Śrīla Prabhupāda was very upset with this absurdity and said, "They will allow importation of dry meat, three hundred years old. That is not infectious, but fresh mango, very nice mango, they will not allow. We started in Mumbai at night and we arrived here this morning—and it has become poisonous!" He looked at me and shook his head.

There was no temple in Perth. It was a refreshing city on the West coast of Australia with a climate similar to Los Angeles. It was a place that Śrīla Prabhupāda could rest as they were preparing the temple in Melbourne. Only three devotees stayed with us in the cottage they had rented; Amogha, Jayadharma and Gaṇeśa.

I always liked Australia. They had first class milk products and it provided a good opportunity to make nice Prasādam. Every day we were able to enjoy maha prasādam along with sour cream and yogurt to our full satisfaction.

One day, after honouring large amounts of lunch prasādam we were all sleeping soundly for about two hours. Śrīla Prabhupāda noticed the quiet when he walked past our quarters on the way to the bathroom and was aware we were all sleeping.

Finally I heard the ringing of the bell from his room. I went into Śrīla Prabhupāda's room and offered obeisances. I tried to remain on the floor longer than usual because I knew my face showed the modes of ignorance that were still affecting me. It was unusual for me to sleep so much in the afternoon but today I had really blown it. I tried not to look directly into Śrīla Prabhupāda's eyes, foolishly thinking he might not notice. It did not help. His first words were, "I've been ringing this bell for hours, trying to wake you. So what is going on? You are sleeping like dead men in there. Why do you need so much sleep? You have become worse than karmīs! Karmīs do not sleep as much as you. They do not sleep during the day. They are all working. You are simply sleeping."

He continued for a few minutes letting me know the māyā we were in. I sat there without saying a word. I never offered excuses, as that only made it worse. I would sit and pray for it to be over. However, he continued, "This is not a good sign. This is too much sleeping. You have nothing else to do but sleep?" I weakly responded, "Yes, I have things to do." Śrīla Prabhupāda then inquired, "Then why you are just sleeping? Go back to sleep, if you have nothing else to do, go back to sleep."

There was no question of sleep now. My blood was flowing quickly through my veins. I sat there not knowing what to do next. Then Śrīla Prabhupāda said, "Call in Paramahaṁsa! Get everyone, bring them here." I offered obeisances and left the room as quickly as I could, unable to look at His Divine Grace. When I went into the room everyone was still fast asleep. I woke everyone and told them "Prabhupada wants to see you." I could not explain to them what had happened. I was so devastated from the chastisement that took place I did not even tell them why they were being called to his room. The two young Australian devotees thought it was wonderful to get the opportunity to see Śrīla Prabhupāda. Not even Paramahaṁsa Swami knew what to expect.

We all entered the room together. Paramahaṁsa Swami offered obeisances and sat up with a smile on his face. Before he could ask Śrīla Prabhupāda what he wanted Śrīla Prabhupāda rhetorically asked, "Why are you sleeping like that?" Paramahaṁsa Swami took a different approach than I. He began to explain about jet lag and how the change in time zones made it difficult and he was trying to adjust his sleep patterns. Of course, this had no effect. Śrīla Prabhupāda was never affected as he travelled around the world. He would always be completely regulated to each place he went. He would immediately adapt his eating, sleeping, and morning walks; his entire schedule to his new environment.

Śrīla Prabhupāda quickly responded, "I am awake. I also flew. Why, if I can? I am an old man and you are so young." Then he began telling everyone just as he told me. "You are worse than karmīs. They do not sleep during the day. They are out working very hard." He shook his head in disgust, "But the devotees, the devotees are sleeping. The karmīs are better than you. They are out working hard just for some sex and to maintain their families; but because Kṛṣṇa is supplying us a little money, then 'Ah! That is all right! Kṛṣṇa is sending, we can spend, eat and sleep!'" Then he told all of us, "All right. You can go. Go do whatever you like. Go and sleep like dead men!"

We all left the room with our heads down. Of course no one went back to sleep. It seemed like hours had gone by when the bell rang, however it was only a few minutes later. I immediately went back into Śrīla Prabhupāda's room and offered obeisances. He looked at me compassionately and said, "So, everyone can come. We will have a class. We can read from one of our books." I nodded happily in agreement and went to the next room and told them of our good fortune. We all took turns reading the 'devotional ecstasies' from one of

Śrīla Prabhupāda's books. It was the perfect medicine for all of us and our spiritual master was the expert physician who knew how to cure us of our disease. His love for us was apparent. We sat in the spiritual world at the lotus feet of Śrīla Prabhupāda for about half an hour.

168

"Where is my coat?"

May 19, 1975 Melbourne, Australia

Śrīla Prabhupāda arrived in Melbourne on the evening of the 17th. The weather in Melbourne was much cooler then in Perth. It was officially winter. I never considered that he would require a coat when we were in Australia. I was wrong. On the morning of the 18th Śrīla Prabhupāda went for his first morning walk in Melbourne. He stepped out of the car and it was very cold. He took a few steps, looked at me and asked the question, already knowing the answer, "Where is my coat?" His coat was full length, pink coloured wool, hand made by Jai Śrī Devī . It was hooded, with a peacock tassel hanging on each side. It was well known amongst all the devotees, being seen in many pictures while Śrīla Prabhupāda was on his morning walks.

My heart sank. I forced the words out of my mouth, knowing I was again a source of inconvenience and discomfort to my spiritual master. "It isn't here Śrīla Prabhupāda. I left it in London the last time we were there." His response was for me, the worse type of chastisement. He looked at me angrily and said nothing. I was devastated not knowing what to do. His secretary, Paramahaṁsa, seeing my anxiety immediately came up with a solution. He told Śrīla Prabhupāda he would contact Haṁsadūta and have it sent by express courier. The coat arrived the next day. On that very day Śrīla Prabhupāda wrote Haṁsadūta a letter and in it said: "Your pair of slippers is very nice. Thank you very much. Thank you for sending my coat to Melbourne. It is a little cool here." Śrīla Prabhupāda never brought the matter up again.

It was not long before I was in difficulty again. Śrīla Prabhupāda always liked to take his morning massage in the sunlight. While in Melbourne the place with the most sunshine was in a common area that was used as a sewing room because the sun shone directly through the window. It had multiple doorways. One of them was left open, while the door that belonged there was leaning against the wall. The open doorway led to the brahmacārīni ashram. For the first few days, while giving Śrīla Prabhupāda a massage, you could hear the ladies talking through the opening. I asked someone if they could do something so Śrīla Prabhupāda had more privacy and quiet. By the third day the door was placed into the opening. I was happy to see it was there and noticed it was quieter.

Śrīla Prabhupāda and I entered the room for massage. Before I even had time to put the mat on the floor there was a deafening crash. I was in shock. The large, heavy, wooden door came crashing down behind him and missed him from his head down to his lotus feet by no more than quarter of an inch. I did not know the door had been leant against the wall but was not on the hinges. A few of the ladies were on the other side of the door hoping to hear something from Śrīla Prabhupāda during his massage. Somehow the door fell over.

I almost jumped out of my body when I heard the sound. Śrīla Prabhupāda sat there, composed but visibly angry at the negligence. He asked gravely, "How is this? What has happened?" I had no answer. Again, he looked at me with that penetrating stare that was so difficult for me to deal with. He was silent and very grave. He did not say another word but remained quiet throughout the massage. After the traumatic incident, I nailed the door in place and Śrīla Prabhupāda never mentioned it again. Even though I had no way of knowing the situation, I felt responsible. Whenever there was a disruption to Śrīla Prabhupāda's service I considered myself at fault. It was my duty to be aware of all his needs and to 'do the needful' whenever required.

Śrīla Prabhupāda, you have always treated me with kindness and compassion, even when chastising me. You never belittled me in the process. When you wrote Haṁsadūta you thanked him for sending the coat so quickly. You did not mention I had forgotten to take it. You never found it necessary to speak about a disciple's difficulty or fault to others, and if you did it was only for their instruction. You desired to save all living entities, what to speak of those who were assisting you in spreading Lord Caitanya's movement. You were always a perfect example to follow. You never made anyone feel guilty, nor did you discourage them by finding fault in their weaknesses. You only encouraged them to progress from whatever their position might be.

See no. 106 for another similar story.

169

"A sannyāsī's business ..."

May 23, 1975 Lautoka, Fiji

Śrīla Prabhupāda had just spent over two weeks in Australia and now he was headed for Fiji. The flight went from Melbourne, with a stop in Sydney. We arrived in Fiji late in the evening of the 22nd. By the time we got through the airport procedures it was very late.

Śrīla Prabhupāda was given comfortable facilities by one of his Indian followers, who was very eager to see an ISKCON centre established there. We were settled in our quarters around midnight. We had not eaten for several hours and, although it was Ekādaśī on the 23rd, when we were offered prasādam that included grains Śrīla Prabhupāda said it was okay and that we should take it. We all ate a full meal even though it was very late in the evening.

We took rest around 1:30 am and got up at 4:00 am. The morning schedule went on as usual, with Śrīla Prabhupāda taking his walk around sunrise. Paramahaṁsa and I went with him along with a few of the local people. We all had breakfast around 8:00 am After breakfast both Paramahaṁsa Swami and I both felt tired and laid down to take some rest.

I heard Śrīla Prabhupāda ring the bell at around 9:00 am I went into his room and offered obeisances. Immediately he asked me, "Why are you sleeping?" I made a big mistake, thinking we had only two hours of sleep that night, I responded, "Well, we did not get much sleep, Prabhupada." He looked at me and said, "But so much...Now is not the time to be sleeping. And Paramahaṁsa, he is a sannyāsī. Why he is sleeping so much?"

The focus turned from me to Paramahaṁsa, but I felt no better. I sat before him with my head down. I did not think I had done anything wrong but I had clearly displeased him. He continued, "I also saw that Paramahaṁsa, so late at night he ate so much." His voice still raised, he said, "Call him here!"

I went and woke my dear god-brother. I had no words, but said, "Prabhupada wants to see you." I was sorry to say this. I decided to go in with him. I knew Śrīla Prabhupāda was going to chastise him severely. I could have avoided it but I thought we were together in this and I wanted to be with him for it.

Śrīla Prabhupāda looked at him and spoke, "You are a

sannyāsī, you shouldn't be eating so much. You shouldn't be sleeping so much." Like I had done, Paramahaṁsa tried to defend himself saying, "I did not eat so much and I hardly slept last night." Śrīla Prabhupāda was not receptive to his reasons. "Never mind." He said, "You are a sannyāsī. You require so much sleep? A sannyāsī's business is to minimize this eating and sleeping."

Śrīla Prabhupāda spoke a little more about the duties of a sannyāsī and then told us we could go. We knew we had displeased him. We both decided to eat less in future so that we did not require so much sleep. We remained there for two more days. Śrīla Prabhupāda was as graceful as ever. The chastisement was over. The instruction was there and his love and protection for us and our safety in Kṛṣṇa Consciousness was always apparent.

Dear Śrīla Prabhupāda so many of my memories are filled with joy, feeling your care and compassion for me. However, with some remembrances I have had it was difficult for me to realize your sweetness. But it is not difficult anymore. I was so young and careless. I did not understand what you were saying. I did not realize how strong māyā is, and how tricky.

Every moment we get to make a conscious choice. You always showed us how to make the right choice. In your association sometimes, when it was obvious we did not make it, you would try so hard to protect us from our lack our lack of Kṛṣṇa Consciousness and point out how we were slipping away. Your chastisement was never out of anger. It only came from your pure love of Kṛṣṇa and for us. Please forgive me for failing to recognize your Divine love. I pray that I cherish it always as I do now.

170

"I already have a watch"

May 24, 1975 Lautoka, Fiji

Śrīla Prabhupāda spent over two weeks in Australia and then travelled to Fiji for three days. This was Śrīla Prabhupāda's first trip there although preaching work had been going on there since around 1970. Śrīla Prabhupāda knew that it was a place that would take to Kṛṣṇa Consciousness very quickly because there was a large Hindu population.

At this time there was still no temple in Fiji and Śrīla Prabhupāda going there was instrumental in its being established. While there, Śrīla Prabhupāda took the time to visit a business of one of the local Indian men. It was a jewellery shop. Paramahaṁsa and I accompanied Śrīla Prabhupāda.

From the time I joined the movement in 1971 devotees were always detached and austere. We never ate anything unless it was prepared in the temple and we never wore karmi clothes. We went everywhere wearing our tilaka, dhoti and our heads were shaved. Only when book distribution appeared did devotees begin to wear shirt and pants and that was only while they were selling books.

In 1972 most ISKCON men wore dhotis that were nothing more then a cutting from a bolt of cloth. A genuine Indian kurta was also rare. By 1975 some of the devotees in ISKCON had developed a liking for articles of jewellery. Fancy watches in particular became popular with a small but growing number of western devotees. Paramahaṁsa and I were not immune to this weakness. It was the one item you could put on your wrist to accompany the nice dhoti and fancy kurta that devotees were now able to get from India. Seiko watches in particular were very popular. Rolex watches were most desired but almost no one could afford one of them.

Śrīla Prabhupāda's disciples would sometimes bring offerings to him when they visited, occasionally a watch. If he liked the watch he would keep it and eventually give his old one to a disciple as prasādam. Paramahaṁsa and I also liked the idea of having a nice watch. Of course we had no money to buy one, but we had a simple plan. If someone asked if Śrīla Prabhupāda needed anything, we would say he could use a new watch. We thought there was a reasonable chance one of us would get his old one.

Now Śrīla Prabhupāda was in a jewellery shop, owned and managed by this wealthy Indian man. He was a well wisher of ISKCON and happy to have Śrīla Prabhupāda come to bless his business. Śrīla Prabhupāda graciously stood in the store as the gentleman went behind his glass counters filled with shiny gold in various forms. Paramahaṁsa and I stood off to the side and looked about.

Śrīla Prabhupāda walked up to the counter where the man was standing and told him he had a very nice shop. The counter that was between the two of them was filled with watches. Rolex watches! After talking for some time Śrīla Prabhupāda indicated that he was ready to go. The man said, "Prabhupada, let me give you something from my shop before you leave. Can I please give you one of these watches?" Śrīla Prabhupāda smiled and said, "No thank you." Paramahaṁsa and I looked at each other as the conversation continued. Again the man said, "Prabhupada, please take one of these watches. I want you to have one. Śrīla Prabhupāda again smiled and declined. A third time he asked, "Please, Prabhupada take one of these watches". Śrīla Prabhupāda smiled and extended his arm saying, "No thank you. I already have a watch and it works very nicely".

Paramahaṁsa and I stood their motionless. It was our one and only opportunity and Śrīla Prabhupāda casually refused. Some of the watches were worth more then $10,000 at that time. Śrīla Prabhupāda always exhibited his sublime qualities.

He held Kṛṣṇa within his heart. What need did he have for anything? The man then thanked Śrīla Prabhupāda for coming and took us all back to our residence. Paramahaṁsa and I briefly discussed our missed chance for a watch and then got back to our service.

Thank you Śrīla Prabhupāda for always being a perfect example to me. I know you were always aware of my weaknesses. You let me see them and showed me how to give them up. I witnessed it many times. You would make a philosophical point in such a way that I never had to feel it was being directed towards me. This was another feature of your compassion and mercy. You dealt with your disciples in a way that minimized the possibility of committing an offence. You spoke on philosophical terms. There was never a 'do this or else'!

In 1971 you sent a letter to Upendra dāsa. He and his wife helped establish Kṛṣṇa Consciousness in Fiji and he was there at the time. In the letter you told him, "Yes, progress of devotional service becomes choked up when there is gross offence to the spiritual master. So far I am concerned, you have no offence. You are carrying my order so faithfully in a far distant place. So you always have my blessings and Lord Caitanya's blessings. Do not think otherwise. Even if you think you have committed offences, it is like kicking of the small child, which is taken pleasingly by the parents. So do not worry about it. Kṛṣṇa will give you all protection. I'm so pleased upon you that on my order you have gone to distant places and faithfully served the cause. I thank you for this attempt." Upendra had the great fortune to again serve Śrīla Prabhupāda personally in Vṛndāvana in his final months with us in 1977.

Śrīla Prabhupāda you have saved the whole world and all your followers one at a time. Fiji yatra developed very slowly until your arrival in 1975. After you put your lotus feet on the soil things changed very rapidly. You travelled around the world to so many towns and cities benedicting them with the touch of your feet. Because of that Kṛṣṇa Consciousness spread around the globe.

I left your personal service in 1975. From that time whenever I was asked what I wanted for my birthday I would say, 'a Rolex watch'. I finally became free of the desire for one in the year 2001. It took a long time. One year later my son, Ātmārāma, gave me one. Laughing is a Vaisnava activity.

171

"Go into the kitchen and get some chapati dough,"

May 25, 1975 ISKCON Honolulu, Hawaii

New Navadvīpa was the site of a very peculiar pastime. When we first arrived, Śrīla Prabhupāda used the bathroom in his quarters, but the toilet did not flush. Yasodalal, a devotee who had plumbing experience, came and fixed it. He explained to Śrīla Prabhupāda that because the plumbing had not been used for some time, it had not flushed properly.

"So, now it is working?" Śrīla Prabhupāda asked.

"Oh, yes, Prabhupada. It is working well," Yasodalal said.

Śrīla Prabhupāda did not seem convinced. "So, how do you know it is working?" he asked.

"I flushed it and the water went down," Yasodalal replied.

Śrīla Prabhupāda was not satisfied. "Go into the kitchen and get some chapati dough," Śrīla Prabhupāda instructed. "Make some balls and put them in the toilet and if they go down then we will know for sure that it is working."

The young brahmacārī complied with Śrīla Prabhupāda's instructions and we were all very happy to hear that everything worked as it should.

Śrīla Prabhupāda, being with you was never boring. You showed me that one should not be taken in by the words of another. You often said, "The proof of the pudding is in the tasting." I pray that some day I may perform some useful service to you.

172

"In that Vṛndāvana, one takes birth ..."

June 10, 1975 ISKCON Honolulu, Hawaii

While in New Navadvīpa, Śrīla Prabhupāda made a statement about taking birth in India. My god-brothers and I became concerned, so I asked Śrīla Prabhupāda about it on a morning walk.

"Śrīla Prabhupāda," I said. "You said the other day that Govinda dasi asked you if, in general, we would have to take birth in India before going back home and you said, 'Yes.' So, we were wondering how that's possible that we have to take birth in India because we haven't seen many strict Vaisnavas there."

My god-brothers began to laugh, knowing my strong dislike for India.

"The land is there, just like this land," Śrīla Prabhupāda compassionately said. "Vaisnavas are there. This land is not meant for spiritual culture, but still Vaisnavas are here.

Similarly, in India, no, there are many Vaisnavas there. The masses of people in India are all Vaisnava."

We still required clarification.

"So, by joining this movement, we come to the platform where we can take birth in India in a nice brahmana family?" Paramahaṁsa asked.

"No, you can go directly also, if you want to finish your business," Śrīla Prabhupāda replied. "*śucīnāṁ śrīmatāṁ gehe.* This is a consideration, one who fails in executing. But, if you become successful, then you go directly where Kṛṣṇa is there. Kṛṣṇa is there in some universe. So those who are completely liberated, they go to that universe. Just like when Kṛṣṇa comes here. In each and every universe there is a Vṛndāvana. So, in that Vṛndāvana, one takes birth, then goes to original Vṛndāvana."

Paramahaṁsa was still concerned about taking birth in India.

"Those who are not able to maintain the Kṛṣṇa Consciousness principle, then they may have to go to India next lifetime?" Paramahaṁsa continued.

"Yes," Śrīla Prabhupāda replied. "Śrīmatam, Śrīmatam sucinam. So, Śrīmatam. You can get here. Śrīmatam means rich, rich family. Here you get many families, Ford family... but, Śrīmatam and sucinam. So, if you are creating so many brahmanas, so if this cult is permanent, then there will be many brahmana families here in the West also."

Śrīla Prabhupāda kindly satisfied our restless minds and the conversation quickly changed.

Śrīla Prabhupāda, I am lost without your guidance. I have come to understand that I must follow in your footsteps. I feel embarrassed recalling my offensive mentality. How dare I not recognize Vaisnavas in the land of Vaisnavas? You gently corrected my disrespectful attitude without chastising me. You described how it is possible to take birth in this country if "this Kṛṣṇa Conscious cult remains permanent." Your optimism in our ability to become Kṛṣṇa Conscious in this life gives me hope. I pray that someday I will see all living entities as devotees, as you have shown by your example.

173

"How is this? No one to do it?"

June 14, 1975 ISKCON Honolulu, Hawaii

Usually the grounds in New Navadvīpa were very nice, but one time Śrīla Prabhupāda arrived and they had not been maintained.

"Why this garden isn't taken care of?" Śrīla Prabhupāda asked while touring the property.

"Śrīla Prabhupāda," the temple president said. "There is no one to do it."

At the time, there were approximately twenty devotees walking with Śrīla Prabhupāda.

"How is this?" Śrīla Prabhupāda asked looking around at his disciples. "No one to do it?"

This scenario happened on different occasions. When Śrīla Prabhupāda noticed something was not getting done. He wanted any person to do any task, however menial it appeared. He once chastised a GBC representative while touring the Deity kitchen because the pots were not clean. He told him if necessary he should do them himself.

To make advancement in devotional service one must facilitate the pleasure of the spiritual master. By doing so one gets the grace of Kṛṣṇa. We are dāsa dāsa anu dāsa.

Jai Śrīla Prabhupāda!

꧁ 174 ꧂

"Look what the Machine has done."

June 16, 1975 ISKCON Honolulu, Hawaii

One morning Śrīla Prabhupāda did something that was most unusual. He rang his bell at about 1:30 am. Normally, Śrīla Prabhupāda went out of his way to see that I was not disturbed while taking rest. In some places, such as Kṛṣṇa Balarāma Mandir, he would have to go through the servants' quarters to use the bathroom. I always awoke hearing the shuffling of his feet as he passed by my head. I instinctively offered my obeisances. Sometimes he became disturbed with me and said, "No, no take rest."

On the morning he called me at 1:30 am I was half asleep when I entered his room and offered my obeisances. I lifted my head to the sight of Śrīla Prabhupāda with a beautiful, childlike smile. I was also faced with a pile of recording tape on his desk. He had been translating and somehow or other, the tape machine malfunctioned. I do not know what happened, but there was tape everywhere. He offered no explanation. With a moving smile he said, "Look what the machine has done. Can you fix it?"

For the next half hour I hand rolled the tape back onto the reel and loaded it into the Uher Dictaphone machine. Upon completion of this transcendentally tedious task he replied lovingly, "Okay, go take rest."

I got the feeling from his mischievous smile that he helped make the pile of recording tape bigger, trying to fix it without waking me. I could not say 'without disturbing me from my sleep' because any opportunity to perform some service to Śrīla Prabhupāda was a blessing, not a disturbance.

Śrīla Prabhupāda, living without service to you in

this material world is painful for me. I pray to always hear you ring the bell to call me into your room so that I may fall at your feet and rise up to see your smiling face.

꧁ 175 ꧂

"I do not like to change my servants."

June 20, 1975 ISKCON Honolulu, Hawaii

In February, I left with Śrīla Prabhupāda and travelled with him, Paramahaṁsa Swami and Nitāi. We went with Śrīla Prabhupāda around the world and four months later we were all back in Hawaii, where I had left my wife and infant son. So much had happened, as it always did, but there were many changes to take place.

Paramahaṁsa Swami had been with Śrīla Prabhupāda for over a year as his secretary. One year was a long time to be in Śrīla Prabhupāda's entourage. I had travelled with him for just over two years in total. He had a total of about 10 personal servants in the period from 1966 to 1977.

Before we arrived in Hawaii Paramahaṁsa was talking to me about going on a preaching tour. When we got to Hawaii he discussed it with Śrīla Prabhupāda. It was a very spectacular plan. He told him he wanted to travel to all the islands in the South Pacific aboard a sailboat with a crew consisting of devotees. Śrīla Prabhupāda asked him where he would get all these devotees to man his craft. He did not think it was very practical but he encouraged him and there was a letter sent out to different temples in the West asking for brahmacārīs to come aboard.

I had to deal with my own circumstances. We were back in Hawaii, where I left with Śrīla Prabhupāda just four months before. At that time, in February, he asked me what I wanted to do as he was about to leave on another tour. I decided to leave my wife and four month old son in the care of the temple and go with him as his personal servant.

We all arrived here from Fiji on May 25th and remained here for a month. I had the opportunity to spend some time with my family. As he was preparing to leave the islands, I was again facing the same dilemma. My son was now eight months old and I had strong family attachments. I was also attached to travelling with Śrīla Prabhupāda.

As the days passed my desire to stay in Hawaii grew stronger. I did not speak about it to anyone but internally I was having a huge battle. Just days before my twenty-fourth birthday, Śrīla Prabhupāda's travel plans were fixed and he was about to leave New Navadvīpa. On my own I decided what I would do, although it was not very well thought out. I nervously walked into Śrīla Prabhupāda's room, where he sat alone behind his desk, and offered my obeisances.

I sat up and looked at him, still afraid to reveal my mind to him. Finally I said the only thing that seemed to make sense to me. Of course it made no sense at all. I blurted out, "Śrīla Prabhupāda, I want to change my service. I feel the need to preach." It was the most difficult thing I had ever done. He looked at me lovingly and responded immediately. I will never forget these words. "My preaching is not good enough?" he asked. It was a question he did not need to ask. It was his gentle way of telling me I should do my service without making any demands I was unable to follow.

I sat there with sweaty palms, covered by my illusion. I was unable to think clearly. I did not know what to say. He looked at me with such compassion. He then softly said the words that will echo in my head forever.

"I do not like to change my servants." Silently, I sat before my most loving, caring spiritual master. He made it clear he wanted me to stay with him, but never told me I must. Out of kindness he gave me the choice, so that my offence would not be so great.

Being the most expert spiritual master he cut through my layers of illusion and brought me to the point of facing what was really going on. Up to this point I could not even admit it to myself. But he brought me to the stage of telling him. I timidly stated, "I want to remain in Hawaii and be with my family." He smiled at me and with kindness in his voice said, "That's all right."

> *Śrīla Prabhupāda, my most merciful master, I will always regret my decision. I was such a foolish boy. I did not know you were going to leave so quickly. I thought you would be with us until you were at least hundred years old. I was with you for over two years. At the time it seemed like a long time to be with you. Now it seems like only a moment in time.*
>
> *It is the only time I felt properly situated. It was the most natural service for me. You were my only father. My father died when I was three and I have no memory of him. Until you mercifully appeared in my life in 1971 I had no reason to live.*
>
> *Shortly after I left your personal service I became the temple president in Hawaii. I quickly turned one area of the property into a "Prabhupada Garden". My hope was that you would soon return and I could again have your personal association. It did not happen. Soon after you left this world I gave up that service. I have been wandering around aimlessly not knowing what to do without you. So many years have gone by; still I do not know what to do. My only solace is talking about you to your followers. Their love for you gives me a reason to take my next breath.*

Sometimes in a lecture you would stop and look at your watch. Looking at us youngsters you would tell us that no matter how much money you have it is impossible to buy back that moment in time. I was so young and foolish. I never understood what you meant. I always thought, 'we are eternal, what difference does it make?' Now millions of moments are going by, and I am without you. How many more moments must go by until I see your lotus feet again? It is unbearable in this world without you.

Epilogue

"Upendra and my last days with Śrīla Prabhupāda."

Śrīla Prabhupāda, today I am coming to terms with the passing of your dear servant, Upendra prabhu. It always amazes me how little I have learned in Kṛṣṇa Consciousness. I spoke with Upendra often this last summer. He told me about his condition and that he was likely to die in the next year. Although I was aware of his illness, still I thought, "No, he won't be leaving us so soon." I am faced with my inability to acknowledge death, and my dear friend, Upendra is now gone.

It reminds me of when I visited you in August of '77. I was the president of New Navadvīpa temple in Hawaii. I left for Vṛndāvana with Madhudviṣa prabhu to spend some time with you, Śrīla Prabhupāda. When I arrived and saw your condition I was greatly disturbed. You had lost so much weight and were so physically weak. Yet, you greeted both of us with enthusiasm. You were charming and effulgent as ever, always encouraging us. You said to Madhudviṣa Prabhu, "So remain as grihasta and render your service. There is no harm. If one could not proceed, it doesn't matter. Failure is the pillar of success. Then try. Again you shall try. Where is Śrutakīrti? How are you?" I replied, "Very well thank you." Śrīla Prabhupāda said, "Śrutakīrti is also grihasta. So jointly you can work and improve this movement. That is our ambition. *Gṛhe bā banete thāke, hā gaurāṅga bole ḍāke, narottama māge tāra saṅga.* 'Either he remains at home or as a sannyāsī if he is devotee of Lord Gaurāṅga, I want his association.' That is Narottama Thakura's... *Gṛhe bā banete thāke, hā gaurāṅga bole ḍāke, narottama māge tāra saṅga.* So follow the principles, and whichever position is suitable. Do not be carried away by the waves of māyā. Capture Caitanya Mahāprabhu and you'll be saved. Is that all right? Do not leave us. You are quite... At least you made advance. You are one of the important devotees. So do not lose that position now. Manage in the position you want to remain. Now Gaurasundara has also come. So I'm glad to see that you are... Your bunch of hair is long. Yes. Cut it. So give them place to stay nicely." Tamāla Kṛṣṇa said, "Prasādam." Śrīla Prabhupāda replied, "Take prasādam and remain here for some time. Of course, according to my horoscope, these days are my last days. But if Kṛṣṇa saves, that is a different thing. They have calculated eighty-two years and two days?"

Tamāla Kṛṣṇa said, "Eighty-one years, five months, and twenty-eight days." Śrīla Prabhupāda continued, "That is according to calculation of my horoscope. Eighty-one years will be completed, and eighty-second year will begin. It doesn't matter I leave this body. Even in death I'll live. One year before or one year after... Now as far as possible, I have trained you. Try to follow the principles. And go ahead. Do not be set back by māyā's tricks. Go ahead, forward, at any cost. Bhaktivinoda Thakura said... So many obstacles are coming. Māyā is strong. And still, we are going forward. That's all right."

I spent the next two weeks at the Kṛṣṇa Balarāma Mandir. Upendra massaged you and gave you sponge baths. He allowed me to perform this wonderful service with him. By your mercy and the mercy of Upendra prabhu, again I got to touch the body of my most transcendental spiritual father. It was the service I was most attached to and having Upendra at my side made it sweeter still. He was such a marvellous servant. He kindly shared the nectar service with me, knowing fully that by sharing you with others his own ecstasy increased.

When I was getting ready to leave for New Navadvīpa, Upendra gave me the sponge that we used to bathe you as a going away present. It was fragrant with the scent of your body and the powder that we used during the massage. I gave most of it away but managed to keep a tiny square and put it in a small picture frame. It is on your altar in our temple room.

Foolishly, I left Vṛndāvana much too soon. I could have stayed with you if my desire was stronger but thinking I was indispensable as temple president, and not realizing that I would not get to see your lotus features again, I left. It is a decision that I will regret for eternity. Suddenly, you were gone. I never thought it would happen. You taught me so much about the temporal nature of this material world and yet I have heard so little. When will I learn what you have painstakingly taught this foolish servant? There is nothing more valuable in this world than the association of devotees of the Lord. How long will it take me to realize that the only wealth in life is associating with Kṛṣṇa's devotees?

Śrīla Prabhupāda, I identify with Upendra so much. He is affectionately known for being your personal servant. He was very sentimental. After your leaving he was mostly known for his difficulties in following the Kṛṣṇa Conscious path. My condition since your departure has been similar. You have mercifully taken your servant, Upendra by the hand and aided his passing to the next world. I do not claim to know where he has gone, but I am sure that despite all of his shortcomings, you have carefully guided that passage. You show all of us just how compassionate and caring you are. You never acknowledge our bad habits as you graciously show appreciation for the service we do, no matter how tiny.

Śrīla Prabhupāda, I am very fallen and lazy. I can not feel your presence since your leaving this world. My attachment to you is sentimental and I am unable to perform any worthwhile service. Please take me away from this horrible place so that I may massage you with my god-brother, Upendra prabhu. Glance upon me lovingly and save me from myself.

You live forever in your instructions and your presence can be seen in your disciples following those instructions, if we have the eyes to see. Please, remember me as you do Upendra. Grant me the joy of having my god-brothers' and god-sisters' association at the time of death. I pray to be chanting the holy names of guru and Gaurāṅga as I leave my body following in the footsteps of my most fortunate friend and god-brother Upendra prabhu.

"Do not try to make a faction."

14 December, 1972 Ahmedabad, India

Letter to: Tuṣṭa Krsna Byron's Bay, Australia

The following is one my favorite letters written by Śrīla Prabhupāda. He dictated it to his secretary three months after I became his personal servant. In it he responds to all of the questions asked. More than that, he shows his profound loyalty and compassion for his disciple.

My dear Tusta Kṛṣṇa,

Please accept my blessings. I am in due receipt of your letters dated November 18, November 22, and December 3, 1972, and I have heard that you are having some difficulties, so I have sent Siddhasvarūpa there to help you. Now try to keep a cool head under all circumstances and always remember that Kṛṣṇa will protect you in any case, you haven't to worry anything. I think that without you the New Zealand affair will not go on, but now you are leaving there to live on some farm in Australia. Of course, our serving Kṛṣṇa is voluntary affair, so what can I say? If you think that is the best choice, I must agree, otherwise you might go away altogether. Anyway we shall discuss in detail if I come there in future.

Regarding your questions in the letter of November 18, 1972, you have asked me if the spiritual master is ultimately Kṛṣṇa, so the answer must be that if you think that way then everyone is Kṛṣṇa. So why we should think like this? śaktyāveśa-avatāra. means a living entity, but he is specially empowered. Not that he is Kṛṣṇa. But on account of his exalted position he is honoured as much as Kṛṣṇa. Not that he is Kṛṣṇa. That is mayavadi. He acts in the position of Kṛṣṇa, but he is not Kṛṣṇa, he is very dear to Kṛṣṇa. That is explained: (here the verse was quoted: yasya prasādād bhagavat-prasādat. . .) The spiritual master is acting in the position of Kṛṣṇa because he is the most confidential servant of Kṛṣṇa.

Your next question, after leaving this material realm does the devotee remain forever with his spiritual master? The answer is yes. But I think you have got the mistaken idea in this connection. You speak of pure devotee, that he is ? śaktyāveśa-avatāra, that we should obey him only--these things are the wrong idea. If anyone thinks like that, that a pure devotee should be obeyed and no one else, that means he is a nonsense. We advise everyone to address one another as Prabhu. Prabhu means master, so how the master should be disobeyed? Others, they are also pure devotees. All of my disciples are pure devotees. Anyone sincerely serving the spiritual master is a pure devotee, it may be Siddhasvarūpa or others, a-Siddhasvarūpa. [devotees other than Siddhasvarupa]. This must be very clearly stated. It is not only that your Siddhasvarūpa is a pure devotee and not others. Do not try to make a faction. Siddhasvarūpa is a good soul. But others should not be misled. Anyone who is surrendered to the spiritual master is a pure devotee, it doesn't matter if Siddhasvarūpa or non-Siddhasvarūpa. Amongst ourselves one should respect others as Prabhu, master, one another. As soon as we distinguish here is a pure devotee, here is a non-pure devotee, that means I am a nonsense. Why you only want to be in the spiritual sky with Siddhasvarūpa? Why not all? If Siddhasvarūpa can go, why not everyone? Siddhasvarūpa will go, you will go, Śyāmasundara. will go, all others will go. We will have another ISKCON there. Of course, Mr. Nair must stay.

And if somebody does not go, then I shall have to come back to take him there. One should remember this and every one of my disciples should act in such a way that they may go with me and may not have to come back to take another birth.

As for your next question, can only a few pure devotees deliver others, anyone, if he is a pure devotee he can deliver others, he can become spiritual master. But unless he on that platform he should not attempt it. Then both of them will to go to hell, like blind men leading the blind.

Next you ask if I am present in my picture and form?

Yes. In form as well as in teachings. To carry out the teachings of guru is more important than to worship the form, but none of them should be neglected. Form is called vapu and teachings is called vani. Both should be worshiped. Vani is more important than vapu.

Your next question is, should we love Kṛṣṇa or love the spiritual master: You cannot go to Kṛṣṇa directly, loving Him. It is common sense that if Kṛṣṇa is the object of your love, His pet dog is also the object of your love. Friends meet friends and if the friend is with his dog the gentleman pats his dog first, is it not? So the man becomes automatically pleased, his dog being patted. I have seen it in your country. The conclusion is this: Without pleasing the spiritual master he cannot please Kṛṣṇa. If anyone tries to please Kṛṣṇa directly, he's fool number one.

Hoping this meets you and your good wife, Kṛṣṇa Tulasī dasi, in good health and devotional mood.

Your ever well-wisher,

A. C. Bhaktivedanta Swami

My dear Śrīla Prabhupāda, in my final prayer I can not ask you for anything. You have already given me everything and answered all my questions. I can only offer my heart and soul to you in service, eternally. As you told me years ago, "Service is love. You do your service and everything will be all right." What is the difficulty?

All glories to Śrīla Prabhupāda!

Appendices

Two Hours in the Daily Life of Śrīla Prabhupāda's Personal Servant

At Any ISKCON Temple

The process for preparing Śrīla Prabhupāda's lunch was usually the same. About a half-hour before I was to massage Śrīla Prabhupāda I made a chapati dough, chopped various types of vegetables and placed them in the middle tier of Śrīla Prabhupāda's famous three-tiered cooker. I put cauliflower and potatoes or some other vegetable combination in the bottom tier with some water to become a wet vegetable. In the top tier I put a small two-part tiffin. I put split dahl in the bottom with water and rice with water in the top. More vegetables were placed around the tiffin in the top tier of the cooker. I then placed Śrīla Prabhupāda's cooker on the stove with the heat set at a medium-low flame. Then I left the kitchen to massage Śrīla Prabhupāda.

Usually, his massage lasted one to two hours. The trick in using the cooker during the massage was not to let the water dry out in the bottom. Śrīla Prabhupāda showed me how to use the cooker with dahl on the bottom. A few times the dahl started to burn during the massage. That was a great source of anxiety for me. I never wanted to leave Śrīla Prabhupāda in the middle of his massage, but sometimes we would smell the dahl burning.

"What is that smell?" Śrīla Prabhupāda would ask me. He knew it was his lunch.

After rendering this service for about eight months and burning a few lunches, I came up with the idea of cooking a wet subji on the bottom and steaming the dahl and rice in the top tier. That eliminated my anxiety because the wet vegetable did not thicken and burn like dahl.

When completing Śrīla Prabhupāda's massage I always poured a small amount of mustard oil into the palm of his hand to oil the gates of his body. Then he walked to the bathroom to bathe. This gave me about twenty minutes to complete the rest of my service.

First, I neatly laid out his dhoti, kurta and kaupina (underwear) on his bed. I buttoned the bottom two buttons of his kurta, so Śrīla Prabhupāda would have only two more to close. I then raced to his sitting room and prepared his desk for applying tilak which meant opening his mirror. It was round like that of a powder compact, with a piece of carved ivory on the lid. I always made sure that his small silver lota (about the size of a golf ball) had water in it. A small silver spoon was placed next to the lota. Finally, I placed the ball of tilak at the centre of his desk.

After that, I ran to the servants' quarters to finish preparing lunch. I removed the cooker from the stove and put a wok on the fire in order to make a large chaunce. If needed, the lid of the cooker was used for this purpose. Some of the chaunce was poured into the wet vegetable in the bottom tier and a little was put into the dahl in the top tier. Then, I poured the assorted vegetables into the remainder of the chaunce in the wok. If bitter melon was available, I sautīed it in ghee and turmeric. I prepared another chaunce to cook the remaining vegetables. I placed all of the preparations on Śrīla Prabhupāda's plates along with a katori of plain yogurt and another with milk sweets. With Śrīla Prabhupāda's plate almost ready, it was time to roll and cook a chapati.

Hopefully, all of this was done at about the same time His Divine Grace finished chanting Gāyatrī mantra. He did not mind waiting a few minutes, but I got scared if he had to wait longer than that. I put the plates down on his choki, offered my obeisances, and ran back to my room to cook another chapati. After he finished eating chapatis he opened the small tiffin filled with rice. Śrīla Prabhupāda usually ate three to six chapatis with his meal. More often than not, he ate three or four chapatis. He enjoyed the remainder of his meal with steaming hot rice.

> *It was wonderful to cook for you, Śrīla Prabhupāda. I pray to become an expert cook, like my god-sister Yamunā Devī, so I can offer you sumptuous foodstuff life after life.*

Acknowledgments

I would like to thank all the devotees who offered their help selflessly in the production of this book. I started writing over ten years ago and it was first made accessible on the Internet for Srila Prabhupada's Centennial and edited by Kusa dasi. Editing and proofreading was later done by Sangita dasi, Sailendriya dasi, Krsnavesa dasi, Dinadayatma, Anasuya and Vandna Synghal.

I am very grateful to Sakshi Gopal and Nitesh Vaghadia for designing the beautiful cover and arranging the photos and captions. My appreciation to Ekanatha at Bhaktivedanta archives for putting the unedited memories on Vedabase and to Ranjit for his kindness in providing all the photos in a timely manner. The layout and graphics were beautifully done by Raj Gope, Yogendra Sahu and Bhawesh Shah. Grahila dasa made a thorough index on short notice.

I am indebted to Vidyananda and Sita Rama prabhus for working together in the production of this book and doing whatever was necessary to bring it to completion. My sincere gratitude goes to Rādhānatha Maharaj for being a loving Godbrother. I will always be grateful to my dear friend Ambarisa for his kindness and support over the years. I would not have finished the book without the assistance of Amekhala dasi. She chose all the photos, edited, encouraged and assisted me every day.

I ask the forgiveness of anyone I have omitted from this list. I have been given encouragement and help by many to complete this book over the years and I hope that they are happy with the result.

About the Author

Srutakirti dasa (Vincent Fiorentino) was born in Philadelphia, Pennsylvania on June 29, 1951. His father died when he was three years old and his mother raised him and his two older sisters in the Catholic faith. He was an altar boy in elementary school and went to Father Judge High School. He attended LaSalle University for two years where he majored in business and sociology.

He found the highest fulfillment of his service attitude when he met the devotees on April 22, 1971 and joined the Hare Krishna movement of Srila Prabhupada. After a one year of training at New Vrndavana, his first devotional home, his commitment to service culminated in even more service -- a week of cooking for sixteen hours a day. He cooked three meals a day, in a small farmhouse kitchen, for 350 guests who had come to hear the Bhagavata Dharma discourses from Srila Prabhupada. He missed the discourses while serving the guests.

Unknown to him his service attitude would soon payoff with the most intimate service possible. At the end of the week Kirtanananda Maharaja asked him if he wanted to become the personal servant of Srila Prabhupada.

Simultaneously, thrilled but retaining his simple, humble demeanor he accepted, with the grace he would be known for throughout his life. This service resulted in the book you now hold. After leaving Srila Prabhupada's personal service he remained in Hawaii and managed Govinda's restaurant and was the temple president there in 1976 and 1977. He also managed Govinda's restaurants in Los Angeles and Laguna Beach.

From 1984 to 2001 he lived in New Jersey with his family. He has three children, two sons, Atmarama and Mayapurcandra (named by Srila Prabhupada in 1974), and a daughter Nitya Lila. He owned a small automotive parts business in New Jersey during that time.

He currently lives in England, near Bhaktivedanta Manor with his wife and spends several months a year traveling to different ISKCON temples and spreading the glories of Srila Prabhupada. He tells all who will listen how much Prabhupada cared for them. Through this work he is helping to solidify Prabhupada's mission throughout the world.

He speaks about his memories of two and half years of personal service for Srila Prabhupada. He enjoys inspiring others to maximize their internal mood of devotion. He has taken a stand encouraging all persons to strive for the change of heart that will lead them to find happiness by serving the Lord and all His children.

Glossary

Acarya – an ideal spiritual master who teaches by example,

Accha – an expression of greeting, questioning, acknowledgement, surprise

Bhajan – personal worship of the Lord by hearing and chanting His glories.

Bhakti – devotional service performed by a bhakta

Bhaktisiddhanta Sarasvati Thakura – the spiritual master of Srila Prabhupada

Bhaktivedanta Manor – large estate temple North of London donated by George Harrison

Bhaktivinoda Thakura – the grand-spiritual master of Srila Prabhupada. The father of Bhaktisiddhanta Sarasvati Thakura

Brahma Muhurta – auspicious pre-dawn meditation hour

Brahmacari – a celibate monk studying under and serving a spiritual master;

Brahmacarini – a celibate unmarried lady devotee (see Brahmacari)

Brahmana – order in society that worships the Lord, studies the scriptures and populace

Brijbasi – a resident of Vrndavana, India

Camara – yak-tail whisk

Caturmasya – a vow of austerity accepted during the four months of the summer rainy season

Chaddar – a shawl-type cloth primarily used to cover the upper body for worship services, warmth,

Chapati – whole-wheat unleavened flat bread cooked on a hot, dry griddle.

Chaunce – flavourful spices combined in a hot pan with a little ghee then added to cooked vegetables

Choki – a small rectangular table on 6" to 10" legs.

Damodara – name for Krishna in His pastime as an infant

Danda – usually the 5' to 6' staff carried by swamis (renuncients

Dandavats – "falling rod"; respectful obeisances offered by falling on the ground like a stiff rod.

Darsana – audience with the Supreme Lord in any of His various forms or His devotee

Dhama – "abode"; place of the Lord's residence.

Dhoti – a single piece of cloth about a yard wide and 4-5 yards long.

Dahl – bean soup

Dvaraka – One of Krishna's homes in the state of Gujarat, India

Ekadasi – twice monthly fast day (eleventh day of the waxing and waning moon)

Gamcha – a short cotton cloth wrapped around the lower body

Gaudiya matha – mission and temples founded by Srila Bhaktisiddhanta Sarasvati Thakura (the spiritual master of Srila Prabhupada) to spread Krishna consciousness in the whole world.

Gayatri – a transcendental vedic prayer chanted silently three times a day by brahmanas

GBC – Governing Body Commission, the administrative authority of ISKCON

Goshala – "farm"; (fields and barn) where cows are tended

Gosvami – a swami, a title for a renuncient (a sannyasi), one who is fully able to control his senses.

Grihasta – regulated householder life, the second order of Vedic spiritual life (brahmacari, grihasta, vanaprastha, sannyasa).

Guru, Gurudeva – spiritual master

Jagatguru – "guru of the universe"; applied to gurus of gurus

Janmastami – birth on the eighth day, Krishna's birthday celebration just before the new moon in August/September.

Kachori – stuffed, deep-fried savoury pastries.

Karmis – one engaged in karmic (fruitive) activities

Kartals – brass hand-cymbals used in bhajan and kirtan

Kartika – the best month to visit Vrndavana for spiritual purification. Occurs every fall in Oct./Nov. (calculated by the lunar calendar.

Katori – small stainless steel cup for serving individual dishes at a meal. Usually, many are used together in a thali.

Kichari, kitri – wholesome stew made with dahl and rice

Kirtana – the melodious devotional chanting of Krishna's holy names. Also, any glorification of Krishna.

Ksatriya – "warrior"; or administrator, the second vedic social order.

Kurta – long, loose shirt (often a pullover) worn over a dhoti by males

Kuruksetra – place of pilgrimage near Delhi, India.

Kutir – a private room for worshipping and glorifying the Lord, often called bhajan kutir or literally chanting place.

Lila – "pastime"; usually refers to the transcendental activities performed by the Supreme Lord

Limca – lemon-lime soft drink in India

Lota – hand-sized pot for carrying/drinking water, about sixteen ounce capacity.

Maha Bhagavata – great devotee, first-class devotee

Maharaja – 'great king', also applied to renuncients (swamis, gosvamis)

Mandir – a temple of the Supreme Lord

Mataji – "mother"; all women, except one's wife, should be addressed as mataji

Matha - See Gaudiya matha

Maya – "illusion"; delusional desires of all living entities in the material world

Mayapur – birthplace of Lord Caitanya, about 100 miles northwest of Kolkata, India.

Mayavadi – an impersonalist philosopher who conceives of the Supreme Personality of Godhead as being without form and personality.

Mistris – "worker";

Mleccha – "uncivilized human beings"; acting outside the Vedic system of society, generally meat-eaters.

Mrdanga – a sacred two-headed clay drum used to accompany congregational chanting to glorify Krishna.

Mudra – hand positions, forms, used symbolically in ritualistic worship.

Murti – a sculpted Deity form of Lord Krishna.

Navadvipa – a town in West Bengal near the birthplace of Lord Caitanya.

Nitya-siddha – "eternally liberated"; refers to eternally liberated souls that descend to earth to bring souls back home, back to Godhead.

Pandal – "large tent"; also refers to the programs held in such tents. Can accommodate thousands of pilgrims.

Paramahamsa – (parama-ultimate + hamsa-swan) "perfect swan."; refers to the wonderful swan-like qualities of someone in the highest stage of perfection in life. The fourth and last order of renunciation (sannyasa)

Parampara – authorized line of disciplic succession coming from Krishna Himself to distribute knowledge of Him in this world.

Parikrama – circumambulation of holy places by walking.

Pera – sweet milk fudge loved by all

Puja – "worship"; according to authorized rituals performed with love and devotion

Puris – soft flatbread puffed by deep-frying and eaten with spiced vegetables or sometimes sugar.

Pujari – "priest"; engaged in worship of the deity of the Lord

Rasgulla – sweet juicy curd-balls. Curdled milk, smoothed and formed into balls is soaked in sugar water.

Rathayatra – annual summer festival of the chariots. Lord

Sadhu – a saintly or Krishna conscious person

Samadhi – "trance"; complete absorption in God consciousness

Samosa – vegetable-filled, triangular, flaky-crusted, savoury pastries.

Sandesa – fresh cheese fudge, may be flavoured or plain.

Sankirtan – congregational chanting of the name, fame, pastimes of Krishna. The approved yoga practice for the Kali yuga (age of Kali) guaranteed to deliver suffering souls.

Sannyasa – the renounced order of life for spiritual culture, the fourth order of life (ashrama). Free from family relationships and with all activities dedicated to pleasing Krishna.

Sastra – "revealed scripture"; vedic literature.

Slokas – a Sanskrit verse

Srila – honorific prefix used for great devotees

Subji – a cooked vegetable preparation

Thali – flat metal dinner plate with a two centimetre vertical lip. Usually used in concert with several katoris to serve a multi-prep meal.

Tilak – auspicious clay markings placed on the forehead and other places (at least twelve) on their body by devotees sanctifying that their body as a temple of God.

Tulasi – "sacred basil"; plant, most dear to Lord Krishna, without which no food offering is accepted, and worshipped daily by His devotees.

Upma – savoury semolina preparation made with vegetables, butter and spices. Great on a cold morning!

Vaikuntha – "without anxiety"; the eternal planets of the spiritual world.

Vaisnava – a devotee of Lord Visnu an expansion of Krishna.

Vraja – "Vrndavana"; the home of Krishna and His friends and cows.

Vrndavana – Krishna's eternal personal abode, a village in India near the Taj Mahal where Krishna performed his sweet pastimes with His dearest associates the cowherd boys and girls and the cows and calves.

Vyasasana – the honoured seat of the spiritual master, the representative of Vyasadeva (the literary incarnation of Krishna who wrote the Srimad Bhagavatam).

Yajna – "sacrifice"; work done for the satisfaction of Krishna

Yavanas – "meat-eaters"; especially cow meat, lower class human beings (see also Mleccha)

Yogapitha – "pious temple"; birth site of Lord Caitanya Mahaprabhu located at Sri Mayapur Dhama.

Yuga – ages of time in the life of a universe, repeated in a cycle of four from creation until dissolution – billions of years.

Guide to Sanskrit Pronunciation

The system of transliteration used in this book conforms to a system that scholars have accepted to indicate the pronunciation of each Sound in the Sanskrit Language.

The short vowel **a** is pronounced like the **u** in b**u**t, long **ā** like the **a** in f**a**r, and short **i** like the **i** in p**i**n. Long **ī** is pronounced as **i** in p**i**que, short **u** as in p**u**ll, and long **ū** as in r**u**le. The vowel **ṛ** is pronounced like the **ri** in **ri**m. The vowel **e** is pronounced as **ey** in th**ey**, **ai** as in **ai**sle, **o** as in g**o**, and **au** as in h**ow**. The anusvāra (**ṁ**), which is a pure nasal, is pronounced like the **n** in the French word bo**n**, and visarga (**ḥ**), which is a strong aspirate, is pronounced as a final **h** sound. Thus **aḥ** is pronounced like **aha**, and **iḥ** like **ihi**.

The guttural consonants—**k**, **kh**, **g**, **gh**, and **ṅ**-are pronounced from the throat in much the same manner as in English. **K** is pronounced as in **k**ite, **kh** as in Ec**kh**art, **g** as in **g**ive, **gh** as in di**g h**ard, and **ṅ** as in si**ng**. The palatal consonants—**c**, **ch**, **j**, **jh**, and **ṇ**-are pronounced from the palate with the middle of the tongue. **C** is pronounced as in **ch**air, **ch** as in staun**ch h**eart, **j** as in **j**oy, **jh** as in he**dgeh**og, and **ñ** as in ca**ny**on. The cerebral consonants—**ṭ**, **ṭh**, **ḍ**, **ḍh**, and **ṇ**-are pronounced with the tip of the tongue turned up and drawn back against the dome of the palate. **Ṭ** is pronounced as in **t**ub, **ṭh** as in ligh**t h**eart, **ḍ** as in **d**ove, **ḍh** as in re**d-h**ot, and **ṇ** as in **n**ut. The dental consonants— **t**, **th**, **d**, **dh**, and **n**-are pronounced in the same manner as the cerebrals but with the forepart of the tongue against the teeth. The labial consonants—**p**, **ph**, **b**, **bh**, and **m**- are pronounced with the lips. **P** is pronounced as in **p**ine, **ph** as in u**ph**ill, **b** as in **b**ird, **bh** as in ru**b h**ard, and **m** as in **m**other. The semivowels—**y**, **r**, **l**, and **v**-are pronounced as in **y**es, **r**un, **l**ight, and **v**ine respectively. The sibilants—**ś**, **ṣ**, and **s**-are pronounced, respectively, as in the German word **s**prechen and the English words **sh**ine and **s**un. The letter **h** is pronounced as in **h**ome.

Index - Srila Prabhupada speaks:

Index - Prayers by Śrutakīrti:

www.ingramcontent.com/pod-product-compliance
Lightning Source LLC
Chambersburg PA
CBHW070327090426
42733CB00012B/2385
* 9 7 8 1 8 8 0 4 0 4 3 3 1 *